The History of Reading, Volume 3

Other publications by Palgrave Macmillan in association with the Institute of English Studies

Brycchan Carey et al. (eds.), *Discourses of Slavery and Abolition: Britain and Its Colonies, 1760–1838*

Gail Marshall and Adrian Poole (eds.), *Victorian Shakespeare*, Vol. 1: *Theatre, Drama and Performance*, Vol. 2: *Literature and Culture*

Andrew Nash (ed.), *The Culture of Collected Editions*

Jerome McGann, *Radiant Textuality: Literary Study after the World Wide Web*

Elizabeth James (ed.), *Macmillan: A Publishing Tradition*

Elizabeth Maslen, *Political and Social Issues in British Women's Fiction, 1928–1968*

Angelique Richardson and Chris Willis (eds.), *The New Woman in Fiction and Fact: Fin-de-Siècle Feminisms*

Warren Chernaik, Martin Swales and Robert Vilain (eds.), *The Art of Detective Fiction*

Rebecca D'Monte and Nicole Pohl (eds.), *Female Communities 1600–1800*

Isobel Armstrong and Virginia Blain (eds.), *Women's Poetry in the Enlightenment: The Making of a Canon, 1730–1820*

Isobel Armstrong and Virginia Blain (eds.), *Women's Poetry, Late Romantic to Late Victorian: Gender and Genre, 1830–1900*

Warren Chernaik and Martin Dzelzainis (eds.), *Marvell and Liberty*

Andy Leak and George Paizis (eds.), *The Holocaust and the Text: Speaking the Unspeakable*

Warwick Gould and Thomas F. Staley (eds.), *Writing the Lives of Writers*

Ian Willison, Warwick Gould and Warren Chernaik (eds.), *Modernist Writers and the Marketplace* (1996)

John Spiers (ed.), *George Gissing and the City: Cultural Crisis and the Making of Books in Late Victorian England*

Mary Hammond and Shafquat Towheed (eds.), *Publishing in the First World War* (2007)

Mary Hammond and Robert Fraser (eds.), *Books without Borders, Volume 1: The Cross-National Dimension in Print Culture* (2008), *Books without Borders, Volume 2: Perspectives from South Asia* (2008)

Gina Potts and Lisa Shahriari (eds.), *Virginia Woolf's Bloomsbury, Volume 1: Aesthetic Theory and Literary Practice* (2010), *Virginia Woolf's Bloomsbury, Volume 2: International Influence and Politics* (2010)

Robert J. Balfour (ed.), *Culture, Capital and Representation* (2010)

John Spiers (ed.), *The Culture of the Publisher's Series, Volume 1: Authors, Publishers and the Shaping of Taste* (2011), *The Culture of the Publisher's Series, Volume 2:* (2011)

Shafquat Towheed and W.R. Owens (eds.), *The History of Reading, Volume 1: International Perspectives, c.1500–1990*. Katie Halsey and W.R. Owens (eds.), *The History of Reading, Volume 2: Evidence from the British Isles, c.1750–1950*. Rosalind Crone and Shafquat Towheed (eds.), *The History of Reading, Volume 3: Methods, Strategies, Tactics*

The History of Reading, Volume 3

Methods, Strategies, Tactics

Edited by

Rosalind Crone
The Open University

and

Shafquat Towheed
The Open University

Foreword by

Simon Eliot

In association with the Institute of English
Studies, School of Advanced Study, University
of London

First published 2011 by
PALGRAVE MACMILLAN

Palgrave Macmillan in the UK is an imprint of Macmillan Publishers Limited, registered in England, company number 785998, of Houndmills, Basingstoke, Hampshire RG21 6XS.

Palgrave Macmillan in the US is a division of St Martin's Press LLC, 175 Fifth Avenue, New York, NY 10010.

Palgrave Macmillan is the global academic imprint of the above companies and has companies and representatives throughout the world.

Palgrave® and Macmillan® are registered trademarks in the United States, the United Kingdom, Europe and other countries.

ISBN 978–0–230–24756–7

This book is printed on paper suitable for recycling and made from fully managed and sustained forest sources. Logging, pulping and manufacturing processes are expected to conform to the environmental regulations of the country of origin.

A catalogue record for this book is available from the British Library.

A catalog record for this book is available from the Library of Congress.

10 9 8 7 6 5 4 3 2 1
20 19 18 17 16 15 14 13 12 11

Printed and bound in Great Britain by
CPI Antony Rowe, Chippenham and Eastbourne

In loving memory of Ian Stuart Robinson, Henrietta (Ettie) Smart, Joyce Pamela Williams and Helen de Wit

Contents

List of Figures

List of Tables

Foreword

Simon Eliot

> People say that life is the thing, but I prefer reading.
> (Logan Pearsall Smith, 1865–1946)

> To pass her time 'twixt reading and Bohea,
> To muse, and spill her solitary tea,
> Or o'er cold coffee trifle with the spoon,
> Count the slow clock, and dine exact at noon.
> (Alexander Pope, 1688–1744)

> Laudant illa sed ista legunt.
> (They praise those works, but read these.)
> (Martial, *c*.AD 40–104)

Little that is commonplace registers in history. Until relatively recently history has been a record of the exceptional, of change, of difference, or of contrast. To reverse the cliché, it's always been about the elephant in the room, and never about how the room was furnished or its other, less striking occupants. Essential commonplaces such as eating, casual conversations in the street, and the street itself, fudge into a fuzzy background against which sharp change or notable differences are brought into focus. In most history the ordinary is at best out of focus or, more commonly, invisible. The quotidian is never quoted, the ordinary is frequently ignored, and 'the same old, same old' is worn out before it is ever recorded.

In most literate societies, reading is usually this sort of prosaic activity. Most of us do it most of the time. It is not necessarily a matter of settling down to spend a few hours with *On the Origin of Species* or catching up with the latest vogue novel; it is more often a matter of reading a cornflakes packet for want of anything better, or reading a 'use by' date on something dubious from the fridge, or a timetable, or a free newspaper, or an email, or an advertisement, or a street name, or a menu, or the instructions on a bottle of aspirin.

However, the reading that we tend to remember, and the reading that much more frequently gets recorded, is of the exceptional sort: the book, the chapter, perhaps even just the sentence, which strikes home, which affects us in some profound way, which sometimes even transforms us. One should never underestimate the power of reading to surprise with joy, shock with facts or reason, or force us to see things from a disturbingly different point of view, and doing so commonly against our will and inclination. Samuel Johnson's experience, while he was an undergraduate at Oxford, of taking up Law's *Serious Call to a Holy Life* on the assumption that he might laugh at it, only to find Law 'an overmatch for me' is an example of such unexpected and sometimes unwelcome power. Reading, as so many other human experiences do, often relies for its impact on the law of unintended consequences.

Now, there is a natural and understandable tendency of those, particularly in literary studies, to prioritize this exceptional form of reading. After all, what is the use of studying something if it does not have a huge potential power to change and to convert? To study something that merely entertained, or diverted, or allowed escape or, worst of all, simply passed the time, is somehow demeaning. What we want are roads to Damascus: the flash, the crash, the conversion.

But if most, or even a significant minority, of reading experiences were of this transformational sort, we as readers would soon be exhausted by it, like Mr Brooke in George Eliot's *Middlemarch*, endlessly buffeted from one set of opinions to the next as he read one pamphlet and then another.

There is, of course, a middle type of reading between the entirely functional and the disconcertingly transcendental. This consists of reading for entertainment (escapist or otherwise), for instruction and information – and for confirmation. The first two are self-explanatory, but the third may need some unpacking. Although we are occasionally subject, often accidentally, to a reading experience that is transformational, we do spend a lot of our reading time trying to avoid such experiences. For instance, we usually choose for our newspaper one that tends to parallel our own views, and we naturally gravitate to other texts that are disposed to assure us that our opinions are the correct ones, and to provide us with further examples to back up our own prejudices. To provide the 'And I am right, and you are right' reassurance is one of the necessary and comforting functions of reading. Much of the content of even the most modern forms of communication, the text and the tweet, are devoted to variations on the theme of 'I'm OK, and you're OK'. It was ever thus: many of the clay tablets exchanged between Assyrian monarchs and their civil servants performed a similar function.

We must not forget that the act of reading or, at least, the act of appearing to read, is also an invaluable social tool. For those wishing to promote themselves as studious, for those wanting to avoid social contact or (even worse) eye contact, for those wishing to create space around themselves in a crowded place, reading is a godsend. How many of us, in dining alone in a restaurant, have taken a book or a newspaper not merely for entertainment, but in order to indicate that we are certainly not sad and lonely people?

Finally, there is the history of implied reading; that is, of reading we have not done but either implicitly or explicitly claimed to have done. The unread books borrowed from libraries, the un-perused books on our tables and bookshelves, all those monuments to our good intentions. Or, equally common, the books we bluff about, the allusion to a text that we hope will impress without being picked up by someone who has actually read the book to which we have casually referred. That this is both not new and all too human is attested by the quotation from Martial at the beginning of this foreword.

The history of reading is as much about the reader as it is about what is read. It is about the cocktail of motives and circumstances that leads us to select one text rather than another, and about the texture of our personalities and the nature of our predicament that determine how we react to that text. In our various attempts to recreate the humanity of the world we have lost, the study of the reading experiences of those in earlier centuries is an important and worthwhile endeavour. The essays that follow are part of a heroic project to explore one of the most significant of the intellectual experiences that we share with the past.

Acknowledgements

The editors would like to thank the Arts and Humanities Research Council for funding The Reading Experience Database, 1450–1945 (RED) project, established at The Open University in collaboration with the Institute of English Studies, University of London. Among the outcomes of the RED project was an international conference, 'Evidence of Reading, Reading the Evidence', held at the Institute of English Studies in July 2008, from which many of the essays in these three volumes emerged. Thanks are also due to Adam Mathew Digital, The Bibliographical Society, the British Academy, *History Today*, The Open University and the Royal Historical Society, who provided additional financial support for the conference, and to all the colleagues at the Institute of English Studies and The Open University who helped with its organization, in particular Dr Karen Attar (Rare Books Librarian, Senate House Library), curator of the accompanying exhibition. We thank colleagues and students at the University of Cambridge, The Open University, the University of Stirling, and the School of Advanced Studies, University of London, for helpful comments and suggestions. Permission to reproduce 'Cross References' by Jonathan Wolstenholme on the cover of this volume was kindly granted by Bridgeman Education. We would also like to thank the following for permission to quote or reproduce material in individual chapters: Reading University Library; John Burton of the George Eliot Fellowship; and Rebecca Walker of the Nuneaton and Bedworth Art Gallery and Museum (Chapter 2); The Lilly Library, Indiana University, Bloomington, Indiana for the postcard by N. Lubschutz (Chapter 4); Kajsa Dahlberg for pages from her copy of *Ett eget rum/Tusen bibliotek* (Chapter 7); ANVIL, Ateneo de Manila University Press, Valerie Barcinal, Camille Maria Castolo, Mark Andrew Lim, Sherwin A. Mapanoo, Jason Tabinas and Melissa Villa for images of Filipino blogs (Chapter 10); and The Huntington Library, San Marino, California, for the illustrations in texts by Ramelli (RB47853), Shreck and Chen (RB713373) and Grollier (RB714532), (Chapter 11). Every effort has been made to trace all copyright holders, but if any have been inadvertently overlooked, the publisher will be pleased to make the necessary arrangements at the first opportunity.

Notes on Contributors

Hanna Adoni is currently teaching at Sammy Ofer School of Communications Interdisciplinary Center, Herzliya, Israel. She is Professor Emeritus and Danny Arnold Professor of Communications from the Hebrew University at Jerusalem. She has written numerous articles and books including *Social Conflicts and Television News* (1990 with A. Cohen and C. Bantz), *Media, Minorities and Hybrid Identities* (2006 with A. Cohen and D. Caspi) and *Readers' Voices* (2007 with Hillel Nossek).

Daniel Allington is Lecturer in English Language Studies and Applied Linguistics at the Open University, UK, with interests in the history and sociology of culture, language and texts. He has written extensively on discourse analysis and reception study, with papers appearing in such journals as *Poetics Today* and *Social Semiotics*.

Stephen Colclough is a Lecturer in the School of English at Bangor University, Wales. He is the author of *Consuming Texts: Readers and Reading Communities 1695–1870* (Palgrave Macmillan, 2007) and co-editor (with Alexis Weedon) of *The History of the Book in the West: 1800–1914* (2010).

Rosalind Crone is Lecturer in History at The Open University, UK, and Co-Investigator on The Reading Experience Database, 1450–1945 (RED) project. She has published widely on popular culture, crime and literacy in the nineteenth century and is author of *Violent Victorians: Popular Entertainment in Nineteenth-Century London* (forthcoming 2012).

Mats Dahlström is an Associate Professor at the Swedish School of Library and Information Science, within the universities of Borås and Gothenburg. His research concerns bibliography and scholarly editing as well as digitization, text encoding and digital artefacts.

Simon Eliot is Professor of the History of the Book at the Institute of English Studies, School of Advanced Study, University of London. He has published on quantitative book history, publishing history, the history of lighting and library history. He is General Editor of the new multi-volume *History of Oxford University Press*.

Kate Flint is Professor of English and Art History at the University of Southern California. She is author of *The Transatlantic Indian 1776–1930* (2009), *The Victorians and the Visual Imagination* (2000), *The Woman Reader 1837–1914* (1993) and *Dickens* (1986), as well as many articles on nineteenth- and twentieth-century literature, cultural history and art history.

Simon R. Frost is External Lecturer at the University of Southern Denmark. Co-editor of *Moveable Type, Mobile Nations* (2010), his book history publications also include 'The Good in a Little Fiction: Conrad, Consumer Readers and Commodity Culture', in *English in Africa*, 35 (2008), pp. 45–66.

Alan Galey is Assistant Professor in the Faculty of Information at the University of Toronto, Canada where he also teaches in the Book History and Print Culture program. His research focuses on theories of the archive and prehistories of digital scholarly editing. More information may be found on his website: individual.utoronto. ca/alangaley/

Hillel Nossek is Professor of Communication at the School of Media Studies of the College of Management Academic Studies, Israel. He is the co-author of *Readers' Voices* (2007 with Hanna Adoni) and co-editor of *Media and Political Violence* (2007 with Annabelle Sreberny and Prasun Sonwalkar), and is the author of various articles and book chapters on these topics.

Sadiah Qureshi is a Research Fellow with the Cambridge Victorian Studies Group based at the University of Cambridge, UK. Her book, *The Tribes of Hyde Park Corner: Human Exhibitions, Empire and Anthropology in Nineteenth-Century Britain* is forthcoming in 2011.

Jonathan Rose is Kenan Professor of History at Drew University, USA. He was the founding president of the Society for the History of Authorship, Reading and Publishing. His publications include *A Companion to the History of the Book* (2007 edited with Simon Eliot), *The Intellectual Life of the British Working Classes* (2001), *The Holocaust and the Book* (2008), and (forthcoming) *The Literary Churchill*.

Barbara Ryan teaches in the University Scholars Programme at the National University of Singapore. She is the author of *Love, Wages, Slavery* (2006) and *Reading Acts: U.S. Readers' Interactions with Literature, 1800–1950* (2002 co-editor with Amy M. Thomas). She is currently co-editing a collection of essays about receptions of *Ben-Hur*.

Joan Swann is a Senior Lecturer in the Centre for Language and Communication at the Open University, UK. Recent books include *The Routledge Companion to English Language Studies* (2010, co-edited with Janet Maybin), and *Creativity, Language, Literature: The State of the Art* (Palgrave Macmillan, 2011, co-edited with Rob Pope and Ron Carter).

Vernon R. Totanes is a Ph.D. candidate at the University of Toronto, Canada. His publications include 'History of the Filipino People and Martial Law', *Philippine Studies*, 58 (2010); and 'Borrowing Privileges: Tagalog, Filipinos and the Toronto Public Library', in *Spectres of In/visibility* (2011).

Shafquat Towheed is Lecturer in English at the Open University, UK, and Co-Investigator on The Reading Experience Database, 1450–1945 (RED) project. He is co-editor of *The History of Reading: A Reader* (2010) and *The History of Reading, Vol. 1: International Perspectives, c.1550–1990* (Palgrave Macmillan, 2011).

Introduction

Shafquat Towheed

A student reads her textbook in preparation for a class, while another passenger, engrossed in the music on his personal music player, casually reads the advertising hoardings inside the train's compartment. One passenger is occupied in reading the business section of a bought broadsheet paper, reading perhaps for profit, while another picks up a free copy of a daily tabloid left behind by an earlier reader, to while away the travel time with trivial entertainment. While one commuter reads a downloaded short detective story using a 3G mobile phone as an e-book reader, another uses a smart phone to access a social networking account and contribute to a discussion about a book read recently by a friend, adding inexorably to the wealth of collective and individual responses to reading available on the Internet. Reading for information, a couple of tourists board the train clutching their guide book and consulting a map, while a local reads and responds to a series of SMS messages, perhaps sent from another location or time zone far away. One passenger is reading their way through a lengthy nineteenth-century novel in daily, sequential instalments, while another discontinuously reads a seemingly random section of a holy book, offering themselves a thought or prayer for the day.

This is a scene which is replicated on a daily basis in the public transport systems of London, New York, Delhi, Beijing, Mexico City, Cairo or any other large metropolitan centre across the world. It is so routine an activity that few of us even notice it, and yet it is a perfect example of the textually super-saturated world that we inhabit. In an increasingly – almost universally – literate world, reading matter

1

is everywhere. Text is ubiquitous and all pervasive, and readers are mobile, numerous and multifunctional. How then, in this dense forest of reading matter, can we study the behaviour of readers, and their individual signs of engagement (or refusals to engage) with the printed or digitized word? Can work on the history of reading in earlier periods inform future research? What sort of methodological approach should we consider? And how might readers themselves leave a trace (whether accidentally or deliberately) of their reading choices?

To answer some of these questions, the eleven chapters in this volume bring together the work of thirteen scholars based in seven different countries, and from a diverse range of academic disciplines and intellectual perspectives: literary studies, history, bibliography and librarianship, linguistics, sociology, art history, information science and literary theory. All these chapters engage directly with the central issues concerning the three volumes of *The History of Reading*: how do we accurately assess who read what? How do we recover the experiences and responses (textual or otherwise) of readers through history? How do we interpret these findings, and extrapolate trends and patterns of reading practice from the data? And finally, how do new modes of reading change both our modes of enquiry *and* interpretation in recovering the behaviour of contemporary readers? Unlike the chapters in *The History of Reading, Vol. 1: International Perspectives, c.1500–1990* and *The History of Reading, Vol. 2: Evidence from the British Isles, c.1750–1950*, the chapters in this volume are not exclusively concerned with either a particular historical period, or the examination of a discrete case study of a reader or reading communities. Rather, they are more explicitly focused on the appropriateness of a specific methodological perspective for their field of study, advocating particular tactics for finding and interpreting data, and exploring whether their adopted strategies offer valuable possibilities for mapping broader trends in reading practices across time or space. Indeed, all contributors to this volume posit the reading of multifarious texts (and not just books) within the wider context of a mixed- and/or multi-media environment. Reading does not (and has not) ever existed in isolation from a variety of other different forms of communication, whether in the visual arts, mass media, advertising, merchandise, social networking or the pervasive oral/aural culture of conversation.

This volume opens with two contrasting and compelling chapters, the first drawing upon historiography and the second literary theory, in order to explore broader perspectives in the history of reading (Part 1, 'Perspectives'). In 'Altick's Map: The New Historiography of the Common Reader', distinguished book historian Jonathan Rose revisits Richard D. Altick's pioneering study in the history of reading, *The English Common Reader* (1957) half a century later, and argues that the collective efforts of book historians gathering data from a wide range of primary source materials in the last three decades have started to fill in the gaps that Altick had earlier identified and mapped out. Rose persuasively argues that the study of ordinary readers – the overwhelming and often critically neglected majority of the reading public – necessitates the gathering of a wide range of data: 'police reports, wills, booksellers' ledgers, sociological surveys, the minutes of literary societies, the memoirs of common readers, letters to newspaper and magazine editors, fan mail to authors, book canvassers' reports back to the home office, marginalia, and library records'. Rose's position is in opposition to the rise of literary theory – the so-called 'theory wars' – that raged across the campuses of America and Britain in the 1970s and 1980s. While he is dismissive of 'theory-spinning in a vacuum', he is measured in his assessment of the 'hard' data upon which enumerative bibliographers and historians of the book have often relied: 'there is no such thing as a wholly trustworthy source . . . all documents have distinctive epistemological strengths and weaknesses, and that therefore we must use the broadest possible repertoire of source materials to reconstruct the experience of the reader', he cogently reminds us. Rose's espousal of the use of a diversity of sources is in contrast to his commitment to a quantitative, evidence based, historically contextualized methodology. For Rose, the new historiography of reading cannot and must not simply speculate or theorize about reading, but should instead painstakingly map out the territory with corroborative data from multiple sources, from which we can begin to identify patterns and trends. Quantitative and qualitative data takes precedent over theoretical agendas.

In contrast, Simon R. Frost's 'Commodity Readers: An Introduction to a Frame for Reading' views reading as intimately related to a wide range of forces (especially economic ones) evident in the public sphere. Approaching the subject from a European humanist scholarly tradition, and drawing upon both literary theory and philology, Frost's perspective is the inverse of Rose's: he uses a range of theoretical perspectives and discourses (Kant, Adorno, Appadurai, Culler, etc.) to inform his interpretation of the material artefacts and reading communities around a single text, George Eliot's *Middlemarch* (1871–2). Frost makes a powerful appeal for historians of reading to examine not only the textual (and other) records left behind by readers, but also to assess the influence of socio-economic forces upon the act of reading: 'if we are to understand the relationships between readers and pages, then we must understand what other forces are at play at any particular historical moment', he notes. Using the mid-nineteenth-century theories of William Stanley Jevons as an interpretative jumping-off point, he notes the interplay between goods and texts, plotting the rise of the 'George Eliot Cycle' and 'George Eliot Mushroom Ketchup' against successive, increasingly illustrated editions of *Middlemarch*, and noting the lexical usages of the terms 'good' and 'goods' in the novel. Texts are commodities and readers are consumers who chose to engage with particular literary works from a range of other material objects. Frost's approach reminds us that literary works are themselves commodities existing within a matrix of evolving socio-economic market forces: something that historians of reading, working around the confines of an increasingly doctrinaire global free-market order ought to acknowledge.

The next three chapters (Part 2, 'Methods and Tactics') illuminate three distinct methodological approaches, all informed by the disciplinary background of their investigators, to recovering and interpreting the evidence of reading in both contemporary and historical frameworks. Hanna Adoni and Hillel Nossek's 'Between the Book and the Reader: The Uses of Reading for the Gratification of Personal Psychosocial Needs' (Chapter 3) summarizes the results of a 2001 comparative survey of media consumption habits (books as well as radio, television and the Internet) amongst 616 adult Israelis from a deliberately diverse and representative demographic catchment. As social scientists, Adoni and Nossek draw upon the functionalist paradigm of the 'uses and gratification' school and the technological displacement school (proposed by Marshall McLuhan amongst others) to interpret reading preferences within the wider consumption of different types of media. Using both quantitative (telephone questionnaire) and qualitative (focus discussion group, recorded and transcribed) methodology in their study, Adoni and Nossek propose a new model, that of 'interchangeable functionality', for interpreting how consumers engage with different types of media. Is reading books displaced by other types of media content (film, television, radio, the Internet), or is its particular functionality not easily substituted? For twenty-first century Israeli readers and viewers, Adoni and Nossek surprisingly found that the lowest level of interchangeability was between television viewing and reading books. Adoni and Nossek's work provides concrete quantitative and qualitative evidence from their survey sample indicating that the rise of new visual media, far from heralding the demise of print, has created new spaces for the reading of books (especially fiction). In a mixed-media world, reading books still provides greater psychological and emotional satisfaction (while perhaps demanding greater engagement) than other (broadcast) forms of cultural consumption.

While Adoni and Nossek use the interview and focus group model to investigate individual responses to reading, in 'The Mediation of Response: A Critical Approach to Individual and Group Reading Practices' (Chapter 5), linguists Daniel Allington and Joan Swann appropriate ethnomethodology to closely examine the social construction of reading through verbal discourse. Contesting Rose's advocacy of the primacy and self-sufficiency of the textual evidence of reading found in autobiographies, diaries and correspondence, Allington and Swann study one specific reading group in the south of England over the course of nearly a year (2007–8) to demonstrate that their reading experiences (and eventual textual records of their reading) were shaped by the discussions that took place at successive reading group meetings. In closely examining the discourse of reading groups, Allington and Swann demonstrate that the reading of any given work is often constructed and re-negotiated through discussions with other members of a group, and that the final textual record of a reading experience may give us a misleadingly absolute outcome for what is in fact an iterative and constantly mediated process. In fact, the process of mediation and meaning construction, rather than the eventual record of reading, might be more worthy of our attention as historians of reading, as Allington and Swann provocatively argue: 'the attempts to discover readers' real responses to texts are ultimately less interesting than attempts to understand the practices that mediate response'.

Whereas Adoni and Nossek and Allington and Swann examine twenty-first century Israeli and British readers respectively, Barbara Ryan in 'One Reader, Two Votes: Retooling Fan Mail Scholarship' (Chapter 4) returns to the evidence yielded up by her investigation of a late nineteenth and early twentieth-century reading phenomenon: Lew Wallace's bestseller, *Ben-Hur* (1880), later made into a popular Hollywood film. Ryan's chapter persuasively reconceptualizes the relevance of readers' fan mail to authors, a previously critically derided but very rich source for the evidence of reading. Carefully mapping the physical and imaginative trajectory of a single piece of fan mail, a postcard from N. Lubschutz to Lew Wallace, Ryan demonstrates the extent to which fan mail represents both an unsolicited plebeian engagement with the public sphere, and uncontested evidence of the completion of the feedback loop between authors and readers, seen in Robert Darnton's 'communications circuit'. Ryan notes that fan mail can be a demonstration of partisanship, as well as an active engagement in advocacy; it records a type of reading and response specifically designed for further public consumption, even though archives have often deliberately marginalized it as ephemeral, or excluded it as critically unconsidered and therefore irrelevant. All three chapters in this section demonstrate that the continued attachment of readers to the printed book in an increasingly multimedia world has potentially profound implications for assessing the practices of future readers, a topic that we return to in the last section of this volume.

If Part 2 outlined three different (and highly contingent) methodological tactics for locating or generating data about or around reading, Part 3 ('Interpretative Strategies') showcases two highly original and distinct strategies for interpreting primary source material. In 'Representing Reading Spaces' (Chapter 6), Stephen Colclough directly engages Roger Chartier's agenda that recovering the various spaces for reading, and with it, the 'forgotten habits and gestures' of the readers who inhabited them, can provide us with valuable information about reading as a material, bodily act. Reading, Colclough reminds us, is always a material act occupying a physical space (humans are not, and cannot become, dematerialized readers), and in his examination of both public and private reading spaces in Britain in the period from *c*.1780–1850, he outlines a phenomenological interpretation of data. Small provincial circulating libraries, the numerous subscription coffee houses catering for working-class newspaper readers, mechanics' institutions and mutual improvement societies all provided public spaces (albeit often cramped and ill-lit) for the consumption of print. The prevalence of reading spaces and the particular practices that they engendered were not only public, but private too. Examining the journal of teenage reader Emily Shore (1819–39), Colclough notes the complex interdependence of reading alone, reading aloud collectively, and writing (both solitary and collaborative) undertaken by the Shore family in their living room as a kind of daily shared performance within a domestic reading space. How a text was read aloud by members of the family circle had a direct impact upon their reception of the work, as did existing domestic power relationships; Shore's journal reveals the extent to which both her father and uncle attempted (not always successfully) to determine her teenage reading. Domestic reading spaces, Colclough reminds us, are every bit as contested and contingent as public ones.

Reading spaces are not just the physical spaces where readers consume texts, but the paratextual or extratextual spaces suggested (and often filled) by the book itself. In 'A Book of One's Own: Examples of Library Book Marginalia' (Chapter 7), Mats Dahlström investigates contemporary Swedish conceptual artist Kajsa Dahlberg's anti-edition of Virginia Woolf's *A Room of One's Own* (1929). Dahlberg's approach places the original text at the very bottom of the analysis of reader response. Intrigued by the marginal notes inscribed on a library copy of Woolf's masterpiece, Dahlberg embarked upon a project to gather together every marked copy of *A Room of One's Own* held at libraries across Sweden; the result was the compilation of an edition of the work which gave priority to the marginal notes made by the many anonymous readers over the single authored original text. In Dahlström's account of Dahlberg's performance of reader response, it is the readers through their marginal marks who quite literally, fashion the text and make it their own. Although both Colclough and Dahlström draw upon practices from other disciplines (material culture/social history and performance art respectively), their application of these strategies to help answer important questions in the history of reading is highly productive.

If Kajsa Dahlberg's project applies ideas from performance art to investigate the collaborative reading of a single text, the two chapters in Part 4 ('Reading the Visual') explore the complex relationship between text and image through the filter of the technological progress in mechanical reproduction. The expansion of cheap print in nineteenth-century Britain transformed the walls of the cities and towns as bill-stickers advertised products and more often entertainments; however, very little attention has been paid by historians to the ways in which ephemera was read *in situ* by the fast growing (and increasingly literate) urban masses. In 'Reading Ephemera' (Chapter 8), Sadiah Qureshi shows how the ephemera (posters, handbills and catalogues, pasted on walls and distributed to paying customers) accompanying touring exhibitions of foreign peoples in London allowed audiences to more readily interpret the displays that were presented to them. Ephemera accompanying exhibitions was not created in a vacuum: passages were borrowed from seemingly more authoritative texts such as travel books and newspapers, and vice versa, so that these ephemeral materials, especially when read during the performances, shaped attitudes to racial difference. The production of ephemera was dependent on technological developments in printing and illustration: steam presses, lithography and lower taxes on paper created both readers of print, and viewers of images. Nineteenth-century readers inhabited a world in which word and image coexisted and were often co-dependent. Nowhere is this relationship more evident than in this vast and relatively neglected hinterland of ephemeral material, designed specifically to support visual (non-textual) spectacles and performances.

While Qureshi's chapter considers textual material read while accompanying a visual spectacle and often discarded afterwards, Kate Flint's 'Books in Photographs' (Chapter 9) reverses our gaze, and closely scrutinizes the representation of reading in photography.

The history of photography, Flint convincingly demonstrates, is inseparable from the history of reading. From its very inception as a mode of reproduction, photography has utilized books as props, as visible signs of cultural capital and social aspiration, and as objects to keep photographic subjects still and occupied during long exposures. Indeed, the seeming photographic reality of a putative reader holding open a book and apparently engaged in an act of reading was often something very different; as Flint observes, 'the co-presence of a human photographic subject and a printed text does not, by any means, guarantee that reading has taken, or may take, place'. Instead of asking whether the presence of a book in a photograph was incidental or contrived, Flint argues we should instead regard the image as evidence of 'prevalent attitudes towards reading and the spaces in which it is conducted'. Long exposure times and the sensitivity of early photography to light helped to create its own circumstances for the representation of reading, often at odds with reality. Fox Talbot's 'A Scene in a Library', Flint observes, gestures towards earlier visual registers (such as the still life), rather than capturing a *mise-en-scène* of the reading act. Despite this, the photographic representation of a book interpolates the act of reading into the image. Flint perceptively comments that 'because it is *of* a book, its metatextuality is foregrounded: we are propelled into considering the types of reading in which we engage when we interpret a photograph'.

Finally, in Part 5 ('Reading in the Digital Age') Vernon Totanes and Alan Galey focus squarely on the increasingly digital (and digitized) access to reading matter and evidence of reader response in the twenty-first century. In 'Filipino Blogs as Evidence of Reading and Reception' (Chapter 10), Vernon Totanes examines personal blogs that respond to reading two influential works on Filipino popular movements and the nationalist leader José Rizal (1861–1896): Reynaldo Ileto's *Pasyon and Revolution* (1979) and Ambeth Ocampo's *Rizal Without the Overcoat* (1990). The spread of personal computers, the rise of Internet cafes, and above all, the ubiquity of 3G mobile phones has meant that even in relatively poor developing countries, a significant proportion of the population have access to the Internet. In the case of the Philippines, nearly 30 million people, (30 per cent of the population) are now online, which means that the country has the seventeenth highest number of Internet users in the world (more than Spain, and just behind Italy). The spread of the Internet and the rise of blogging has largely democratized the publication of critical comment on books, though the proliferation and transience of personal blogs poses new challenges for the interpretation of reader response. As Totanes demonstrates, bloggers' comments on books need to be read alongside evidence provided by the ways in which individuals have customized their sites. While bloggers discuss the various texts they have read, the practice of reading blogs pushes the boundaries of readership studies even further. A large proportion of our reading is now conducted in a digital environment, and as the prevalence of literary blogs demonstrate, a significant proportion of our responses to reading of analogue printed matter (as in the case of these two books on Rizal) is now expressed digitally. The book and the blog have become increasingly interdependent modes of cultural mediation, much as the manuscript and the diary were in earlier centuries. To successfully chart the readership and reception of a book published in our digital twenty-first century, we must be conscious of the digital mediation of readers' responses.

Historians of reading in the twenty-first century also need to be aware of the interface itself as an agent that mediates both reading and response, and can provide valuable evidence of individual reading practices. In 'Reading the Book of Mozilla: Web Browsers and the Materiality of Digital Texts' (Chapter 11), Galey argues that while browsers are meant to impose order on the unquantifiable number of texts available on the World Wide Web, the inherent instability of digital texts seems to defy any attempt at a rational understanding of the information available on a particular subject. Moreover, as demonstrated by other authors in this volume, Galey shows that texts cannot be analysed outside the systems that surround them, be they social or mechanical. Internet browsers like other interfaces (lending libraries, bookshops, the codex, etc.), offer additional tools for analysing reading; these have so far been largely overlooked, but are in desperate need of concerted scholarly attention. Galey draws important parallels between the understanding of texts and the process of reading in the past and the present. For instance, Galey encourages us to consider browsing, whether onscreen or in the library, as 'a readerly activity, one which links humanists of the past and the present'. Whether in Renaissance Europe or Qing Dynasty China, the book wheel serves as a post-Gutenberg, pre-Microsoft metaphorical and conceptual precursor to our own incessant (web) based browsing.

Both Totanes and Galey interrogate new methods of assessing reader engagement and response through digital media (blogs and browsers respectively) while also looking at historical content (Totanes) and earlier historical models (Galey). Matthew G. Kirschenbaum's award winning study *Mechanisms: New Media and the Forensic Imagination* (2008) and N. Katherine Hayles's groundbreaking *Electronic Literature: New Horizons for the Literary* (2008) have demonstrated the complex interpretability and inherent fragility (how do we now recover and 'read' a first generation floppy diskette?) of new, 'digital born' media, while at the same time offering penetrating analyses of how digital texts are composed, stored, distributed, consumed and effaced. Drawing upon the implications of these and other production and distribution focused studies, Galey and Totanes offer insightful approaches to the consumption of texts through and via digital interfaces by examining reading practices in an increasingly digital world.

The range of methodological and intellectual perspectives offered in this volume is rich and diverse, but not entirely exhaustive. Other academic fields, especially in the social and empirical sciences, are also beginning to research and interpret the act of reading. Recent pioneering research on reading by neuroscientists and developmental psychologists has shown how the brain processes and interprets the visual representation of language that is text, and has demonstrated how the acquisition of reading as a skill significantly increases the plasticity of the human brain and our capacity to learn. Maryanne Wolf's *Proust and the Squid: The Story and Science of the Reading Brain* (2007) and Stanislas Dehaene's *Reading in the Brain: The Science and Evolution of a Human Invention* (2009) have argued that despite the ability to read not being an evolutionary requirement or an inherited trait, reading is itself a biological effort that has a intrinsic effect on the physical development of the brain: the act of reading is both physically and psychologically transformative. Such discoveries have profound implications for historians of reading; but while Wolf and Dehaene have cogently argued for the importance of reading on human neural development, they have not been able to explain individual or social differences in reading practice or preferences, nor have they examined the extent to which readers (who are also often themselves writers) shape their own engagements with textual matter. Readers, no matter who they are, where they live or what language they read in, have considerable agency: they can chose what to read, or not to read at all.

The study of reading, and especially the location and interpretation of readers and reading communities, has both a historic hinterland and many (some as yet uncharted) future frontiers. The eleven chapters in this volume offer a representative sample of different methodological perspectives to assess and interpret the multiple, co-extensive reading practices that have developed (and are continuing to develop) over the last two centuries. In the last five thousand years, reading and writing have gone from being the highly specialized skills jealously guarded by the few, to an essential engagement for almost all. Increasingly, humans construct their understanding of the wider world and negotiate their social relations with others through their reading and engagement with multifarious texts in a variety of forms. Reading and technology cannot be separated as the rise of a new generation of e-readers, such as Amazon's Kindle, testifies; but reading has always been far more than simply ingesting the words on a page or a screen. Reading, the process by which text is deciphered and meaning is produced, is conditioned by the circumstances in which it occurs: the physical attributes of the text, the space in which it is consumed, the practices or bodily postures adopted by the reader, and the related events which follow. E-readers such as Amazon's Kindle represent a significant development as a tool which will change publishing and distribution patterns. However, claims that it will spark a reading revolution are almost certainly overstated. Kindle will not spark a reading revolution, because in fact the key to its success lies in its ability to draw upon the methods, tactics and strategies that have been employed by a wide range of readers for many centuries. Many of those, as well as the relationship between the past and present, are explored by the authors in this volume. Lest we forget the sometimes absolute importance of the circulation of textual material and the process of reading and writing, the 33 miners trapped in the San José gold mine in Chile's Atacama Desert on 6 August 2010 have sent us a telling reminder. 'Estamos bien en el refugio los 33' (All 33 of us are alive and well), read the capitalized hand-written note in red marker pen that was attached to the drill shaft that reached them 17 days after they were trapped. For those miners, cut off 700 metres underground, the act of writing and its consummation through reading – the completion of textual circulation – verified their existence and offered them their only prospect of rescue.

Part 1
Perspectives

1
Altick's Map: The New Historiography of the Common Reader

Jonathan Rose

When Elizabeth Long began investigating women's book groups in the mid-1980s, her research plan provoked two profoundly different sets of reactions. Women, who had themselves participated in such groups, as well as men whose mothers and grandmothers had done so, immediately grasped the importance of her project: 'You will never know what a difference it made' was the phrase she heard again and again. But among her academic colleagues, common readers 'occupied a zone of cultural invisibility. They were not of interest to literature departments, whose major focus is on books and authors, not readers. They were not of interest to sociologists or political scientists because women's reading groups do not pursue activities with any obvious relationship to formal political processes' – though Long went on to show that such groups had mobilized the women's suffrage and Progressive movements at the grass roots. 'Scholars of popular culture had not found reading groups interesting because the groups read canonized fiction and did not transform their cultural consumption into a "resistant" subcultural style': it had not yet occurred to them that canonical literature can be immensely popular and devilishly subversive. 'Communications departments had not researched them because reading groups were not engaged with the mass media,' as if books were not a mass medium. 'Leftists were uninterested because book group participants were middle class and clearly not part of pro-letarian or potentially revolutionary culture', though David Vincent's *Bread, Knowledge and Freedom* (1981) had already demonstrated the importance of reading in inspiring working-class consciousness in early nineteenth-century Britain. As a sociologist, Long concluded that the really important question that needed answering was *why* academics did not care about readers.[1]

Of course, Richard Altick cared a great deal. Stuck in Lancaster, Pennsylvania during the Great Depression, he filled four commonplace books – a total of 1248 single-spaced typewritten pages – with comments on his insatiable reading. In the first volume he recorded a traumatic encounter with a classic tale of a common reader:

> Began *Jude the Obscure* and read a hundred pages before I decided, in view of the deep pessimism which is supposed to pervade it, to postpone it for another time. My state of mind is such that I require stimulation and hope, and not any more food for despair. Particularly since Jude yearned for the scholarly life, and so do I; and there are so many real obstacles to my path to that goal that I do not now want to discover any more by reading of the gods' sport with Jude.[2]

He lived for another 70 years, but he could never bring himself to open Hardy's novel again.

Compared with most Americans in the 1930s, Altick was not so badly off. He had a BA from Franklin and Marshall, a solid liberal arts college founded in 1787, and he soon entered the doctoral program in English at the University of Pennsylvania. That department, as he recalled, was shockingly mediocre and inbred, hiring only its own PhDs. It was in fact 'the academic branch of the celebrated Old Philadelphia Establishment'. In all probability, no member of the faculty ever voted for Franklin D. Roosevelt. A few did real research, but more typical was this unnamed professor: 'With no discernible record of scholarly activity, he read his lectures on American literature from tattered pages, and he glowered at us from the lectern as if he blamed us for his having to be there.'[3] Today the postmodern academy has its own share of clubbiness and pedantry, of inflated reputations and blinkered orthodoxies, but we shouldn't imagine that it was preceded by some kind of golden age.

Graduate students who go on to do innovative work are usually not the worshipful protégés of eminent professors, but those who see the shortcomings of their mentors and therefore look for new methodologies beyond the bounds of their discipline. Early on, Altick realized that social history could provide the essential context for literary studies – in fact 'the social history of literature' is a very good definition of what would later be called 'book history'. 'My initial focus was the audience', he recalled late in life. 'If, as I believed, a literary work was best studied as a transaction between an author (an individual man or woman) and a reader (multiplied into an audience) which occurred in time (historical context), then I had to relate literature to social history, reflected as it was in the growth of a mass readership.' Altick was familiar with the pioneering studies of the English common people by G.M. Trevelyan and J.L. and Barbara Hammond. He read H.L. Mencken's *The American Language* (1919) and immediately recognized it as 'a classic not only of philology but of sociology as well, because in essence it is not a book about words at all, but a broad survey of American cultural traits. The whole wide field of American social history is reflected in these pages.' He knew Amy Cruse's *The Englishman and His Books in the Early Nineteenth Century* (1930) and *The Victorians and Their Reading* (1935),[4] though he found them 'over-chattily presented and maddeningly undocumented'. He also read Q. D. Leavis's *Fiction and the Reading Public* (1932),[5] but was repelled by her 'deep-seated social prejudice and . . . equally deep-seated ignorance. Consequently, I developed a mission, to rescue the study of English reading tastes and habits from Cruse's amateurism on the one hand and Leavis's crippling snobbery and lack of dependable information on the other.'[6]

Altick understood that a history of reading could not focus on reading alone. It would have to explore the whole of 'what I might have called the food chain of literature, where social history had its greatest impact on literary history: the unbroken but often accident-prone sequence of events – the fortunes of a novel, say, or a book of poems, from author's pen to publisher and printer and thence, via bookseller or circulating library, to the reader'.[7] In tracing the life cycle of books from creation to consumption, Altick anticipated by 25 years the 'communications circuit' sketched by Robert Darnton in 1982.[8] In fact *The English Common Reader* (1957) devoted only one chapter to reading experiences, mainly because Altick had access to few of the primary sources that are available to historians of reading today. In that sense he did for book history what Charles Babbage (1791–1871) had done for the computer: he understood how it would work long before the necessary technology had been developed.

When it was first published, *The English Common Reader* was not one but two generations ahead of its time, and profoundly at odds with the prevailing climate of academic literary studies. The year was 1957, the high noon of the New Critics, who did not see the relevance of the history of literacy, public libraries, newspapers, publishing, bookselling, or the ordinary reader. In the 1980s they would be elbowed aside by an assortment of literary theorists: deconstructionists, New Historicists, Lacanians, semioticians, postcolonialists, feminists, and reader-response critics. All of them (especially the last) generalized broadly about 'the reader', usually without studying this creature. 'I might have been expected to welcome and perhaps even join the school of reader-response critics', Altick reminisced:

> The truth is, their conception of the literary encounter left me cold. It was too hypothetical and schematic, having nothing to do, as far as I could see, with actual experience; the interaction between an 'ideal' reader and a text occurred only in the sophisticated imagining of the critic. Or, to put it another way, they regarded literature as the site of an endless series of social or political power plays between author and reader, predetermined antagonists rather than like-minded friends. No actual reader ever chronicled any such confrontation. Speculation on such a high level of abstraction, unsupported by any kind of empirical evidence, was not my cup of tea.[9]

Elizabeth Long thought her research might interest a senior colleague who was trying to secure an endowed chair for Stanley Fish, the dean of the reader-response school, but his eyes glazed over as soon as she moved the discussion from theory to real book discussion groups ('Oh, my wife's in one of those').[10] As Heidi Brayman Hackel observes, literary critics 'often ignore actual readers in favor of theoretical constructs, variously described as "mock", "ideal", "model", "implied", "encoded", "informed", and "super" readers. Even the tendency to refer in the singular to "the reader" obscures the diversity of individual readers and the range of reading practices available at any one historical moment'. Feminist critics may address women's reading, but they tend 'to slide into transhistorical notions of an essentialized female reader'.[11] And that slide, as Julie Sloan Brannon recognizes, effectively keeps the reader at arm's length: 'The uncomfortable truth behind this impulse in literary criticism is that the common reader is, in fact, the Other: the marginalized spectre against which literary critics define their own position in literary culture.'[12]

Altick had introduced *The English Common Reader* as 'a preliminary map of the vast territory, still virtually unexplored, which awaits the researcher'.[13] But thirty years later he protested to me – with good reason – that 'not much has been done to expand the scope of the *ECR*. . .[or] to fill in the map I outlined'.[14]

However, all that was about to change – dramatically. In 1986 Robert Darnton published his cautiously optimistic manifesto 'First Steps Toward a History of Reading'.[15] Five years later the Society for the History of Authorship, Reading and Publishing (SHARP) was founded. In the heyday of theory, SHARP offered literary scholars a haven where 'empirical' was not a dirty word. They were joined by librarians eager to prove that they were more than warehousers of books: studies of reading offered them a chance to make an important contribution to cultural history. And when social historians dismissed intellectual history as 'elitist' and promoted the study of the everyday lives of ordinary people, intellectual historians like Darnton adopted the methods of social history – and reminded their critics that no complete history of everyday life can ignore the experience of reading. As a result, the historiography of reading took off in the 1990s and accelerated in the new century. One measure of that progress was registered in the greatly expanded bibliography in the second edition of *The English Common Reader* (1998).[16]

As Altick and Darnton admitted, a lack of source material had always presented a serious obstacle to writing a history of reading. But this book and its companion volumes demonstrate that in recent years scholars have, with considerable ingenuity, located and used a wide range of raw materials that allow us to fill in the vast blank spaces on Altick's map. We find our evidence in police reports, wills, booksellers' ledgers, sociological surveys, the minutes of literary societies, the memoirs of common readers, letters to newspaper and magazine editors, fan mail to authors, book canvassers' reports back to the home office, marginalia, and library records. Reader responses are set down in commonplace books and in their modern incarnation, the scrapbook, as revealed in Ellen Gruber Garvey's work on reading during the American Civil War.[17] Ronald and Mary Zboray were able to gather together the letters and diaries of more than 900 readers in antebellum New England, which became the basis of their book *Everyday Ideas*.[18] Family archives may be saturated with information about books: Claire White Putala used the 358 boxes of Osborne

Family Papers at Syracuse University to reconstruct a literary micro-culture among a group of nineteenth-century middle-class women.[19] Records of educational institutions reveal a great deal about literacy acquisition and early reading habits, especially when those agencies served disenfranchised readers: for example the Workers' Educational Association in Britain, or the Freedmen's Bureau archives for Heather Andrea Williams's *Self-Taught: African American Education in Slavery and Freedom* (2005).[20] And the methodology of oral history has given us two recent studies of Oprah's Book Club.[21]

The *Reading Experience Database* (www.open.ac.uk/Arts/reading/) offers an ever-growing bank of recorded reader responses in Britain between 1450 and 1945, with more than 30,000 entries as of May 2010; all are searchable by date, class, age, gender, religion, occupation, author, and title, among other dimensions. The 'What Middletown Read' project (www.bsu.edu/middletown/wmr/) has constructed a database from the borrowing records of the public library in Muncie, Indiana, a 'typical' American town that has been intensively studied by sociologists. It records more than 400,000 loans of 13,000 books to 6,000 individuals between 1891 and 1902. These two tools, easy enough for undergraduates to use, could become valuable (not to mention fun) teaching resources for the Google Generation. Similar projects have been launched in Canada, Australia, New Zealand and the Netherlands. And why should we not develop databases to investigate *Lesen im Mitteleuropa*, or what the Middle East read?

Apropos of electronic sources for the history of reading, we should not overlook the search possibilities opened by the Internet itself. Some years ago one of my doctoral students, Robert McParland, proposed to write a dissertation on Charles Dickens's American readers. But where would we find them? The methodology that David Vincent and Martyn Lyons and I had used for our studies – trawling a large body of autobiographies for references to reading – could be used to reconstruct the literary diet of a group of readers, but it could not efficiently focus on responses to a single author. Nor was fan mail an option: Dickens had burned all of his. Ultimately we sent out queries over listservs for SHARP members, librarians, and archivists. The flood of responses suggested that nearly every archive, special collections library, and local historical society in the United States had one or two letters, diaries, newspaper clippings, or literary society minutes books that discussed Dickens. And that accumulated mass of documents made possible McParland's book, *Charles Dickens's American Audience* (2010).[22]

Given all this new scholarship, it is fairly astonishing to recall that just twenty years ago, the history of the common reader was widely believed to be unrecoverable. Now no one doubts a wealth of primary sources exists. The only question (a debate which has engaged William St. Clair, Jan Fergus, Stephen Colclough, myself, and others) is which sources are most reliable – publishers' records or booksellers' ledgers or readers' memoirs?[23] And we all know how that debate must end: we will inevitably conclude that there is no such thing as a wholly trust-worthy source, that all documents have distinctive epistemological strengths and weaknesses, and that therefore we must use the broadest possible repertoire of source materials to reconstruct the experience of the reader.

Of course the fact that we do think seriously about our sources, their reliability and their ambiguities, indicates that historians of reading are not 'anti-theory'. Occasionally an inexperienced researcher in our field will ferret out of the archives a lot of individual reading experiences, and then go nowhere with them. But most of us do draw larger conclusions from our data, and when we do that, we theorize. We do object to theory-spinning in a vacuum: even recent theoretical approaches to reading, like Karin Littau's, are weakly grounded in his-toriography.[24] We do insist that theory be tested against research, and we have accumulated enough research to make that possible. You can no longer theorize about canonization without taking into account the passion for 'great books' among British domestic servants, French workers, and African Americans in the nineteenth and early twentieth centuries.[25] Postcolonial theorists have to recognize that the same kind of self-improving readers were found by Stephanie Newell in the Gold Coast (modern day Ghana) and by Isabel Hofmeyr among the Shakespeare-quoting leadership of the African National Congress.[26] 'Charles Dickens and John Ruskin were the favourites of colonial educators and *also* of ambitious, but socially powerless, African young men', Newell points out. *Wuthering Heights* and *The Pickwick Papers* were not 'thrown like a punch at Ghanaian society, knocking existing interpretive practices out of action', rather they were 'dropped like a pebble into a pool of existing literacies and narrative conventions, sending ripples through the multiplicity of reading practices which operated already in local cultures'.[27] Yes, we must open our minds to the possibility that non-Western readers may have deployed distinctively non-Western reading methods: see Germaine Warkentin on deciphering aboriginal sign systems in Canada,[28] and Charlotte Eubanks on the 'circumambulatory reading' of Buddhist scrolls.[29] But often paradigms of 'appropriation' and 'poaching', developed to explain European reading responses, work very well in non-European contexts, as Sari Kawana discovered in her recent study of younger readers in wartime Japan.[30]

And before we theorize women's reading, we should make sure that we know what women actually read: according to Mary Kelley, William St. Clair, Kate Flint, Christine Pawley, and Clarence Karr, it often wasn't very different from what men were reading.[31] Some long-standing assumptions about the female audience for eighteenth-century novels were recently upset by Jan Fergus, who mined the records of provincial booksellers to discover that the buyers and borrowers of novels were mainly men, even if we discount for the possibility that some of them were obtaining books for their wives and daughters. Even novels written by women were requested more often by male customers than female customers, by a ratio of as much as five to one. All this calls into question the business of sorting complicated human beings into the simple categories of identity based criticism: race, class, and gender are each weak predictors of reading tastes because readers are influenced by so many other factors. Jan Fergus's telling conclusion should be mounted on the desks of all historians of reading: 'Audiences are multiple, shifting, and intersecting, and each reader belongs to many.'[32]

This kind of history is finding an audience well beyond academia. One measure of the success of our field is the proliferation of pop histories of reading by Alberto Manguel, Steven Roger Fischer, and Nicholas A. Basbanes.[33] The 2003 winner of the Pulitzer Prize in theatre, Nilo Cruz's *Anna in the Tropics*, was a dramatization of the history of reading. The play is set in a 1929 Tampa cigar factory, where the employer hires a *lector* to read aloud to his workers, as a kind of literary fringe benefit, and they find an epiphany in Tolstoy's *Anna Karenina* (1877). Consider also the phenomenal popularity of Allan Bloom's *The Closing of the American Mind*, David Denby's *Great Books*, Anne Fadiman's *Ex Libris: Confessions of a Common Reader*, Harold Bloom's *How to Read and Why*, and Azar Nafisi's *Reading Lolita in Tehran*.[34] Guides to reading have been with us for centuries, but it is probably unprecedented (and certainly thrilling) to see so many books about reading on the bestseller lists, to have millions of common readers debating what we should read.

And yet, at the same time, academic literary studies became ever more ingrown, fractured into mutually unintelligible theoretical sects, disengaged from the lay reading public, and (in the United States) losing undergraduates to business courses. Elizabeth Long found that her book club members, who were obviously passionate about literature, laughed off the criticism they learned in their college courses 'as an arcane, demanding, and even manipulative game,' where you won points for reading into the text whatever the professor wanted. One discussion of *Huckleberry Finn* (1885) led 'to uproarious reminiscences about the tribulations of searching for symbols in English literature classes and everyone's favorite trick for getting A's. One member said that the ocean was his favorite symbol: "It could mean death, sex, rebirth – you could do anything with the ocean."'[35]

The problem, as Stephen Greenblatt put it in his 2002 MLA presidential address, is not that literature professors are only writing for other literature professors. If only they were. The painful reality is that these professors are no longer buying and reading each other's books. University presses, consequently, often cannot sell the few hundred copies needed to break even on a scholarly monograph. Greenblatt was somewhat at a loss for a solution, except to suggest that no one leave the MLA convention without buying a book from the publishers' exhibits.[36] If we assume that every MLA member has published a book, that strategy would increase the sales of each on average by one copy. Clearly, something more radical needs to be done. I second a modest proposal offered by Julie Brannon: that literary studies reengage students and the general public by turning its attention to the ordinary reader in history. 'Our scholarship depends in part on understanding just who reads the works under examination, and why they read them', Brannon argues. 'Such an understanding will allow us to see how our own work functions in the discourse of Literature: in tandem with, not opposition to, readers outside of academia. We have an obligation in that dyad to continue the vital work of scholarship for the benefit of all who read literary works, to keep literature a vibrant part of our larger cultural discourse, and to ensure that what we do is indeed credible to readers both in and out of academia.'[37]

The MLA may be arriving at last at that conclusion. According to a reporter covering their January 2006 convention, 'Literary scholars have made a startling discovery: Books are objects that people actually read.' Shannon McLachlan, an editor at Oxford University Press, affirmed that 'The main trend that's beginning to be important is an interest in print culture', which is 'bringing literary scholars back into physical contact with archives, with books, with the ways people have interacted with and used books in their lives'. She saw 'the pendulum swinging away from theory' and toward readers: for example, studies of Thomas Jefferson's library and nineteenth-century scrapbooks. 'We sort of had to rediscover how people read historically', said John Guillory of New York University's English department, which has lately hired quite a few specialists in print culture.[38] 'Broadly speaking, the past two decades have seen a move back toward historicism from the purely rhetorical realms of deconstruction', observes William Deresiewicz, specifically toward historicizing the book and its readers.[39] It has taken fifty years, but it is gratifying to know that the cutting edge has finally caught up with Richard Altick.

Notes and references

1. Elizabeth Long, *Book Clubs: Women and the Uses of Reading in Everyday Life* (Chicago and London: University of Chicago Press, 2003), pp. ix–x.
2. Richard D. Altick, *A Little Bit of Luck: The Making of an Adventurous Scholar* (Philadelphia: Xlibris, 2002), pp. 41–2.
3. Ibid., pp. 51–5.
4. Amy Cruse, *The Englishman and His Books in the Early Nineteenth Century* (New York: T. Y. Crowell, 1930) and *The Victorians and Their Books* (London: Allen & Unwin, 1935).
5. Q. D. Leavis, *Fiction and the Reading Public* (London: Chatto & Windus, 1932).
6. Altick., *A Little Bit of Luck*, pp. 164–7.
7. Ibid., p. 168.
8. Robert Darnton, 'What is the history of books?' in *The Kiss of Lamourette* (New York: W. W. Norton, 1990), ch. 7.
9. Altick, *A Little Bit of Luck*, p. 170.
10. Long, *Book Clubs*, p. 225.
11. Heidi Brayman Hackel, *Reading Material in Early Modern England: Print, Gender, and Literacy* (Cambridge: Cambridge University Press, 2005), pp. 6–7.
12. Julie Sloan Brannon, *Who Reads* Ulysses? *The Rhetoric of the Joyce Wars and the Common Reader* (New York & London: Routledge, 2003), pp. 1–5.

13. Richard D. Altick, *The English Common Reader: A Social History of the Mass Reading Public, 1800–1900* (Chicago: University of Chicago Press, 1957), p. 9.
14. Correspondence with the author, 2 May 1988.
15. Originally published in the *Australian Journal of French Studies,* 23 (1986), 5–30. Reprinted in his *The Kiss of Lamourette* (New York: W. W. Norton, 1990), ch. 9.
16. Richard D. Altick, *The English Common Reader: A Social History of the Mass Reading Public, 1800–1900,* 2nd edn. (Columbus: Ohio State University Press, 1998), pp. 413–27.
17. Ellen Gruber Garvey, 'Anonymity, authorship, and recirculation: a Civil War episode,' *Book History,* 9 (2006), 159–78.
18. Ronald J. Zboray and Mary Sracino Zboray, *Everyday Ideas: Socioliterary Experience among Antebellum New Englanders* (Knoxville: University of Tennesee Press, 2007), p. xxi.
19. Claire White Putala, *Reading and Writing Ourselves into Being: The Literacy of Certain Nineteeth-Century Young Women* (Greenwich, CT: Information Age Publishing, 2004). See also M. Jeanne Peterson, *Family, Love, and Work in the Lives of Victorian Gentlewomen* (Bloomington and Indianapolis: Indiana University Press, 1989), pp. 41–5.
20. Heather Andrea Williams, *Self-Taught: African American Education in Slavery and Freedom* (Chapel Hill: University of North Carolina Press, 2005).
21. Kathleen Rooney, *Reading with Oprah: The Book Club that Changed America* (Fayetteville: University of Arkansas Press, 2005); and Cecilia Konchar Farr, *Reading Oprah: How Oprah's Book Club Changed the Way America Reads* (Albany: State University of New York Press, 2005).
22. Robert McParland, *Charles Dickens's American Audience* (Lanham, MD: Lexington Books, 2010), p. 272.
23. Jan Fergus, *Provincial Readers in Eighteenth-Century England* (Oxford: Oxford University Press, 2006), introduction; Stephen Colclough, *Consuming Texts: Readers and Reading Communities, 1695–1870* (Basingstoke: Palgrave Macmillan, 2007), ch. 1; William St. Clair, *The Reading Nation in the Romantic Period* (Cambridge: Cambridge University Press, 2004), passim; Jonathan Rose, *The Intellectual Life of the British Working Classes,* 2nd edn. (New Haven and London: Yale University Press, 2010), preface.
24. Karin Littau, *Theories of Reading: Books, Bodies and Bibliomania* (Cambridge: Polity Press, 2006).
25. Rose, *Intellectual Life*; Martyn Lyons, *Readers and Society in Nineteenth-Century France: Workers, Women, Peasants* (Basingstoke: Palgrave – now Palgrave Macmillan, 2001); and Elizabeth McHenry, *Forgotten Readers: Recovering the Lost History of African-American Literary Societies* (Durham: Duke University Press, 2002).
26. Isabel Hofmeyr, 'Reading debating/debating reading: the case of the Lovedale Literary Society, or why Mandela quotes Shakespeare,' in *Africa's Hidden Histories: Everyday Literacy and Making the Self,* ed. Karin Barber (Bloomington and Indianapolis: Indiana University Press, 2006), pp. 258–77.

27. Stephanie Newell, *Literary Culture in Colonial Ghana: 'How to Play the Game of Life'* (Bloomington: Indiana University Press, 2002), pp. 2–3.

28. Germaine Warkentin, 'In search of "The word of the other": Aboriginal sign systems and the history of the book in Canada,' *Book History,* 2 (1999), 1–27.

29. Charlotte Eubanks, 'Circumambulatory reading: revolving Sutra libraries and Buddhist scrolls,' *Book History,* 13 (2010), 1–24.

30. Sari Kawana, 'Reading beyond the lines: young readers and wartime Japanese literature,' *Book History,* 13 (2010), 154–84.

31. Mary Kelley, 'Reading women/women reading: the making of learned women in antebellum America,' in *Reading Acts: U.S. Readers' Interactions with Literature, 1800–1950* (Knoxville: University of Tennessee Press, 2002), p. 56; St. Clair, *Reading Nation in the Romantic Period*, 119; Clarence Karr, *Authors and Audiences: Popular Canadian Fiction in the Early Twentieth Century* (Montreal and Kingston: McGill: Queen's University Press, 2000), ch. 10; Kate Flint, *The Woman Reader 1837–1914* (Oxford: Clarendon Press, 1993), esp. ch. 8; and Christine Pawley, *Reading on the Middle Border: The Culture of Print in Late-Nineteenth-Century Osage, Iowa* (Amherst: University of Massachusetts Press, 2001), pp. 108–11.

32. Fergus, *Provincial Readers*, pp. 41–52.

33. Alberto Manguel, *A History of Reading* (London: HarperCollins, 1996); Stephen Roger Fischer, *A History of Reading* (London: Reaktion, 2003); Nicholas A. Basbanes, *Every Book Its Reader: The Power of the Printed Word to Stir the World* (London: HarperCollins, 2005).

34. Allan Bloom, *The Closing of the American Mind* (New York: Simon & Schuster, 1987); David Denby, *Great Books: My Adventures with Homer, Rousseau, Woolf, and Other Indestructible Writers of the Western World* (New York: Simon & Schuster, 1996); Anne Fadiman, *Ex Libris: Confessions of a Common Reader* (New York: Farrar, Straus & Giroux, 1998); Harold Bloom, *How to Read and Why* (New York: Scribner, 2000); Azar Nafisi, *Reading Lolita in Tehran* (New York: Random House, 2003).

35. Long, *Book Clubs*, pp. 147–8.

36. Stephen Greenblatt, 'Presidential Address 2002: "Stay, Illusion" – On Receiving Messages from the Dead,' *PMLA*, 118 (May 2003), 417–26.

37. Brannon, *Who Reads* Ulysses?, pp. 9–10.

38. Jennifer Howard, 'At the MLA, publishers discuss what's new,' *Chronicle of Higher Education*, 13 January 2006, A17.

39. William Deresiewicz, 'Professing literature in 2008,' *Nation*, 11 March 2008.

2
Commodity Readers: An Introduction to a Frame for Reading

Simon R. Frost

In the history of human conduct, the studied readings of national philology form only a fragment, for reading does not always comprise literary critical interpretation and aesthetic judgement. In the custody of other habits, other types of reading are clearly possible. So what kinds of other readings have occurred? Empirical studies have begun investigating reading evidence, gathered in searchable databases, but they remain largely evidential fragments and for the most part remain mute on the performance of 'a reading'. To conduct a reading of a work, no matter how alternative, might risk sending the empiricist back into the domain of criticism, thus staking out the 'reading' as the fault line that separates histories of the book from comparative literary study.

One alternative discourse to scholarly aesthetics is economics. Exclusion of the moneyed interest appears in the aesthetic theorization of Kant, its repercussions flowing into Adorno and Horkheimer's accusations of 1944.[1] The apparent opposition appears as a *cause célèbre* in much subsequent criticism of the Frankfurt school.[2] Ignoring for a moment that all texts published by the booktrade involve a commercial element, it is still reasonable to assert that any reading undertaken within a discursive frame of economics should reproduce an experience of the text ungoverned by accepted literary-critical criteria. In this chapter, therefore, I will consider one such way of reading, which I have coined 'a commodity reading'. I will examine its historical pertinence, how it differs from reception theory, how commodity decoding contrasts to literary hermeneutics, and the relevance of free indirect discourse and framing. I will introduce the idea of 'goods' or satisfactions the commodity reader can decode when treating the work as a bibliographic and linguistic resource. Finally, I offer a résumé of a commodity reading of George Eliot's *Middlemarch* (1871–72). However, rather than remain within theory, I explore the commodity reading's plausibility by comparison: to the few extant remarks of contemporary readers, and to the satisfactions foregrounded in rival print products as well as rival spin-off products, from Eliot bicycles to Eliot ketchup.[3] Besides the literary-aesthetic value of *Middlemarch*, concomitant commodified appeals can be identified that are exploited by the material book and by other rival products, explaining why such a work finds an enduring appeal in a commodity culture. The commodity reading, therefore, is only useful in that it provides a plausible articulation of appeals made by a group of products and that it offers a fragment of theorization back to a larger empirical project.

Historical pertinence

The term 'commodity' is extremely specific. As Arjun Appadurai indicates, commodities predate industrial and even monetarized societies. A commodity, 'refer[s] to things that, at a certain *phase* in their careers and in a particular *context*, meet the requirements of commodity candidacy'; this applies equally to the necklaces and arm-shells used in the kula exchange system of the Western Pacific, 'the best documented example of a non-Western, preindustrial, nonmonetized, translocal exchange system', as to any item from a class of industrialized manufactured goods.[4] To paraphrase Appadurai, the question is not 'what is a commodity?' but what contexts justify the term 'commodification'.

For commodification, all that is required is material, human intervention and exchange. Material must be worked upon and exchanged in an economy, which can be characterized in any number of ways, such as a barter economy or a mercantile or free-trade economy. Marx's definition of the commodity follows these lines, in proposing that the value commodities supply to be the disembodied labour that has gone into the commodity's production; all of which is a simplification of Marx's discussion of commodities in *Capital*.[5] All kinds of published writing, therefore, from incunabula to T. S. Eliot qualify as commodities.

Commodity culture, however, although conceptually possible, is hard to imagine without industrialization. Thomas Richards finds commodity culture emerging in Britain from the second half of the nineteenth century,[6] a period of increasing affluence among the labouring classes necessary for the large-scale consumption described by W. H. Fraser in *The Coming of the Mass Market 1850–1914*.[7] Richards deploys the term first for the Victorian middle classes and later to the labouring classes, when and where enough surplus income and leisure time allow for goods to be purchased. Frank Trentmann, in *Free Trade Nation* (2008), identifies a period from the late 1870s until the First World War in which the policy of free trade (and consumption in general) was seen as a driving force in a popular democratic project to further the welfare of the British people. Any delineation of commodity culture in Britain, Trentmann notes, places its emergence when 'Free Trade culture played a decisive role in launching a whole new self-conscious interest: the "consumer".'[8]

Commodity culture is not a useful term for all places and all people; even today, there may be pockets of a subsistence economy where commodity culture has yet to penetrate. The term 'commodity culture' appears in a number of literary studies, including Christoph Lindner's *Fictions of Commodity Culture* (2003), Catherine Waters' *Commodity Culture in Dickens's Household Words* (2008) and Andrew Miller's *Novels Behind Glass: Commodity Culture in Victorian Narrative* (1995).[9] Often the definition is loose: 'By the mid-nineteenth century, the increasing influence of capitalism on everyday life generated in Britain what has come to be known as "commodity culture."'[10] However, life influenced by capitalism could easily be discussed in terms of market logic, without recourse to culture. Instead, I propose defining commodity culture as a description for the praxis of a body of people who attempt to satisfy private wants through the acquisition of commodities, and not through collective political or religious action. The drive to satisfy human wants, from the most mundane to the most existential, does not lack profundity; commodity culture is the cultural condition in which we read now, whatever the age of the literary work, and, if the prophets of neo-liberal globalization are to be believed, then quantitively more so. This, then, is the sketch of a boundary within which the commodity reading takes place.

Reception

Rezeptionsästhetik is inadequate for a commodity reading, for reasons of both materiality and readerships. First, materiality: as textual criticism asks constantly, which version comprises the text? The manuscript, first published or last authorized version, or a subsequently edited scholarly edition? Which document provides an adequate witness for the work? All documents collectively, or each partially, but inadequately by any single one? For a sociology of texts, the material work involves more than lexical signs alone. Format (serialization, parts, multiple or single volume) and dimensions (its bibliographic code) provide signs, important enough for publishers to invest in, to say nothing of signs accumulated from price, distribution and sales. The gaps that appear between writers, printers, distributors, readers and retailers, as Chartier says, 'is rightly the space in which meaning is constructed, [it] has too often been forgotten not only by classical literary history . . . but even by *Rezeptionstheorie*.'[11]

Rezeptionstheorie also reduces audiences into monolithic ideas of readership. It is ill-placed to explain differences of gender, race and demographics, with the same subtlety sometimes reached by marketing. Unlike a marketing department, reception theory supposes interpretation primarily according to literary history: to interpret text doubly, both as an immediate experience of the text and in interaction with texts previously read. Interpretation becomes a play of literary conventions, and the reader's memory of them, but the commodity reader's personal, private experience (*Erfahrung* of life) is much broader than this frame of literary conventions. A shopper's experience is not something wholly construed by texts (though advertisers wish they were), and the shopper's choice is complex. Some would reduce the audience into poachers and therefore game-keepers, but within the commodity frame we should note, along with G. H. Lewes (George Eliot's partner) writing anxiously to Blackwood's business manager about the sales of *Middlemarch*, 'but 'tis an incalculable animal the general reader!'[12]

Decoding, hermeneutics and textual unity

Literary hermeneutics involves interpretation, but to what degree? In *Psychonarratology* (2003), Bortolussi and Dixon differentiate between degrees of the interpretive act.[13] A simple cognitive operation to decode a sign differs from discourse processing. Conversely, to process a discourse by generating meanings from interactions between semantic units in a narrative (such as via knowledge discrepancies between narrator, focaliser and focalized) is something different from a sophisticated literary hermeneutic investigation of a formal unity.

Common to all literary hermeneutics is a loyalty to the text as something irreducibly singular, i.e. that the text, however that may be defined, should be considered as a unified whole. Literary interpretation directs itself at a textual unity, whether the signs include paratext or other signs from the material surface, or not (the New Critical variant simply 'reads' an autonomous lexical text, freed of historical or biographic contexts). The commodity reader, on the other hand, has no such loyalty to unified form, and is apt to pick and mix. A commodity reading might explain how an individual decodes textual fragments in order to generate not meanings, but a list of potential benefits. When read for the commodity, the work is best described as an open list of benefits perceived by an individual user, rather than a formal unity.

George Acorn (1911) when unhindered by belt-buckle fights and numbing poverty, found that 'George Eliot in those days I read solely for the story. I used to skip the parts that moralized, or painted verbal scenery, a practice at which I became very dexterous.'[14] George Holyoake, former chartist, cooperative socialist and the last man to be jailed for atheism in Britain, found an unlikely socialist role model in *Middlemarch's* fictional Caleb Garth.[15] A diary entry for Sarah Jewett states 'Perhaps I read my Middlemarch too late in the evening but I find very dull stretches in it now and then. But think of Mr Casaubon being but forty five at the time of his marriage!'[16] The key point of such 'readings' is their selectiveness, coupled to a willingness to decode textual fragments according to the contexts of private wants. By judiciously selecting from the same work, Acorn, Holyoake and Jewett manage to find a good story, a role model for socialism and gossipy drama respectively.

Free indirect discourse and framing

Like literary hermeneutics, the commodity reading is also an interpretation. However, the work under consideration is conceived only as a supplier of goods and benefits, quite different from meanings: commodity reading is directed towards an inventory of goods worth acquiring. The list is in principle endless, limited only by the capricious interpretative abilities of actual readers. The experience that determines which item is valuable lies not within texts but within commodity culture, itself primarily a matter of social relations; the

identity of valuable items will change along with changes in commodity values. What is valuable in one year, to a particular audience,
has a different kind of stability shaped by different kinds of forces,
than the values of the literary critical heritage. Both the commodity
and critical reading involves hermeneutics, but of a different order.

A key to the ambiguity of fiction – and hence its potential commercial adaptability – lies in free indirect discourse. An example of this
from *Middlemarch* comes from a description of Joshua Rigg: 'I will add
that his finger nails were scrupulously attended to, and that he [Rigg]
meant to marry a well-educated young lady (as yet unspecified) whose
person was good, and whose connections, in a solid middle-class way,
were undeniable.'[17] If this is read as direct reporting of Rigg's intentions then the sentence neutrally imparts information. We are then
in a position to establish Rigg as a good sign, if we approve of clean
nails, marriage, education and middle-class solidity. If the sentence
is decoded as indirect representation, then the narrator comments
on Rigg's intentions, possibly in disapproving sarcasm; we therefore
discover that Rigg is not supposed to be an index of good. Further
collisions between Rigg and other perceived goods throughout the
narrative form our opinion. The commodity reading avails itself of
Bakhtinian polyphony, although in its reduction of the text to a
finite set of positive values, is by rights, anti-Bakhtinian. Free indirect
discourse allows the commodity reader to align the text with their
own private set of values. The commodity reader reads in their own
favour.

Implied in the commodity reading is a conception of framing.[18]
The discursive frame, whether aesthetic or economic, enables the sign
to signify in the way it can, what Derrida calls the 'parergon'.[19] In
Framing the Sign (1988), Jonathan Culler describes frames as critical,
social and historical contexts, stressing that these contexts are something we produce.[20] David Lodge argues similarly in '*Middlemarch* and
the idea of the Classic Realist Text' that 'the meaning of an utterance
is determined entirely by its context and the interpretative assumptions that are brought to it'.[21] It should therefore be possible for a
reader's interpretation to be enabled by a commodity context, for as
Culler notes, 'meaning is context bound but context is boundless'.[22]
An example might be the verisimilitude of Eliot's writing, especially
the descriptions of her rural Warwickshire childhood. For Lodge's formalist criticism, Eliot's verisimilitude is a key feature in the evolution

of realism. In another context (e.g. for someone marooned in an industrial metropolis in the 1870s), Eliot's truthfulness to geographic location could signify the rare pleasures of a day in the countryside. In the more recent context of twentieth-century urban sprawl, that same verisimilitude might be processed as nostalgia for a world that never was. The frame shifts meanings. What might happen if the alternative is a commodity frame? What sort of readings would this produce?

The history of economic theory proposes the concept of utility and the notion of goods, that an item or service is deemed good if it satisfies some personal need. William Stanley Jevons (1835–82), co-founder of marginalism (the corner stone of current neo-classical economics), described economics as a calculus of pleasure and pain. *Homo-economicus* seeks satisfaction through the acquisition of anything deemed to be good: 'Pleasure and pain are undoubtedly the ultimate objects of the Calculus of Economics. To satisfy our wants to the utmost with the least effort . . . is the problem of Economics.'[23] In normal usage the notion of a good is transferred to solid items, Goods, but the good provided by the product or service does not have to be tangible. The tangible good of 'sitting down' is supplied in a sofa. The good of 'great design', however, is supplied if the sofa is designed by Le Corbusier. The good of a product or service can also be an encouragement, reassurance, inspiration, identity, keys to knowledge, sources of excitement or of wonder or of solace. To apply this insight to a commodity reading, however, requires a sharp left turn into the realm of speculation.

As *The Advertiser's Guide to Publicity* (1887) puts it, 'The usefulness and value of most things depend, not so much on their own nature, as upon the number of people who can be persuaded to desire and use them.'[24] George Eliot, too, said that the greatest benefit we owe to the artist is the 'extension of our sympathies'.[25] In order to find where the commodity-read text seeks to extend our sympathy most, I undertook to search an e-text of *Middlemarch* and create a register of lexical material, and found discernible patterns.[26] The term 'good' was entered and incidents noted where the term was a direct modifier for a second substantive. A total of some 520 hits were registered: noted when occurring at rates of three or above. Approximately 160 did not modify a second term ('no good because a woman', 'how good of him'). Approximately 50 only appear once (good accent, action, audience, corner-to-sit-in and constitution, etc). Idiomatic usage (good day, good morning) was not registered. For textual scholars, the Gutenberg text is extremely unreliable, presenting a corrupt text, carrying no references for source, etc. It is only a rough guide. However, given that users of *Middlemarch* may have come to the work through any number of editions or even abridgements, and that the search is purely a speculative experiment for the purposes of illustration, the method is considered acceptable (see Table 2.1).

The most numerous occurrences by far were good reason and good understanding (20 hits); followed by good fellowship, home, wife, husband (poignantly no good sisters or good mothers), cottages, housing, house, work, marriage and so on, as well as good blood and making a good match. I then compiled a second list of 'Good by association and metaphor' (Table 2.2). I compiled this second list by organizing positive strings. The narrator positively values 'fine yews', 'fine old oaks', 'grassy hills' and 'flowered meadows' (pp. 77, 72, 55, 347). Later, a building's Old English style is admired, which must have 'children, many flowers, open windows and vistas of bright things to be joyous' (p. 72). A string of associations include oak-treed nature, children, joyous homes and Old England. The narrator then tells us that the guardian of Old England's homes is the hard-working Caleb Garth, a man suspicious of intellectual folly. The string

Table 2.1   Lexical good as a direct modifier in *Middlemarch*

	hits
Good reason (18) [and good understanding (2)]	18
Good humour	15
Good fellow/fellowship	13
Good nature/natured	12
Good wife/husband (6) and good brother/father (4): [no good sisters or mothers]	10
Good birth/blood/family	9
Good cottages/house/housing	6
Good food/dinner/drink/cook	6
Good work/day's work	5
Good will	5
Good news	4
Good matches (marriage)	4
Good looks/looking	3
Good income	3
Good berth/position	3

Table 2.2 Inventory of goods by association and metaphor

Gossip	(as character analysis and a response to the epistemological failure of objectivism)
Money	(as a means of payment, not store of wealth or means of exchange)
Food	(nourishing and frugal)
Nature and landscape	(but not sublime)
Light, fire, brightness and seeing	(vistas of knowledge)
Wordless communication	(because words cannot adequately)
Effective words and reliable knowledge	(for strategic use and self education)
Children	(as source and end-goal of good)
Families, extended families and communities	(but not society)
Common values: solidarity, rural simplicity, and hard work	
Good health and true love	(but not unpragmatically)
Improvement	(but not reform)
Small things made great	(the importance of small creatures: squirrels)

expands to include nature, husbandry, homes, family, hard work and scepticism. Such a commodity reading is speculative. Unlike a literary analysis that might select 'goods' in a literary text and present them as thematic keys to the formal structure, the commodity reading offers a loose coalition of decoded positive values, consistent enough to have personal (financial) appeal, with no organizational principle latent to the text.

Table 2.2 draws our attention to freedom from debt, food, both frugal and nourishing, endlessly discussing neighbours, rural, provincial, bucolic values, a productive marriage, private improvement, and so on. An intangible good that *Middlemarch* provides is a piece of worldly advice that urges the 'dear reader' to work hard and pay their debts, to remain intellectually suspicious, and to draw inspiration from nature, glimpsed in the Yeoman's yew trees and grassy meadows. The bundled phrases of *Middlemarch* speak in praise of good health and a happy marriage. The appeal is to pragmatic conservatism, oriented to family and diligence, and perhaps to merciless honesty, which delights in scepticism and the satisfying rejection of absolute knowledge that readers could never enjoy anyway; but *Middlemarch* also signals a desperate need for aphoristic knowledge in what amounts to self-help.

All of these goods belong not only to *Middlemarch* the narrative text but to *Middlemarch* the published product. Eliot's realism is as natural as the careful rural construction on the serial publication's covers,[27] while its intellectualism to console intellectually-battered readers offered 'wise and witty' sayings that readers could not only mine from her text, but purchase in separate publications. Eliot's commitment to her useful realism, what Caleb Garth called a 'sacred occupation' (p. 535) is displayed throughout the Imperial vastness of her eight-book task, for example, in the narrator's 'history of man' (p. 3), and Dorothea's delightful 'little colony, where everybody should work' (p. 452), and above all, through the security of membership in a Middle community of 'dear readers', addressed as 'we' by the narrator.

Is there however any reason for supposing that actual historic readers may have responded to Eliot and Blackwood's publication in such a manner? Does the commodity reading compare to the satisfactions foregrounded by rival print products and services at the time? A major commodification of goods in *Middlemarch* and Eliot appears with Blackwood's and Alexander Maine's two publications of epigrammatic sayings: *Wise, Witty and Tender Sayings, in Prose and Verse* (1872), and *The George Eliot Birthday Book* (1878).[28] In 1870, an essay in *Tinsley's Magazine* wrote that 'the first and chief business of a novel is to give us authentic descriptions of this or that section of the world'.[29] Numerous newspaper reviews, such as those in *The Times*, *The Galaxy* and the regional *Manchester Examiner and Times*, praised Eliot's topographical powers.[30] This quality is also found in Anne Manning's *The Ladies of Bever Hollow* (1858), described by John Sutherland as 'a study of small-town life in the Midlands',[31] in her *Meadowleigh, a Tale of English Country Life* (1863) and *Compton Friars: A Tale of English Country Life* (1872); *Middlemarch* was subtitled *A Study of Provincial Life*. Contemporaneously, Ellen Isabelle Tupper had a *Country Lane, with Illustrations* (1872), there was *Lizzie Blake: Or Scenes from the Life of a Village Maiden* (1872),[32] while Mrs Henry Wood published tales from her childhood in rural Worcester in the *Argosy* (and later in volume form) by 1874.

Bucolic value took centre stage again in 1905 in F. L. Sabatini's *Pictures in Colour of Warwickshire: The Country of George Eliot and Shakespeare*, which utilized new colour print technologies.[33] In 1904, William Sharp published *Literary Geography*, with chapters on 'Brontë

Country', 'Scott Land' and 'The Country of George Eliot'; making capital out of a profound, imaginative landscape inspired by real country, with accompanying drawings.[34] It was precisely this imaginative country that the *London and North Western Railway Company* offered through cheap day returns to Eliot's childhood Warwickshire, together with accompanying guides, the *George Eliot Country* (1900) and *Pictures of Nuneaton & GE Country* (1908).[35]

The children's (and thus family) market was broached by two books, by Kate Sweetser (1906) and Amy Cruse (1913) extolling 'a pretty picture of child life', the 'sober harmonies' of English landscape, and 'the long cow shed, where generations of milky mothers have stood patiently' (Figure 2.1).[36]

This is reiterated in Emily Swinnerton's *George Eliot: Her Early Home* (1891).[37] When rural interest became personal, Guy Roslyn's *George Eliot in Derbyshire: A Volume of Gossip About Passages and People in the Novels of George Eliot* (1876), asserted that Eliot's *dramatis personæ* 'have had a flesh-and-blood existence in the heart of England'.[38] Like-minded titles include William Mottram's mendacious *True Story of George Eliot* (1905)[39] with 86 photographs and illustrations and, following a successful volume for Thackeray, Routledge's *George Eliot Dictionary* (1924), giving the real-life sources of Eliot's characters.[40] L. G. Seguin's *Scenes and Characters from the Works of George Eliot* (1888) prominently carried luxury etchings of interpersonal intimacies (Figure 2.2): a market potential that did not go unnoticed at Blackwood's.[41] Their 1901 frontispiece of *Middlemarch* suddenly eschewed views of rural life (as in all Blackwood publications up until 1874) for drama, namely of Dorothea finding her dead husband in the garden (Figure 2.2). In the vignette from Blackwood's 1901 edition of George Eliot's *Middlemarch* (Figure 2.3) the caption reads, 'She laid her hand upon his shoulder and repeated, "I am ready"'.[42]

Having arrived in Warwickshire on the Great Western, you would need to move around, not by public transport but by private emancipation: the bicycle. By the end of the nineteenth-century, J. N. Birch of Nuneaton produced a range of 'George Eliot Cycles', advertising his machines in the local newspaper (see Figure 2.4). Both cheap and private, bicycles liberated movement; they also became emblems of female emancipation. Robert Buchanan's *Bicycle Song (for women)* (1898), finishes 'This magic Wheel I ride / For now I know God meant

THE GARTHS.

Figure 2.1   Kate Sweetser, *Boys and Girls from George Eliot*, illustrations by George Alfred Williams (New York: Duffield, 1906), p. 138

me / To match Man, side by side!'[43] The emancipation was economic, too: 'They [cyclists] had gained the éclat and independence of riding without the expense and trouble of maintaining a stable.'[44] Literary critics have confined themselves to internal structures of Eliot's texts when arguing over Eliot's feminism. Perhaps Birch's bicycle-buying readers came to firmer conclusions that 'the Eliot' was an emblem, if not of suffragism, then at least of emancipated independence.

Figure 2.2 'Dorothea finds her husband dead in the garden' from Lisbeth Gooch Seguin, *Scenes and Characters from the works of George Eliot: a series of illustrations by eminent artists* (London: Alexander Strahan, 1888)

Figure 2.3 Vignette from Blackwood's 1901 edition of George Eliot, *Middlemarch*

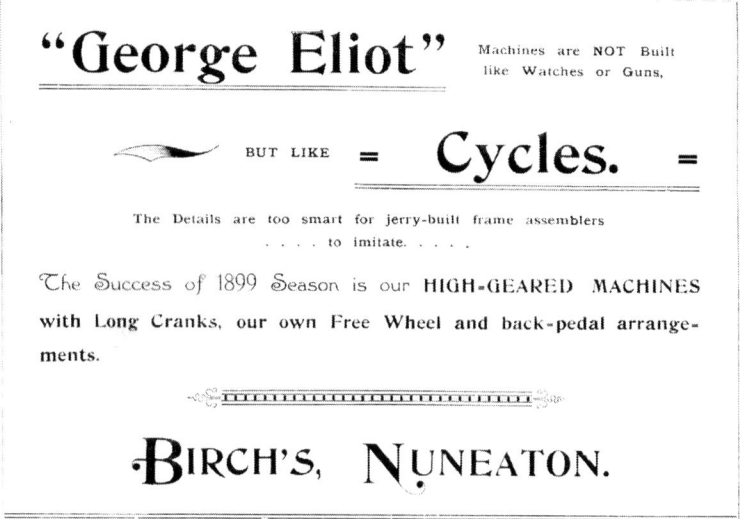

Figure 2.4   Birch cycles from the turn of the century, *c*.1899, Nuneaton and Bedworth Art Gallery and Museum

R. J. Smith of the *George Eliot Sauce Works* in Chilvers Coton, Nuneaton, even produced a 'George Eliot Mushroom Ketchup'. A clue to what was possibly afoot is found in the label. The leaf and berry motif from the cover design of *Middlemarch* in serialization is repeated along with the focus on regional 'leafy' Warwickshire. The label states: 'The ketchup in this bottle is the guaranteed product of real mushrooms, fresh gathered from the meadows surrounding the birthplace of George Eliot.' As Roslyn's book of gossip says in its preface, 'Obvious fidelity to the original sources of inspiration is perhaps more remarkably displayed in this writer than in any other author now living.'[45]

Sharp and Sabatini, Cruse and Sweetser, Roslyn and Seguin, and of course, John Blackwood, knew that Eliot's intangible value lay in English meadows and the people who flourished there, exactly the same site that was a resource for Smith's ketchup. Consider Smith's competitors: HP sauce launched around 1903, again from the Midlands, while Worcestershire sauce sprung from the neighbouring county. Both sauces became worldwide motifs for Englishness, in much the same way as Eliot's Midlands fiction; though in Jevonian economic terms much more effectively.

Literary works – their books and magazine pages, together with their effects on readers – are not solely the custody of national philologies. If we are to understand the relationships between readers and pages, then we must understand what other forces are at play at any particular historical moment. Once those forces are identified, the terms of their discourse can be incorporated into interpretation and thereby generate new theories of reading. There is a methodological advantage in a commodity reading: as a tool to organize large quantities of stubborn empirical material into manageable groups. The commodity reading does not organize solely under the *regis* of literary criticism or of humanities studies alone, but instead incorporates study from the social sciences, such as economics. Crucially, theorization of the commodity reading, regardless of whether or not it maintains internal consistency, should not remain immune as a deduced result. The measure of its worth is not in its internal logic but in its interactions with historical data. Its explanation will suffice until a better explanation comes along. What I am suggesting, here, is that the commodity reading provides a place from which to start.

Notes and references

1. Cf. Theodor W. Adorno and Max Horkheimer, 'Preface (1944 and 1947)', in *Dialectic of the Enlightenment: Philosophical Fragments* (Stanford: Stanford University Press, 2002), pp. xiv–xix.
2. One such criticism pertinent to the history of reading is found in Karin Littau, *Theories of Reading: Books, Bodies and Bibliomania* (Cambridge: Polity Press, 2006), p. 99.
3. I owe a debt of gratitude to Mr John Burton of Nuneaton and to Rebecca Walker of the Nuneaton and Bedworth Art Gallery and Museum, for pointing out the Birch and Smith 'Eliot' products, as well as various Eliot-related publications.
4. Arjun Appadurai, 'Introduction: commodities and the politics of value' in *The Social Life of Things: Commodities in a Cultural perspective*, ed. Arjun Appadurai (Cambridge: Cambridge University Press, 1986) pp. 3–63, p. 6 and p. 18.
5. Karl Marx *Capital: A Critique of Political Economy* [*Das Kapital* 1867–94] trans. Ben Fowkes (Harmondsworth: Penguin, 1976): see Part 1 'Commodities and money', pp. 123–244, herein Chapter 1 'The commodity', section 3 'The value form, or exchange value', pp. 138–64 and Chapter 2, 'The process of exchange' pp. 178–87; see also Appendix, 'Results of the immediate process of production', pp. 949–55.

6. Thomas Richards, *The Commodity Culture of Victorian England* (Stanford: Stanford University Press, 1990), pp. 7–8, 53, 250, and 258–9.

7. William Hamish Fraser, 'The growth of demand' in *The Coming of the Mass Market, 1850–1914* (London: Macmillan, 1981), pp. 3–82.

8. Frank Trentmann, *Free Trade Nation: Commerce, Consumption and Civil Society in Modern Britain* (Oxford: Oxford University Press, 2008), p. 13.

9. Christoph Lindner, *Fictions of Commodity Culture: From the Victorian to the Post-Modern* (Aldershot: Ashgate, 2003); Catherine Waters, *Commodity Culture in Dickens's* Household Words: *The Social Life of Goods* (Aldershot: Ashgate 2008); Andrew Miller, *Novels Behind Glass: Commodity Culture and Victorian Narrative* (Cambridge: Cambridge University Press, 1995).

10. Lindner, *Fictions of Commodity Culture*, p. 3.

11. Roger Chartier [1992], 'Labourers and voyagers' in *Readers and Reading*, ed. Andrew Bennett (Harlow: Longman, 1995) pp. 132–49, p. 138.

12. *The George Eliot Letters*, ed. Gordon Haight, 9 vols (New Haven: Yale University Press, 1978), V, p. 243.

13. Marisa Bortolussi and Peter Dixon, *Psychonarratology: Foundations for the Empirical Study of Literary Response* (New York: Cambridge University Press, 2002), pp. 1–33.

14. George Acorn, *One of the Multitude*, with Introduction by Arthur C. Benson (London: Heinemann, 1911), pp. 49–50.

15. George Holyoake, *The History of Co-operation* (London: T. Fischer Unwin, 1908), p. 348.

16. Sarah Orne Jewett, in *North American Women's Letters and Diaries, Colonial to 1950* (electronic collection) Alexander Street Press, http://alexanderstreet.com/products/nwld.htm [accessed July 2008].

17. George Eliot, *Middlemarch*, ed. David Carroll (Oxford: Clarendon Press, 1986 reprinted 1992), p. 403. Future page references are to this edition, and are included in parentheses in the text.

18. Defined as a set of related mental data that enables human comprehension: Gerald Prince, *A Dictionary of Narratology* (Aldershot: Scolar Press, 1988), p. 33.

19. For a discussion of *parergon* and sources in Derrida, see John Frow, *Marxism and Literary History* (Oxford: Basil Blackwell, 1986), pp. 216–24.

20. Jonathan Culler, *Framing the Sign* (Oxford: Basil Blackwell, 1988), p. ix.

21. David Lodge, '*Middlemarch* and the idea of the classic realist text: revised', in *The Nineteenth Century Novel,* ed. Arnold Kettle (London: Heinemann, 1985), pp. 218–38, p. 233.

22. Jonathan Culler, *On Deconstruction: Theory and Criticism after Structuralism* (London: Routledge, 1983), p. 128.

23. William Stanley Jevons [1871], *Theory of Political Economy*, 3rd edn. (London: Macmillan, 1888), chapter 3, p. 37. See also Preface, v–ix, and chapter 3, pp. 37–45.

24. Cited in Fraser, *The Coming of the Mass Market*, p. 134.

25. George Eliot [1856], 'Natural history of German life' in *Essays of George Eliot*, ed. Thomas Pinney (London: Routledge and Kegan Paul, 1963), pp. 270–1.

26. Search undertaken of George Eliot, *Middlemarch* (Project Gutenberg), online at http://www.gutenberg.org/dirs/etext94/mdmar11.txt [accessed 14 April 2007].

27. See Simon Frost, '"A handsome volume": fra litteraturhistorie til den litterære teksts sociologi' in *Passage: tidsskrift for litteratur og kritik*, 57 (2007), 28–45.

28. Alexander Maine, *Wise, Witty and Tender Sayings, in Prose and Verse* (Edinburgh, London: Blackwood and Sons, 1872) and *The George Eliot Birthday Book* (Edinburgh, London: Blackwood and Sons, 1878). See also Leah Price, *The Anthology and the Rise of the Novel* (Cambridge: Cambridge University Press, 2000), pp. 105–56.

29. 'The uses of fiction' in *Tinsley's Magazine* [1870], reproduced in *A Victorian Art of Fiction*, ed. John Charles Olmstead, 3 vols (New York and London: Garland, 1979), III, p. 8.

30. See Anon [Fredrick Napier Broome] 'Review', *The Times*, 7 March 1873, reprinted in *George Eliot: Critical Assessments*, ed. Stuart Hutchinson, 4 vols (Robertsbridge: Helm Information, 1996), I, pp. 333–7, at p. 333; Anon. [Henry James] 'Middlemarch', *Galaxy*, 15 March 1873, reprinted in Henry James, *The House of Fiction: Essays on the Novel* (London: Mercury Books, 1962), pp. 259–67; the *Manchester Examiner and Times*, cited in Carol A. Martin, 'Revisiting *Middlemarch*', *Victorian Periodicals Review*, 25 (1992) 72–8; 77.

31. John Sutherland, *The Stanford Companion to Victorian Fiction* (Stanford: Stanford University Press, 1989), p. 407. Anne Manning, *The Ladies of Bever Hollow* (London: Richard Bentley, 1858); Anne Manning, *Meadowleigh: A Tale of English Country Life* (London: Richard Bentley, 1863); Anne Manning, *Compton Friars: A Tale of English Country Life* (London: Sampson Low, Marston, Low and Searle, 1872). Ellen Isabelle Tupper, *A Country Lane*, with illustrations by M. E. Tupper (London, Norwich: 1872).

32. Anon., *Lizzie Blake: Or Scenes from the Life of a Village Maiden* (London: Religious Tracts Society, 1872).

33. F. L. Sabatini, *Pictures in Colour of Warwickshire, the Country of Shakespeare and George Eliot with Descriptive Notes* (London and Norwich: Jarrold & Sons Ltd., 1905).

34. William Sharp, *Literary Geography* (London: Pall Mall 1904).

35. *The George Eliot Country, Official Guide of the London North western Railway Company* (Nuneaton and London: The Abbey Press, 1908), and *Pictures of Nuneaton and the George Eliot Country* (Nuneaton and London: The Abbey Press, 1911). Both guides held at the Nuneaton and Bedworth Museum and Art Gallery, Warwickshire.

36. Kate Sweetser, *Boys and Girls from George Eliot*, illustrations by George Alfred Williams (New York: Duffield, 1906), preface: and Amy Cruse, *Stories From George Eliot* (London: Harrap & Co., 1913), pp. 24–5.

37. Emily Swinnerton, *George Eliot, Her Early Home* (London: Raphael Tuck and Sons, 1891).

38. Guy Roslyn, *George Eliot in Derbyshire: A Volume of Gossip . . . reprinted from London Society with Alterations and Additions, and an Introduction by George Barnett Smith* (London: Ward, Lock and Tyler, 1876), p. 8.

39. William Mottram, *The True Story of George Eliot: In Relation to Adam Bede Giving the Real Life History of the More Prominent Characters* (London: Francis Griffiths, 1905).
40. Isadore Gilbert Mudge, *George Eliot Dictionary* (London: Routledge, 1924).
41. Lisbeth Gooch Seguin, *Scenes and Characters from the Works of George Eliot: A Series of Illustrations by Eminent Artists* (London: Alexander Strahan, 1888).
42. George Eliot, *Middlemarch* (Edinburgh, London: William Blackwood and Sons, 1901).
43. Robert Williams Buchanan, 'Bicycle Song (for women)' in *Complete Poetical Works*, 2 vols (London: Chatto and Windus, 1901), II, p. 350.
44. Patricia Marks, *Bicycles, Bangs and Bloomers* (Lexington: University Press of Kentucky, 1990), p. 186.
45. Roslyn, *George Eliot*, p. 5.

Part 2
Methods and Tactics

3
Between the Book and the Reader: The Uses of Reading for the Gratification of Personal Psychosocial Needs

Hanna Adoni and Hillel Nossek

The main question addressed in this chapter concerns the function of book reading in fulfilling personal psychosocial needs, such as knowledge acquisition, aesthetic pleasure, entertainment and escapism in the multi-channel media environment. We will first describe the two main approaches to date exploring communication research – the functionalist and the technological approaches – and then our proposed approach for interchangeable functionality that combines the two. We will then present our empirical findings using this combined approach to study the functions of book reading for Israeli readers and media consumers.

The central approach to communication research grounded in functionalist theory is the 'uses and gratifications' approach that deals with the different psychosocial functions of the media, including books. The underlying assumption is that the existing active consumer audience attempts to satisfy psychosocial needs by means of selective exposure to media and to specific contents.[1] Studies based on this approach found that all of the media specialize in gratifying certain types of needs and that a functional division of labour forms between them.[2] Books were shown to principally assist in fulfilling cognitive needs related to learning and knowledge expansion, and in providing an aesthetic experience. Newspapers, the other print medium, were identified as useful in providing general information and in updating readers regarding political events. Television was found to fulfil information needs but also to enable escapism and leisure time with family and friends. Escapist and aesthetic needs can also be satisfied by books and films, while the need for up-to-date information is provided primarily by the radio. Cinema as well as television encourage social relations and fulfil escapist, aesthetic and entertainment needs. The functional exchangeability between books and television is low, because these two media do not fulfil the same needs.[3] Similar conclusions were reached by Susan Neuman, who investigated the roles of the media using synergy theory and focused on consumers' ability to consume different complementary media, thus maximizing each medium's satisfaction of unique needs.[4]

Criticisms of the 'uses and gratifications' model have been primarily directed at its positivist approach and quantitative methodologies. It was also claimed that it is too psychological, relating solely to the needs of individual consumers, and thus cannot easily explain issues of a more general social nature. An overwhelming majority of such studies have focused on assessing the consumption of different media (television, books, newspapers and so forth) and to a large degree neglect consumers' relations with the varied contents of these media. It has also been asserted that the approach's primary methodological assumption – that individuals are capable of assessing their own media usage – has not been proven sufficiently. Altogether, critics have expressed doubt as to whether the 'uses and gratifications' approach has indeed helped further understanding of the meaning of media consumption for the audience of consumers. After reviewing these critical notions, Dennis McQuail pointed out the contribution of previous studies based on the 'uses and gratifications' approach for understanding consumers' media uses and suggested that there is a renewed interest in assessing the value of this approach and its methodology.[5] He suggested that, as a result of the rapid adoption of new communication technologies, this approach appears especially suitable for the study of media use as social action in the multi-channel media environment.[6]

In contrast to the functionalist approach to the study of communication, the technological approach as formulated by Harold Innis and Marshall McLuhan developed the idea of displacement of one communication medium by another and focused on the social outcomes of the invention of the printing press and later the extensive use of television.[7] In his last work, as Paul Levinson observed, McLuhan refined the original displacement theory and proposed four possible types of interaction between different media: amplification, displacement, retrieval and reversal.[8] McLuhan proposed that the dynamics between these four interactive situations are dialectical, as in the classic model of thesis-antithesis-synthesis. The first two stages of this process are thesis (amplification) and antithesis (displacement). In the third and fourth stages – retrieval and reversal – synthesis becomes the new thesis. Recent developments in computer technology and the Internet make it possible to claim that the final stage – synthesis – could also include convergence between two or more media.

Adoni and Nossek's model of 'interchangeable functionality'

We have proposed a model that integrates the technological and functionalist approaches to communication research.[9] As seen in Figure 3.1, this model presents the interrelations between the different media and

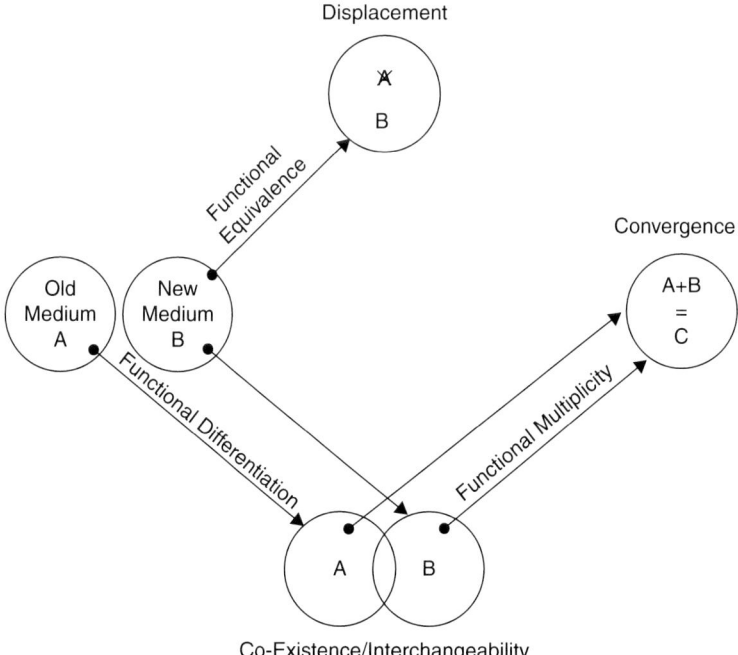

Figure 3.1   Dialectical model of media interactions

their contribution to the survival or disappearance of a medium in a continuously dialectical process. The model presents several alternatives of interaction between new and old media: displacement of the older medium by the new one because of their functional equivalence (telegraph disappears when telephone appears); coexistence of several media when they share a low level of functional interchangeability (books and television coexist simultaneously); and the possibility of a new functional synthesis or even convergence between any given media (e.g. computer and mobile phones).

Following our theoretical model, the main question of our study was how the readers of books use various media consumption activities to satisfy their diverse personal needs in mental, affective and social domains. To what degree are other activities interchangeable with reading in order to satisfy these same needs? Or, in other words, to what degree do book readers believe that reading fulfils unique personal needs or that reading could be substituted by other types of media activities to satisfy these same needs?

Methodology: data collection methods and rationale

We collected empirical data on patterns of media consumption in 2001 from two samples: (a) a representative sample of the adult urban Jewish Israeli population, comprising 520 adults (>21), who were surveyed through telephone interviews; and (b) 96 urban Israeli adults in eight focus groups (12 participants each) that were heterogeneous demographically, socio-economically and culturally, including men and women, younger and older adults, and persons with different levels of education and religiosity. We integrated quantitative and qualitative methods to examine readers' evaluation of the unique contribution of their reading experiences to the satisfaction of their personal needs in intellectual, affective and social domains. The use of a survey questionnaire enabled the examination of large populations and the comparison of different groups. This claim does not detract from the necessity of conducting direct, open discussions with readers on these very same matters, or in other words, the parallel need to apply qualitative methodologies such as focus groups or in-depth interviews. We applied both methods simultaneously, although face-to-face discussions with readers did provide insights not covered by the answers to survey questions.

Telephone survey

In our 2001 study of different patterns of media consumption, we conducted a representative survey of Jewish Israelis using telephone interviews based on a questionnaire containing mostly closed, multiple-choice questions. It is important to emphasize that surveys used in the research of cultural consumption, including reading, may be problematic. In a detailed position paper, Steven Tepper analysed the lack of consistency in survey findings measuring respondents' attitudes among different populations during relatively short periods of time, such as attitudes and patterns of participation in cultural consumption.[10] Tepper quoted the research findings of John Robinson who studied American leisure through systematic comparison of different surveys of participation in cultural consumption activities.[11] Tepper extended and probed these comparisons more deeply and cited a number of factors that may distort respondents' answers and undermine the validity and reliability of the survey. The first factor, according to Tepper, refers to the sequence within the survey's list of questions. When questions about attitudes toward the arts and cultural activity precede questions about reading, Tepper reported that interviewees will seek to maintain consistency with the stances they established earlier and will match their reading responses to what they reported regarding their other cultural behaviour.

Inconsistent wording of the questions is also a factor that weakens the validity and reliability of the survey as a research tool for data collection. Tepper found that even the smallest differences in wording can produce different results. Similarly, some questions, especially those pertaining to cultural consumption like book reading, can arouse social desirability and therefore biased answers. A third difficulty can arise from the context, length and method of the interview itself. An overly long interview can cause interviewee fatigue. Telephone versus face-to-face interviews versus completion of the interview as part of a group may also influence the content of responses.

Finally, sample variation and sampling methods can be problematic. In comparing two representative samples, for example, Robinson found that in one a slight overrepresentation of persons with higher education and income led to its higher frequency of cultural consumption. In a number of activities like book reading, women comprise a larger proportion of the audience; therefore, over-representation or under-representation of one gender group can influence data. Related to sampling is the problem inherent in different groups' varying degrees of response to researchers' recruitment outreach, which can cause bias in sample selections. It may be the case that persons who agree to provide information about their cultural consumption are those who are more interested in such activities. In our studies we tried to avoid some of these pitfalls by using representative, randomly chosen samples.

Focus groups

In an attempt to exploit all the advantages of the survey methodology yet to overcome some of its disadvantages, we also used the focus group method. Each focus group included nine to ten participants who were not subgroups of the survey sample. These groups were heterogeneous in terms of gender, age, socioeconomic status and degree of religiosity. They also included newly arrived immigrants from the former Soviet Union and representatives of Arab communities in Israel. Statements by focus group participants provided an additional view of the way in which readers perceive the meaning of the experience of reading books and its special contribution. The focus groups were conducted by both authors in volunteering participants' homes and lasted for about one hour. Guidelines for discussion were based on the survey questionnaire, providing in-depth examination of their attitudes. The discussions of the focus groups were conducted in Hebrew, recorded and transcribed by the authors and their research assistants. All the quotations below were derived from these transcriptions and translated by the authors.

Results

First, the survey and focus group results will be presented in terms of how the different media meet consumers' intellectual, affective and social needs. Second, we will report on the findings for the interchangeability between reading and other media for fulfilling personal needs.

Intellectual needs: learning, self-enrichment and self-reflexivity

The central finding of our research (Table 3.1) shows that reading books still contributed more than any other media consumption activity to satisfy intellectual curiosity. This tendency was most pronounced among the young, the educated and the religiously observant readers. Similarly, a considerable difference emerged between the proportion

Table 3.1 Percentage of interviewees reporting that media consumption assists them in fulfilling psychosocial needs

Psychosocial need	Media consumption activity			
	Reading books	Reading newspapers	Viewing television	Surfing the Internet
Cognitive:				
Learning and professional study	76	52	55	54
Engaging in self-reflexivity/critique	49	57	53	37
Learning about self and life	72	44	51	35
Affective:				
Being entertained; escaping reality	62	43	76	44
Having aesthetic experiences	63	30	55	28
Instrumental (contacts):				
Contacting persons sharing same interests	47	45	48	46
Being with friends	31	30	48	46
Talking with friends	53	43	46	37
Being with family	44	31	55	22
Talking with family	50	44	50	28

of persons who testified that reading assisted them in learning more about themselves and the proportion who thought that other media were more useful for that purpose.

The focus group data suggested that the connection between study and book reading was grounded in the image that the book has in Jewish society (as well as in secular Israeli society) as the ultimate source for study and knowledge expansion. One female focus group participant (Orna, age 45, with postsecondary education), claimed: 'It is important to read for knowledge enrichment.' Arnon (male, 51, college educated) stated that reading 'develops more thinking about ideas'. Uzi (male, 38, college educated) said that it 'develops the imagination – you have to construct the scene in your imagination'. Uzi reported that when reading a book 'you are with yourself . . . in your own world'. According to Orna, reading a book 'turns you inward and may even cause you to take stock of your life'.

Likewise, Shani (male, 28, college educated) declared that he 'read informative books. When my wife was pregnant I read about pregnancy. Now I am reading about child development.' Other readers who reported using books for guidance included Rachel (54, college educated), who read 'books about travelling abroad, cookbooks; I come across them everyday' and David (39, college educated, immigrated 20 years ago), who reported reading 'different types of atlases, encyclopaedias of the history of the country, a medical encyclopaedia, books used for information'. Another need that emerged from the focus group data was to share information from books with friends. As Uzi noted, 'after I told people about the books such as the one on the topic of cholesterol, they were interested, so I bought them one as a present'.

Beyond book reading, the Internet continued to establish itself as a growing means for providing consumers with information on an exceptionally wide range of topics. Even though the computer was a relatively new medium adopted by only some of the respondents in 2001, half of the research respondents described it as assisting them in study and professional learning – a rate similar to television viewing and reading newspapers. Both television viewing and newspaper reading were perceived to be useful for civic and political participation in a democratic society. More than three-quarters of the research respondents claimed that viewing television and reading newspapers assisted them in keeping abreast of what was happening in the country. Close to two-thirds of respondents used these media to follow the government's functioning and close to half claimed that these activities influenced their decisions to vote for a party or candidate.

Affective needs: enjoyment and pleasure, aesthetic experience, entertainment and escapism

Reading books and viewing television contributed more than any other media consumption activity to respondents' satisfaction of affective needs. According to two-thirds of the respondents, reading books excelled in providing aesthetic experiences, whereas television viewing provided the most entertaining experiences. The emphasis on reading as a private time in which a person has privacy and derives pure personal enjoyment was described by Orly (female, 40, college educated): 'This pleasure is private. I find time to read, devote time to myself. When I am reading a book, it is with me throughout the day. Reading a book is an escape, relaxation, the greatest form of rejuvenation that there is. It is a pleasure. To think about other matters and worlds.' Liora, her friend (female, 50s, postsecondary), emphasized being able to escape from the realities of everyday life: 'It frees me from stress. It is fun. I enjoy it. It lures me into other worlds, sometimes inward.' Tzvia (female, 50s, postsecondary) reinforced these statements: 'You do indeed break away with a book but you return much more connected to reality. There is continuity with it, as I am compelled to share what I read with others. When I am reading – I am cut off from reality and when I return – I am strong and more complete and want to continue.' Aliza (50, college educated) asserted: 'Reading is pure pleasure. It is the added value of my leisure time. I don't see my life without books. Choice is not accidental. You go for a particular type and it is important that I can speak about it afterwards.'

As expected, television viewing, too, contributed to satisfying the need for entertainment and detachment from everyday reality, but differently from reading books. Whereas reading books emphasized the connection with other worlds as well as the return from them, television viewing was described as much more escapist. Tzafrir (male, 27, college educated) described this in the following manner: '[In a] half-hour series you don't have to think too much, primarily in daily reruns from the past such as *MacGyver* or *The A-Team*. You watch it in order to feel like a sack of potatoes.' Reading books also exceeded other activities in providing aesthetic experiences and satisfaction. More women than men thought that reading provided them with an aesthetic experience both in terms of contents and the language of the books that they were reading.

Social needs: relations with family, friends, persons with the same interests

Reading books contributed more topics for conversation among friends and family members than any other media consumption activity; however, reading newspapers and television, too, were an abundant source of topics for conversation. In regard to media fulfilling the need to be in contact with persons who share the same interests, it appeared that surfing the Internet resembled all the other media consumption activities; each activity fulfilled this social need for about half of the respondents.

Focus group participants reported that they participated in conversations about books with friends, parents, children and their spouses.

Orna (female, 45, postsecondary) stated: 'Reading a book is like having a telephone conversation with a friend.' Nelly (female, 40s, postsecondary, an immigrant from former Soviet Union) stated: 'I discuss one book with my mother, the children tell me about other books, and I discuss yet other books with them.' Alex (male, 27, college educated, an immigrant from former Soviet Union) expressed this social interaction as follows: 'My mother recommended a detective story in Russian, one from a series. So I read it – and then the entire series.' Uzi (38, college educated) commented that he 'read it [*Who Moved My Cheese?*] because my wife read it and said that it would change the life of whoever reads it'. Gila (female, 48, college educated) concurred: 'I primarily read books that my 14 year old daughter selects. *Harry Potter* books. The discussions are with her, she is the one who loves books, writes prose and poetry.' Bosmat (female, 32, college educated) explained that her book choices stem 'from friends' recommendations or my mother or I go to shops and get caught up with a bestseller, skim thought it, read the blurb on the back cover, and purchase whatever seems interesting to me'. And Mickey (male, 25, college educated) described his conversations about books with others: 'friends who are interested in science fiction try to get me interested in it and recommend books. The local Rabbi tries to interest me in the latest book by a certain Rabbi.'

Reading was noted as a topic of conversation with workmates and in encounters with friends, as related by the following participants. Ella (40s, postsecondary) declared that she 'read books that people are discussing. I want to be up to date.' Orna (female, 45, postsecondary) discussed 'books that I have read with colleagues at work, friends who read'. Ilana (female, 50s, college educated) was even more involved: 'I also mark interesting sentences in pencil. This is also for activities with friends. Books that I read and enjoy, I recommend to them.' On occasion, family members' recommendations extend beyond literary matters and address the family's identity. Tzafrir (male, 27, college educated) described how reading has connected his family to its history: 'I inherited my father's love of books. When I come home on weekends we exchange books . . . They borrowed a book on my grandfather's community and I read it. It related to the past, the family, and the village there. It wasn't like a book read for pleasure.'

Television viewing, too, was reported as contributing to connections between family members and friends, because viewing is an activity often shared by several people, and because it is easier to find partners for conversation about television programmes viewed than about a book read. Simcha (60s, high school graduate), who had indicated that he did not like to read, stated this very clearly when he observed that it is possible to talk with everyone about television whereas conversations about books are much more limited, taking place on a 'one to one' basis. Simon (60, postsecondary) described the contribution of television viewing to his relationship with his spouse: '[I] see a lot of news. My wife and I love to watch different series together . . . On weekends, if there is an interesting film, we generally watch it together' while Rachel (54, college educated) usually watched television 'with my husband'. Many of the participants engaged in viewing with their children as a way to have a shared experience and supervise their viewing. Shani (male, 28, college educated): 'in the morning I watch animated films and children's programmes because of my 4 month old son'. Yardena (female, 40s, postsecondary) stressed that she was a regular viewer of *The Life of Love* soap opera 'because my 14 year old son likes to discuss it afterwards. It is important for me to be together with him.' Orly (female, 40, college educated) acknowledged that 'because of my children I watch *Seinfeld* and *Friends*', and Tzvia (female, 58, postsecondary), a grandmother, stated: '[I] watch *Chiquititas* so that I can speak with my grandchild'.

As in the case of reading books, television viewing contributed topics for conversations with friends and work colleagues. Iris (38, postsecondary) commented that 'when I used to watch *The Bold and the Beautiful* on television, I would speak about it with friends'. On the popular soap opera, *Touching Happiness*, Orna (45, postsecondary) claimed that she 'felt that it was not right not to watch it'. Bezalel (male, 34, college educated) said he watched '*Sex and the City* because they talk about it at work'. The imperative in religious families to refrain from watching television on the Sabbath is considered to contribute to relations within the family. This stands in opposition to the value expressed by members of secular families regarding the contribution of television viewing during leisure time as strengthening family relations. The first view was stated by Orna (female, 45, postsecondary): 'there is no television on the Sabbath. This is family time.' Use of the computer and Internet were also found to contribute to strengthening relations with friends and family, and even for creating an intergenerational common culture, as described by participants in focus groups. Rachel (42, college educated) stated that 'when you already have a computer at home, you slowly get used to having it there. And, aside from this, if my 6-year-old son is able to use it, why can't I?' And Morit (female, 20s, college educated) remarked that:

> It was very boring for my grandfather and grandmother without a computer. They are in their 70s. We had to write down the instructions about starting the computer for grandfather. He adjusted to it more quickly. He started to play with it first. My grandmother did not have the energy to start learning something new. They play games on it – solitaire is too easy for them now. They are not connected to Internet. This week my mother started to try the Internet for the first time because she was jealous of those who were playing *The Safe* on the net. The grandchildren assisted their grandfather and grandmother.

Likewise, Nelly (female, 40s, college educated, immigrant from Ukraine) related to the Internet: 'it helps me keep in contact with relatives. It is very good for my mother – it is quick, inexpensive.' Yardena (female, 40s, postsecondary) explained: 'my son is on the Internet all the time. It is an exceptional source of information. It is possible to go to magical places. It helps my son prepare homework.'

The use of email for contact with friends was widespread among all age groups, but highest for younger users. For Sarah (22, high school graduate, immigrant from France) it is indispensable: 'I check email, connect with friends who travel abroad.' Orly (40, college educated) noted that 'email is a central part of my communication with friends'. Tzila (female, 55, college educated) explained: 'I signed up for *Friends* and exchange emails with friends from primary school. I exchange emails with 10 people throughout the world who were friends then.'

Interchangeability between reading and other activities for fulfilling personal needs

With the aim of examining the degree of functional interchangeability between uses of different media for satisfaction of personal needs, Pearson correlations were calculated between each pair of media regarding fulfilment of the different needs. The reliability of the correlations between each pairing of media in relation to specific questions was at least $p < 0.5$, but in regard to means no calculations of reliability were undertaken.[12]

For example, the Pearson correlation was calculated between the questions 'To what degree does book reading assist you to escape from the reality of everyday life?' and 'To what degree does television viewing assist you to escape from the reality of everyday life?'

The low Pearson correlations (Table 3.2) are evidence of low inter-changeability between different media activities, suggesting unique functions for each medium. The highest levels of interchangeability emerged between television viewing and newspaper reading, between reading books and newspapers, and between reading books and Internet surfing, while the lowest interchangeability was between television viewing and reading books. The interchangeability between reading books and other activities was especially low both with regard to affective and cognitive needs. A slightly different pattern emerged with regard to strengthening relations with friends and family members, where a higher rate of interchangeability emerged between different media consumption activities. Here the highest level of interchangeability was found between reading books and reading newspapers (use of two print media) and between television viewing and reading newspapers, due to the contents related to current events provided by both sources.

Table 3.2 Interchangeability in satisfying psychosocial needs: mean Pearson correlations between all types of media consumption for satisfaction of intellectual, affective and social needs

Media activity pairs	Types of personal needs			
	Total	Intellectual	Affective	Social
Reading books and television viewing	.17	.15	.12	.26
Reading books and reading newspapers	.24	.24	.17	.32
Reading books and Internet surfing	.23	.27	.17	.25
Newspaper reading and television viewing	.25	.19	.24	.33
Reading newspapers and Internet surfing	.18	.10	.21	.22
Television viewing and Internet surfing	.20	.16	.22	.21
Total (all activities)	.20	.19	.19	.27

Readers' perspective of the book as an object, regarding the aesthetics of its cover and the feeling of holding the book in hand, also revealed that reading books is a very intimate experience in comparison to other media. Orna (female, 45, postsecondary) stated that 'there is serenity in reading. It is impossible to get up and leave a film [in the middle]. You can do that at any time with a book.' Arnon (male, 51, college educated): 'I am not dependent on time with a book, while television restricts me and also gives me what I do not want, such as advertisements. I control my time with a book.' Lihi (female, 42, college educated) noted that 'you finish viewing television in an hour, a film in an hour and a half, while things take much longer in a book. A book activates your imagination. You are with yourself in a book.' Uzi (male, 38, college educated) also related to the feeling of control: 'when you read a book, you build the scenery; you exist in a world of your own. If you leave for a moment or an hour, you return to the same place. That is fun.'

Iris (38, college educated) liked the intimacy of the actual act of reading: 'it is not possible to get into bed with the computer or to put it under your pillow' while Orna (female, 45, postsecondary) found it fun: 'it is fun to read books, but this is not so with computerized books'. Ruth (50s, college educated) indicated how she uses the Internet as a source for information about books: 'I look for recommendations on the Internet, to see if it will be of interest to me, and then I go and purchase it.' Yaron (male, 42, college educated) was perhaps the most explicit: 'you have to be respectful of a book. A book has a binding and perhaps a picture, but computer pages are not a book, not at all.' It is interesting to note the distinction made by focus group participants regarding the interchangeability between computers and books for specific types of information and in-depth study. This distinction was more pronounced by older participants, who used the Internet for more specific information and books for more in-depth understanding, whereas younger participants asserted that they were capable of both retrieving specific information and studying by means of the Internet.

Conclusions

Using the combination of two research methodologies, qualitative and quantitative, we found that book reading continues to serve as an important contributor to the satisfaction of personal psychosocial human needs, even in the era of new media technologies. Book readers claimed that reading assists them in learning more than any other media consumption activity; they testified to the pleasure they received from reading and their unwillingness to relinquish it. Book reading provides readers with possibilities for utilizing their imagination, helps them develop self-reflexivity, and serves as an important means to connect with oneself, or to escape into an imaginary world. The strength and magic of book reading is grounded in the emotional experience it engenders and the freedom it provides for the reader's imagination to roam.

Reading books also fulfils the social needs of connecting with both one's distant and immediate social environments, with friends and people who are interested in similar subjects, with spouses and relatives, and it even creates especially meaningful intergenerational connections between children and parents, and between grandparents and grandchildren. It also provides topics of conversation between good friends and colleagues at work as well as family members, and talking about books at social gatherings serves as an agreed way of displaying cultural capital and affiliation with elite groups.

Both the survey findings and the attitudes of the participants gleaned from the focus groups demonstrated that book reading uniquely fulfils emotional needs and holds a low interchangeability with other media regarding those needs. In their attempts to express the elusive sensation they derived from reading books, the readers often used expressions such as enjoyment, experience, pleasure, imagination, escape, detachment, fortification, relaxation, excitement, insight, serenity, soul searching, meaning of life, privacy, treasure, richness, the real me, self-understanding, pleasure from the richness of language and imagination, pick-me-up, relaxation, benefit. These words were used repeatedly in statements by focus groups participants and in their cautious and hesitant articulations that tried to touch upon the unique experience of book reading.

Notes and references

1. See for example the following stuies: *The Uses of Mass Communications*, ed. by Jay Blumler and Elihu Katz (London: Sage, 1974); Elihu Katz and Hanna Adoni, 'Functions of the book for society and self', *Dlogenes*,

81 (1973), 106–18; Elihu Katz, Hadassah Hass, Shoshana Weitz, Hanna Adoni, Michael Gurevitz and Miriam Schiff, *Tarbut Ha'pnay Be'Israel: Tmurot Be'dfusay Ha'peilut Ha'tarbutit 1970–1990* [*Leisure in Israel: Changes in Patterns of Cultural Activities 1970–1990*] (Tel Aviv: Open University, 2000, Hebrew); Dennis McQuail and S. Windhal, *Communication Models* (London: Longman, 1993, 2nd edn.); and Eric K. Rosengren, P. Palmgreen and L. Wenner (eds), *Media Gratification Research: Current Perspectives*, ed. Eric K. Rosengren, P. Palmgreen and L. Wenner (Beverly Hills: Sage, 1985).

2. See for example, Hanna Adoni, 'Media interchangeability and co-existence: trends and changes in production distribution and consumption patterns of the print media in the television era', *Libri*, 3 (1985), 202–17 and Susan B. Neuman, 'Television, reading and the home environment', *Reading Research and Instruction*, 25 (1986), 173–83.

3. Hilde T. Himmelweit and B. Swift, 'Continuities and discontinuities in media usage and taste: a longitudinal study', *Journal of Social Issues*, 32 (1976), 133–56; Elihu Katz, Michael Gurevitch and Hadassah Haas, 'On the use of the mass media for important things', *American Sociological Review*, 36 (1973), 164–81; and Eric K. Rosengren and S. Windahl, 'Mass media consumption as a functional alternative', in *Sociology of Mass Communications*, ed. Dennis McQuail (Harmondworth: Penguin, 1972), pp. 166–94.

4. Neuman, 'Television, reading and the home environment', pp. 173–83 and Susan B. Neuman, *Literacy in the Television Age: The Myth of TV Effect* (Norwood, NJ: Ablex, 1991).

5. Dennis McQuail, 'With more hindsight: conceptual problems and some ways forward for media use research', paper presented at the 2nd International EJCR Colloquium, University of Nijmegen, The Netherlands, 18–20 October, 2001.

6. K. Renckstorf and Dennis McQuail, 'Social action perspectives in mass communication research: an introduction', in *Media Use as Social Action*, ed. K. Renckstorf, Dennis McQuail and N. Jankowski (London: John Libbey, 1996), pp. 1–17; and K. Renckstorf and F. Webster, 'An action theoretical frame of reference for the study of television news use', in *Television News Research: Recent European Approaches and Findings*, ed. K. Renckstorf, Dennis McQuail and N. Jankowski (Berlin: Quintessenz Books, 2001), pp. 91–109.

7. Harold Innis, *The Bias of Communication* (Toronto: University of Toronto Press, 1951); Marshall McLuhan, *The Gutenberg Galaxy* (Toronto: University of Toronto Press, 1962).

8. Paul Levinson, *Digital McLuhan* (New York: Routledge, 1999).

9. Hanna Adoni and Hillel Nossek, 'The new media consumers: media convergence and the displacement effect', *Communications: The European Journal of Communication Research*, 26 (2001), 59–83.

10. Steven Tepper, *Working paper #4* (Princeton: Center for Arts and Cultural Policy Studies, Princeton University, 1998).

11. John Robinson, 'The polls – a review: survey organization differences in estimating public participation in the arts', *Public Opinion Quarterly*, 53 (1989), 397–414, and 'Arts participation in America: 1982–1992' [Research Division Report #27] (Washington DC: National Endowment for the Arts, 1993).
12. See for example, Elihu Katz and Michael Gurevitch, *The Secularization of Leisure* (London: Faber and Faber, 1976), pp. 230–35.

4
One Reader, Two Votes: Retooling Fan Mail Scholarship

Barbara Ryan

Historians of reading range widely. So much so that, in the last ten years, we have variously decided that 'the main problem' is 'where to uncover evidence', at the same time declaring that it is vital to do some 'serious scholarly retooling' in the interests of organizing 'research that links actual readers not only to texts but to social contexts in which the readers lived and the texts were read'.[1] I address this welter of approaches and demands by retooling our methodology to learn more about reading from fan mail. Others have investigated postal responses to favourite imprints, yet under pressure from Robert Darnton's model of the circuit of print communications, most think data as personalized as fans' effusions 'a weak feedback loop'.[2] Christine Pawley offered this critique in 2009 to urge reading historians toward exploration of 'spaces where activities of reading and writing may intersect'.[3] I share Pawley's interest in 'non-elite' readers, 'noncommercial sites' and 'thick description', but rather than explore, with her, spaces as materialized as libraries, I look to show how fan activity can operate at what Joke Hermes calls a 'meta-level of citizenship'.[4] The model I sketch in this chapter has a broad utility, but I developed it by poring over a single postcard – one written by an N. Lubschutz and archived in the Wallace Family Papers at the University of Indiana. My approach replies to historians who query the use-value of scraps of reaction from days gone by. I show how much can be learned from one scrap by demonstrating how my subject, N. Lubschutz, used a postcard to cast a not-so-secret ballot. Intriguing too is the inference that with this penny postcard, s/he cast two different votes.

First-order understanding of this scrap of reaction is simple: by sharing opinions of each of General Lew Wallace's historical romances, Lubschutz acted as a literary critic. His/her opinions of *The Fair God* (1873), *Ben-Hur* (1880) and *The Prince of India* (1893) qualify as an 'arts' vote. Civic, though, is the vote Lubschutz cast by charging that the conclusion of Wallace's mega-selling *Ben-Hur, A Tale of the Christ* is 'unjust to the Jew's religion'.[5] Emily Satterwhite might ask whether this writing reader took an identitarian stand like one she has pinpointed in fan mail to later US authors.[6] However, as I have not been able to find out much about Lubschutz, I cannot comment on the possibility that that surname marks a Jew with a creedal reason to dislike a romance that ends with its Jewish hero's decision to follow the teachings of the crucified rebbe he hails as the Messiah. By refusing that option, I extend fan mail research that settles for 'an especially intimate portrait of a particular author's reading public'.[7] One reason to choose Lubschutz's 1904 card for study is that it is the single scrappiest bit in Wallace's papers; another is the directive, 'Return this', scrawled in a blank space at the top of its message-side, in darker ink and a different hand (this was ignored presumably because Lubschutz supplied no return address). Historians will note with interest that the directive indicates this postcard's preservation in what Stephen Colclough has dubbed a 'chance survival'.[8] To learn more from this chance survival, I examine the late nineteenth-century social shifts that contextualize Lubschutz's decision to send the card. I also survey ways in which historians of reading have learned from fan mail. These shifts affected how US newspapers engaged potential readers – who were also possible buyers and voters.

First though, let me describe Lubschutz's postcard (see Figure 4.1). The mailing side is to the point: 'General Lew Wallace', states its first line; 'Crawfordsville, Indiana' adds the second. Further information on this side of the card includes a date-stamp that marks its sending at 9.30 a.m. on 23 May 1904. A second date-stamp tells us this card took 29 hours to travel from Louisville, Kentucky to Crawfordsville, Indiana, a distance of 163 miles. In addition to a pre-printed frank that carries an image of a former US President, William McKinley, a second pre-printed emblem features an eagle with wings outstretched. Still on the mailing side, the writing starts in large hand but ends up cramped, as it had to be adjusted to the space allotted.

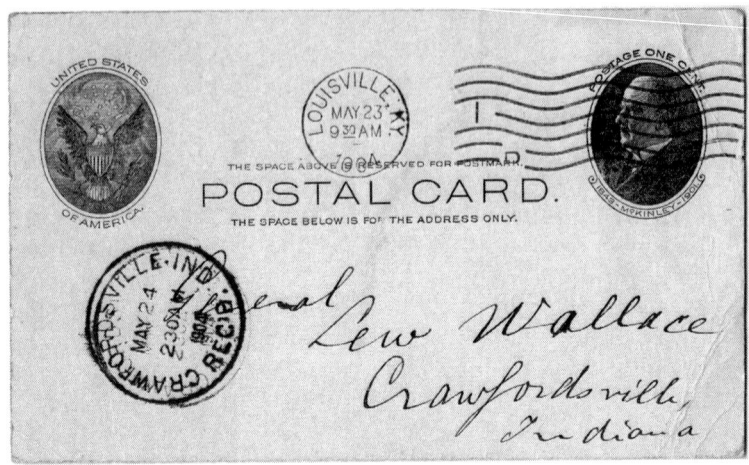

Figure 4.1   Postcard from N. Lubschutz to Lew Wallace, 22 May 1904 (front)

On the flip side, after 'Return this' (see Figure 4.2), is a message in faded, watery ink:

> May 22^d 1904
>
> I just finished reading your Prince of India, the third in order in my reading. Ben-Hur is a work of a genius as a whole although in its last pages it is pueril and unjust to the Jew's religion. A Fair God is a fair novel well sustained throughout. Prince of India is very foolish throughout, inconsistent and weak, relieved only here and there by some flashes of genius.
>
> Respectfully,
> N. Lubschutz

Rare indeed are historians of reading who would smirk about misspelt words in fan mail; however, the failure to recognize Lubschutz as a civic agent is still possible. By finding more than author-reader intimacy in this scrap of reception, I add to reading historians' toolsets. I expect this addition to prove most useful to analysts who consult records as patchy and personal as fan mail.

Fan mail collections can be very patchy, but are they in fact, personal? Theodor Adorno did not think so; in a *Kenyon Review* essay he dismissed fan mail so flatly that it may explain why studies of this form of reception tarry in a preliminary phase. 'In analyzing the fan

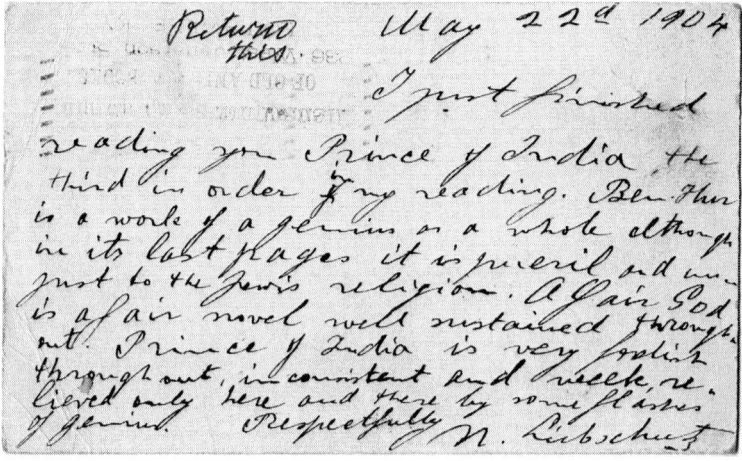

Figure 4.2   Postcard from N. Lubschutz to Lew Wallace, 22 May 1904 (reverse)

mail of an educational [radio] station in a rural section of the Middle West', Adorno avowed, in what was then a high-prestige outlet for new poetry, 'one is struck by the apparent enthusiasm of the listeners' reception, by the vast response'. Alas, while 'exuberant indeed', fans' letters are 'enthusiastic in a manner that makes one feel uncomfortable. It is what might be called standardized enthusiasm', he charged, in that their remarks are almost literally identical: 'Dear X, Your Music Shop is swell. It widens my musical horizon and gives me an ever deeper feeling for the profound qualities of our great music.'[9]

Adorno fails to reflect that people who write to addressees they will never meet have cause to adhere to sanctioned structures. In a richly researched account of 'what mail meant to *users*' in the nineteenth-century USA, David M. Henkins says conventions were favoured by people with less experience of the post.[10] However, they were surely also favoured by many who sent unsolicited opinions to never-met celebrities, regardless of their experience of the mail.

This is one problem with Adorno's dismissal; another drives his act of mimicry. Presumably he slipped from high to low diction ('swell') to suggest the half-understanding of the half-educated. Yet by doing so, he admitted not only that audiences differ but that they can be fervent. That admission does not ease worries (often voiced as certainties) that mass-media (like radio) and mega-selling romances herd audiences like so many sheep. These worries persist despite knowledge gained from 'active reader' research nor will they be eased by scholarship that segregates readers' activities from social structures that guided acts and attitudes. On this basis, I agree with Pawley that historians must find ways to study 'the millions of ordinary readers and writers for whom the technologies and practices of literacy were an indispensable but often taken-for-granted part of their everyday lives'.[11] Adorno recognized the millions by mimicking slang. More illuminating are Henkins's discoveries about 'ordinary' users of the US mail in *The Postal Age* (2007), which gives fans' letters only a passing nod; he makes the vibrant claim that nineteenth-century Americans were consciously proud of a postal technology (also a practice of literacy) that many turned to their own ends. If historians consider this claim in terms of the one-penny frank on Lubschutz's card, they may recall how few readers of 1904 were paid to share their experiences of print. By mimicking fans' slang, Adorno implied that readers who share their opinions, gratis, show a lack of self-restraint that marks them déclassé. Critiquing the attitude that drives that implication, Hermes concluded that 'popular culture links the domains of the public and private' in a way that 'blurs' that 'borderline more than any other institution or practice, for more people – regardless of their age, gender, or ethnicity'; culture that pleases widely 'is the most democratic of domains in our society', she added, whatever 'the commercial and governmental interests and investments that co-shape its form and contents'.[12]

Hermes's input should be considered by all historians who consult fans' letters. Why? Because it indicates how much is lost when we caution that these scraps of reaction 'over-represent enthusiasts and under-represent disgusted or lukewarm readers'.[13] This advice, offered in 2008, is common sense. Prominent, however, in fan research is evidence that the common sense of academic researchers can be contradicted by projects that try to assess how fans see avidity that even their defenders deem 'at least partly scandalous'.[14] The fact that someone tried to banish Lubschutz's expression of disgust from Wallace's papers (hence, posthumous fame), by directing that the card be returned, demonstrates an unexpectedly strong feedback loop. The larger discovery is that talk of over- and under-representation posits only certain kinds of questions. This is a key concern in fan research that demonstrates how enthusiasm for one aspect of a career, or corpus, can lead to indifference for another, while, perhaps, inciting distaste for a third.[15] Variety of this kind is significant because when a fan feels lukewarm about this or that aspect of a favorite's *oeuvre*, that 'lukewarmness' can be far more 'heated' than the indifference experienced by a consumer whose interest is more measured. This approach points out the diversity of Lubschutz's opinions of Wallace's novels. It is right to caution that fan mail is dominated by glowing feedback, but scholars know that especially avid fans can also be severe critics. In Lubschutz's case, it is patently a fan who hails *Ben-Hur* as 'a work of genius'; it is nonetheless as a fan that s/he reports disgust for its conclusion. It is also as a fan that s/he deprecates Wallace's first romance and dismisses his last.

Janice Radway's work with avid readers of mass-market romances may seem a likely source of information on engagements of print as intense as Lubschutz's, but interviews with live subjects offer little to historians who work with scraps of the past. More useful is Robert and Katharine Morsberger's biography of *Ben-Hur*'s author; in *Lew Wallace: Militant Romantic* (1980), they excerpted some of the 30-plus remnants of what Wallace called 'many flattering letters, *Ben Hur* the subject'.[16] They also excerpted a few from detractors, thus offering 'active reader' research *avant la lettre*. Unfortunately fan mail studies have advanced little since the Morsbergers' day. Much can be learned from methods they worked out before Radway conducted her interviews, but much has been lost, too, and cultural historians have been most inquiring in trying to recover these responses.[17]

So far, cultural historians have developed two era-sensitive models of fan mail, both developed in relation to letters written to early nineteenth-century poets. In a study of America's N. P. Willis, published in 1999, Thomas N. Baker developed the model he calls 'sentimental commerce'; eight years later, working with letters to Byron, Tom Mole offered an alternative he labelled 'hermeneutic intimacy'.[18] In 2003, Lisa Spiro showed how Baker's model sheds light on letters to another antebellum poet. This is unusual, however, among historians of reading who bypass opportunities to improve our research tools. I will therefore echo Pawley's praise of historian Joan Shelley Rubin when I say I think Spiro's re-use of Baker's model 'a welcome exception to [the] lack of reflexivity' among historians who acknowledge fan mail.[19] In the case of the postcard to Wallace, I think it vital not only that Lubschutz de-selected sentimental and hermeneutic ways of contacting Wallace but, also, wrote in much the same manner David Paul

Nord descried in letters to the editor of two Chicago papers between 1912 and 1917. By providing 'a glimpse into the past of some actual readers reading their newspapers,' *Communities of Journalism* (2001) showed that letters to an editor might be directed, in truth, to a 'generalized figure of the editor' whose role was to listen.[20]

This is a very interesting charge, with regard to Lubschutz, because it shows how his/her postcard raises this vexed topic: who is qualified to pass arts judgment? This is an arts debate of long standing yet it is a civic conundrum too. Hermes is right to equate cultural citizenship with 'a way of insisting on how politics and pleasure are . . . articulated at the level of the everyday'.[21] Insistence of that sort is on offer in the postcard, intended to remind Wallace that Jews comprised part of the *civitas* in which Judah Ben-Hur was a household name. Lubschutz was not the first to offer this reminder; in 1888 a Jewish paper lamented Ben-Hur's decision to follow Jesus, and this was newsworthy enough to be noted by the *Morning Oregonian* and New Orleans *Daily Picayune*.[22] That is one reason to think Lubschutz's card a civic intervention; another is the decision to proffer an open card rather than a sealed letter. A third reason might be the flattery two fans offered Wallace, apparently without knowledge of each other. 'I would rather be the author of *Ben Hur*', both attested, 'than to be President of the United States.'[23] Tom Mole might smile to think how unlikely anyone was to write, comparably, to Byron. The nexus of art and the *demos* being calculated differently however, in Wallace's and Lubschutz's America, it is relevant that as-civic stands were taken in fan mail sent to W. E. B. Du Bois in response to *The Souls of Black Folk* (1903).[24] If few literary historians have discovered civic effusions in authors' papers, the key consideration may be how they conceptualize their research goals.

That is why it makes sense to develop models for fan mail research which move past sentiment and intimacy. Nord's 'generalized figure' fits this bill. The shortest letter he discusses is a case in point. 'To the Editor of the Chicago Herald', this letter states; 'Sir I am not a writer of any Discriptian, or Speller either, I am only a plain grocery clerk hard working man every day.'[25] This is the entire letter, bar the signature and address. How does it share ground with Lubschutz's less personal card? A hint is found in a passage from another letter Nord quotes. 'You may not give this a thought, or hold it up for ridicule', a woman told the Chicago editor. 'Any way, I feel better for having relieved my mind.'[26] This remark shows none of the emotion of much fan mail, although it echoes Lubschutz's desire to be heard. The same cannot be unequivocally said of marginalia, library records, book-sellers' ledgers, references in private journals, and other sources of information long consulted by historians of reading. All of these sources are informative, but each yields information according to its own tool-set. Nord's research shows how letters to never-met editors may shed light on mail to never-met authors. We might consider how Barbara Hochman's work on ways in which readers in turn-of-the-last-century America struggled to 'get at the author' who seemed distanced by print.[27] Nord's work on a generalized editor-figure may cause us to ask if some readers cared less about intimacy than about securing a platform for self-advocacy. In the collections of literary fan mail I have examined, this possibility looms largest in letters to Du Bois, Charles A. Lindbergh and, surprisingly to me, plant engineer Luther Burbank. Once alerted to its prevalence in these collections, though, by Lubschutz's postcard, I discerned it even in letters that do not seem political, at first.

Nord could have considered an 'electoral' model for the letters he discussed due to realization that journalism is 'the literature of politics', but he stopped short with the conclusion that 'when journalistic conventions change, readers sometimes find themselves unusually perplexed or grumpy'.[28] More attuned to social context is a sociologist he acknowledges. However, Nord acknowledges Michael Schudson's early work rather than the book in which Schudson argued that between 1880 and 1910 'the meaning of the human act of casting a ballot' reconfigured 'the act of reading a newspaper' in the USA.[29] *The Good Citizen* (1998) builds on electoral histories which agree that after the 1860s US political 'campaigns had an intensity that is hard to recapture' because 'electoral politics provided public recreation and entertainment' that was marked by 'impressive, exciting spectacles, offering ample opportunity for public involvement'.[30] Schudson observed that after decades in which local party organizations put huge time, energy and money into electioneering fests scheduled far more often than the once-in-four-years plan that is the norm now, the partisanship evoked by the resultant hoopla was dammed by the abrupt demise of this 'vital democratic theater'.[31] The reason this should interest historians of reading is that the more enthusiastic a partisanship, the more energetically partisans will seek an outlet when avidity is obstructed.

The historical backdrop is simply told. 'Mid-nineteenth-century partisanship was aggressive, demonstrative, contentious, and often vicious', agree electoral historians.[32] Yet political principles were not the main thing at stake while party loyalty meant jobs based on patronage. Instead, '[p]arty membership was a part of men's identity' that required loyalty 'be paraded and asserted in public'.[33] This requirement intrigued Schudson. 'The spectacular political campaigning of the nineteenth century was carried on largely out of doors', he stressed, 'in the streets, with elaborate rituals' such as brass bands, competitive glee clubs, the raising of liberty poles, ribbons in ladies' hats and fisticuffs on certain playgrounds.[34] Festivities that could last all day and into the night, with oratorical flights and torchlight parades, culminated in the public casting of votes. Traditionally, each party printed ballots that flaunted the party's colours, but these listed just the one party's candidates rather than all who were running for office. Under this dispensation, party loyalty was affirmed visually with every ballot cast by men with little, if any, reason to keep their vote secret. That changed when a uniform ballot, listing candidates from all parties, was adopted by 39 states between 1888 and 1896. The shift to a secret ballot was tectonic; most significantly, in Schudson's estimate, it made voting less fun. Freighting this shift further is how urgently the secret ballot fostered newspapers dubbed 'independent' because they lived or died by subscriptions and advertising revenue rather than party funding that wilted as voting privatized. Newspapers had been party functionaries while local elections were paramount; later, they had to go it alone by appealing to as many readers as possible.

Schudson's observation that after this revision of electoral and journalistic norms the 'cognitive demands on the American voter were extraordinary', is more thickly descriptive than talk of grumpy readers.[35] *The Good Citizen* does not stop there, however; instead, it increments the history of fandoms by pointing out that the search for replacement activities, on which dammed enthusiasm could be expended, took Americans to film, dance-halls and car rides. Fan scholars may pause here to recollect Robert A. Stebbins's idea that fandom stands 'at the margins of modern leisure'.[36] More productive is the recognition that before film and cars were invented, vital public displays added meaning to deciding to write to an editor – or author – when ballots grew secret. This depended on editors' willingness to find space for readers' input, as part of their outreach to potential readers who might also be buyers. Neither outreach nor page-space forced Americans to 'take pen in hand', but the importance of being heard, on a public platform, would have been felt deeply by all who had grown to adulthood prizing the civic responsibility of taking a stand. This feeling could have been intensified or fractured by calculations of manliness, Americanness, Whiteness and so on. Clear-cut still is that Lubschutz wrote to Wallace after the demise of 'spectacular political campaigning . . . carried on largely out of doors, in the streets' by citizens who '*enjoyed* politics' they found 'simultaneously serious and entertaining, both intellectually and emotionally satisfying'.[37] The same was true of Nord's letter-writers, but Lubschutz wrote several years closer to the era in which public displays of partisanship brought electoral hoopla to a crescendo.

If we look back now at Lubschutz's postcard, we see more than a *litterateur*. Of course, the card's critical tone highlights Lubschutz's claim to have read all of Wallace's novels even though Lubschutz thought one of them 'fair' only. This nod toward *mesure* sits oddly against the decision to include no hailing as polite as 'Dear General' or 'Dear Sir'. This omission may bespeak knowledge that Wallace's name is writ large on the card's address side. Pertinent to researchers' sense of this will be how they interpret the closing that professes respect, the relatively large blank area where a hailing could have fit, and Lubschutz's insistence on signing a name to opinions so harsh that some would have sent them anonymously. Each of these tactics can be pondered in terms of intimacy, if that term includes shows of anti-intimacy, too. Yet ultimately, that concept is less relevant to this card than is Hermes's sense of the urgency with which cultural citizenship demands attention to how 'reciprocally' politics and pleasure mesh in the ways in which 'we constitute ourselves in relation to society'.[38]

What can historians of reading take from this charge? They may see a rejoinder to William St Clair's concern that scraps of by-gone reception as individualized as fan mail offer 'at best' only 'a tiny randomly surviving, and perhaps highly unrepresentative, sample of the far larger total of acts of reception which were never turned into words in the mind of the reader let alone recorded in writing'.[39] This concern is quite reasonable. But because gapped and filtered collections may hold troves for historians, concern about representative samples must engage counter-arguments as incisive as Nord's explanation why scraps of the past need not be thought 'random'.[40] An electoral model of fan activities can engage in that way, due to its grounding in social contexts.

I note but bypass how this model sheds light on Wallace's crowd pleaser, due to the limited number of researchers who will find that gain compelling. Intriguing to scholars in more fields will be how the electoral model's historical roots rebut psychoanalytic explanations of fandom that drain history from behaviours born in the modernizing West.[41] Equally important, this model's roots in the era of mass education give historians ways (and cause) to find more, in fan mail, than author–reader intimacy. Christine Pawley might remark that searches of that kind affirm uni-directional flows in Darnton's circuit model, but to push her critique further, I will conclude this introduction to the electoral model by sketching a by-product of the damming of electoral energies as the nineteenth century drew to a close. This by-product was a circulation-booster deployed by several US periodicals just before Lubschutz sent the scrap someone tried to remove from Wallace's papers. The simplest way to conceptualize this by-product is to recognize them as book-canvasses that gave the 'ordinary millions' an electoral say.

Canvasses of Americans' favourite, or most respected, books started to appear in US newsprint in the later 1880s. Impelling this surge was a British knight's list of the books 'most often recommended'.[42] Democratic, in contrast, was US editors' deliberative use of readers' selections to compile lists of the greatest books, the best US novels, the top 100 books for a village library, and so on. Edmund Gosse sneered at a frequent result in 1901: 'the presence of "Ben Hur" in a list of "the best books" suggests a grave doubt as to whether the list-makers knew what a good book is'.[43] In the context of a Biblical page-turner, this is supple wit, but in a democratic republic, it could have been a goad to readers who lacked Gosse's easy access to print. Among those readers, Lubschutz represents a cohort whose opinion could be drowned out by majority rule book-lists, compiled from readers' selections, that vaunted *Ben-Hur* in imprints as selective as the *Critic* and *Bookman*, and as mainstream as the *Library Journal*. Printed also in Lubschutz's America were reports of the books checked out most often from public libraries. Filler of this kind in papers based in Massachusetts, Minnesota, New York, Kansas and Washington, DC may seem unrelated to a writing reader in Kentucky. But consider: for-profit periodicals had no incentive to publish opinions like Lubschutz's. *Sniping* about *Ben-Hur*'s artistry might have been welcome, if it incited controversy; barred, though, were *indictments* of the national favorite a California paper called 'the best novel yet produced by an American author'.[44]

I close this chapter with a provocation by a media scholar that returns us to social contexts. 'The point is not whether the audience is active or passive', Nicholas Garnham asserts, 'but rather the fields of action which are opened up or closed down.'[45] One field of research action opened up by the electoral model is the option of de-centring authors to make room for receptors who use a given novel as a platform. Another is reckoning the historical roots of expressions of partisanship in the republic that gave the world Hollywood stars and fan magazines. Yet one more is a mesh of arts and civics avidities, and implications thereof. For all historians of reading – but especially those who think the goal is 'thick description' – the electoral model ushers fan mail studies into an exciting new phase.

Notes and references

1. Sources quoted are, respectively, Teresa Gerrard, 'New methods in the history of reading: "Answers to correspondents" in the Family Herald, 1860–1900', *Publishing History*, 43 (1998), 53–69 (p. 53); Jonathan Rose, *The Intellectual Life of the British Working Classes* (New Haven and London: Yale University Press, 2001), p. 4; and David Paul Nord, *Communities of Journalism: A History of American Newspapers and Their Readers* (Urbana: University of Illinois Press, 2000), p. 268.
2. Christine Pawley, 'Beyond Market models and resistance: organizations as a middle layer in the history of reading', *Library Quarterly*, 79 (2009), 73–93 (p. 75).
3. Pawley, 'Beyond market models', p. 74.
4. Joke Hermes, *Re-reading Popular Culture* (Malden: Blackwell, 2005), p. viii.
5. Lubschutz's card is archived in the Wallace Family Papers, subsection 'Wallace MSS. II' at the University of Indiana.
6. The fullest exposition of Emily Satterwhite's approach, to date, is in '"Resell rural America to Americans": fan mail, migrants, and the pastoral system'. She presented this paper at the Open University and Institute of English Studies Conference, 'Evidence of Reading, Reading the Evidence' (University of London, 21–3 July 2008).
7. Jonathan Rose, 'The history of education as the history of reading', *History of Education* 36 (2007), 595–605 (p. 598).
8. Stephen Colclough, *Consuming Texts: Readers and Reading Communities, 1695–1870* (Basingstoke: Palgrave Macmillan, 2007), p. 9.
9. Theodor W. Adorno, 'A social critique of radio music', in *Mass Communication and American Social Thought: Key Texts, 1919–1968*, ed. John Durham Peters and Peter Simonson (Lanham: Rowman & Littlefield, 2004), pp. 211–14 (p. 213). NB: though 'horizons' may be expected, 'horizon' is *sic*.
10. David M. Henkins, *The Postal Age: The Emergence of Modern Communications in Nineteenth-Century America* (University of Chicago Press, 2007), p. 5.

11. Pawley, 'Beyond market models', p. 90.
12. Hermes, *Re-reading Popular Culture*, p. 3.
13. Rose, 'History of Education,' p. 598.
14. 'Matt Hills interviews Henry Jenkins', *Intensities* 2 (2001), posted at http://intensities.org/Issues/Intensities_Two.htm. Access date: 10 October 2009.
15. Projects that spotlight enthusiasts' selectivity include Steve Bailey, *Media Audiences and Identity: Self-construction in the Fan Experience* (New York: Palgrave Macmillan, 2005); and Daniel Cavicchi, *Tramps Like Us: Music and Meaning among Springsteen Fans* (New York: Oxford University Press, 1998).
16. Wallace's modest remark was published in his *Autobiography* (New York: Harper Brothers, 1906), p. 949. I offer a rough count because some saved letters hover between fan mail and business correspondence.
17. See, for instance, projects as edifying as Amy Blair, 'Main Street reading Main Street', in *New Directions in American Reception Study*, ed. Philip Goldstein and James L. Machor (New York and London: Oxford University Press, 2008), pp. 139–58; and Melissa Homestead, 'Middlebrow readers and pioneer heroines: Willa Cather's *My Ántonia* and Bess Streeter Aldrich's *A Lantern in Her Hand* and the popular fiction market', in *Criss-crossing Borders in Literature of the American West*, ed. Reginald Dick and Cheli Reutter (New York: Palgrave Macmillan, 2009), pp. 75–94.
18. Thomas N. Baker, *Sentiment and Celebrity: Nathaniel Parker Willis and the Trials of Literary Fame* (New York: Oxford University Press, 1999); Lisa Spiro, 'Reading with a tender rapture: *Reveries of a Bachelor* and the rhetoric of detached intimacy', *Book History*, 6 (2003), 57–93; and Tom Mole, *Byron's Romantic Celebrity: Industrial Culture and the Hermeneutic of Intimacy* (New York: Palgrave Macmillan, 2007).
19. Pawley, 'Beyond market models', p. 77.
20. Nord, *Communities of Journalism*, p. 250.
21. Hermes, *Re-reading Popular Culture*, p. 152.
22. Compare 'Hebrew criticism of *Ben Hur*' in the *Morning Oregonian* (10 August 1888), p. 3; and the *Daily Picayune* (12 August 1888), p. 6.
23. Samuel Moore's letter of 1887 is excerpted in Robert E. Morsberger and Katharine M. Morsberger, *Lew Wallace: Militant Romantic* (San Francisco: San Francisco Book Co., 1980), p. 310; cf. the letter, sent in 1885, in which Mother Angela quotes a friend who offered the same tribute.
24. Du Bois's literary executor, and long-time friend, published several fan letters Du Bois had saved which take a civic stand; see *The Correspondence of W. E. B. Du Bois*, ed. Herbert Aptheker (University of Massachusetts Press, 1973), pp. 60, 125–6, 152–3 and 196.
25. Nord, *Communities of Journalism*, p. 251.
26. Ibid., p. 256.
27. Barbara Hochman, *Getting At the Author: Reimagining Books and Reading in the Age of American Realism* (Amherst, MA: University of Massachusetts Press, 2001).
28. Nord, *Communities of Journalism*, p. 270.

29. Michael Schudson, *The Good Citizen: A History of American Civic Life* (New York: Free Press, 1998), p. 147.
30. Mark Lawrence Kornbluh, *Why America Stopped Voting: The Decline of Participatory Democracy and the Emergence of Modern American Politics* (New York: New York University Press, 2000), pp. 63 and 30.
31. Michael E. McGerr, *The Decline of Popular Politics: The American North, 1865–1928* (New York: Oxford University Press, 1968), p. 6.
32. Ibid., p. 13.
33. Ibid.
34. Schudson, *Good Citizen*, p. 155.
35. Ibid., p. 171.
36. Robert A. Stebbins, *Amateurs, Professionals, and Serious Leisure* (Montreal: McGill-Queen's University Press, 1992), p. 55.
37. Schudson, *Good Citizen*, p. 145.
38. Hermes, *Re-reading Popular Culture*, p. 152.
39. William St Clair, *The Reading Nation in the Romantic Period* (Cambridge: Cambridge University Press, 2004), p. 5.
40. Nord, *Communities of Journalism*, p. 251.
41. Psychoanalytic explanations of fandom are important in Matt Hills, *Fan Cultures* (London and New York: Routledge, 2002) and Cornel Sandvoss, *Fans: The Mirror of Consumption* (London: Polity, 2005).
42. Mary Hammond reviews Sir John Lubbock's project in *Reading, Publishing, and the Formation of Literary Taste in England, 1880–1914* (Aldershot: Ashgate, 2006), pp. 93–4.
43. Henry James, Jr.'s literary agent punned in 'The best books', *Lippincott's Monthly Magazine* 68 (December 1901), p. 739.
44. Joseph R. McElrath, Jr. and Jesse S. Crisler quote this judgement-call from the San Francisco *Wave* in 1897. See *Frank Norris: A Life* (Urbana: University of Illinois Press, 2006), p. 336.
45. Nicholas Garnham, *Emancipation, the Media, and Modernity* (Oxford: Oxford University Press, 1999), p. 118.

5
The Mediation of Response: A Critical Approach to Individual and Group Reading Practices

Daniel Allington and Joan Swann

Introduction

In this chapter, we attempt to put into practice Martin Lyons and Lucy Taksa's argument that, when it comes to data, 'the historian's duty is not accumulation, but analysis and interpretation'.[1] With regard to the book historian's traditional materials – sales figures, library records, typefaces, book bindings, etc. – this is fairly self-evident. However, when we deal with the sorts of materials on which it has been proposed that a 'new book history' be built – autobiographical references to reading experiences, and the like – then this principle is sometimes forgotten, because materials of this nature seem to come to us, as it were, *pre-interpreted*.[2] People do not memorize textual encounters and then spew them out unmediated but produce narrative accounts in which these and other events are given a meaning and a form comprehensible within a given cultural context. This means that it can be difficult – in many cases impossible – to get at the reality of narrated events. This has been noted by historians of reading, such as Katie Halsey:

> Memoirs and biographies, like autobiographies, are involved in fashioning an image of the subject they treat. And because the books someone reads can be used as a sort of shorthand to describe the kind of person they were, it is wise to be wary of such descriptions. While they may well be true . . . they may not tell the whole truth.[3]

There are several possible approaches to take in response to such cautionary words. One is to ignore them and proceed as if narrative accounts of reading provided unproblematic access to the stable, objective reality of people's true experiences of reading, perhaps opposing this putative reality to something that we might call theory or interpretation. However, this risks the uncritical importation into one's analysis of the agendas, attitudes and assumptions of one's research subjects.

A contrasting approach pursued by Joke Hermes amongst others, is to take those selfsame agendas, attitudes and assumptions as our objects of interest.[4] The greatest recommendation of this approach, which we might call discourse analysis, is that it enables us to find much of interest and value in what might otherwise seem to be very imperfect data. As William St Clair has shown, pirate editions of *Don Juan* circulated in vast numbers and at prices that a working-class readership could afford.[5] Despite this, and presumably reflecting a lack of mention in his sources, Jonathan Rose is all-but-silent on the matter of *Don Juan*: Byron's *magnum opus* is mentioned only twice in his.[6] This would seem a good illustration of Jacqueline Pearson's maxim that '[e]ven autobiographical accounts . . . may not be the transparent historical record they seem', as '[t]he temptation to suppress facts, even to tell outright lies, was sometimes strong'. Appealing to further autobiographical evidence, Pearson suggests that the reading of this particular work was a 'fact' especially likely to be suppressed.[7] St Clair demonstrates that mentioning *Don Juan* was routinely minimized or avoided by nineteenth-century cultural authorities:

> There are at least eight 19th-century editions of Byron's 'poetical works' which omit *Don Juan* altogether or which confine themselves to a few safe extracts. The lives of Byron which accompany these editions hurry past *Don Juan* in one sentence or, in some cases, omit all mention of the fact that he had written the most widely read long poem of the century. Textbooks and histories of English literature by Victorian professors and educationalists contort their sentences to avoid even naming the book, afraid that even the words 'Don Juan' on a printed page would drive their readers into the arms of perdition.[8]

This situation would seem to have been replicated for the twenty-first century by the new book historical use of nineteenth- and early twentieth-century autobiographical sources. Absences from the source material must become absences from the history that is based thereon unless greater critical distance is established between the two. If work-ing-class autobiographers followed their social superiors' policy of silence on a book, then that policy will be imported into any history of reading that treats autobiography as 'reasonably (if not perfectly) accurate'.[9] Discourse analysis, on the other hand, leaves aside the ques-tion of accuracy, treating autobiographies less as historical records than as historical artefacts – that is, as products of the attitudes, beliefs, etc. that were in circulation within a particular context at a particular time, assembled by reference to genres, registers, modes of speech, etc. also in circulation within that context. If Rose's research has revealed the inaccuracy of a particular class of autobiographical writings with regard to the specific case of *Don Juan*, then perhaps, through close attention, we can find something of interest in the few references to this work that his extensive scholarship has unearthed.

The first of Rose's references to *Don Juan* is simply an item in a list.[10] The second, quoted from the twentieth-century autobiography of 'a housepainter's son who became a Cambridge don', gives us something to work on.[11] Recognizing Lyons and Taksa's principle that, in the writing of autobiography, past reality is reworked for present purposes, we should consider the motives for which an elderly Cambridge don insisted that as the eleven-year-old son of a working-class family, he 'saw nothing in' that infamous work 'but comic adventures, sunny shores, storms, Arabian Nights interiors, and words, words, words'.[12] Of key importance here is the fact that this writer does not simply state that he 'saw' comic adventures, etc., in *Don Juan*, but that he 'saw nothing' else: this implicitly draws attention to the unmentioned *something* that he knew he might have been expected to see. Rather than take this as evidence that a particular reader had read *Don Juan* 'through a prepubescent frame, of course',[13] we might, then, see it potentially as evidence of what it (through opposing) presupposes, ie. the late persistence, in certain circles, of the fear that *Don Juan* would have a corrupting influence on young people, particularly among the lower social orders.[14] Detailed analysis would examine the don's precise lexical choices, such as the studied harmlessness of the adjec-tives 'comic' and 'sunny', or the focus on 'interiors' as the sole aspect of the (also potentially problematic) *Arabian Nights* to be invoked, or the respectably Shakespearean allusion of 'words, words, words' in the context of his book and of other texts produced at the same approximate time. Findings of such analysis might then be usefully incorporated in a larger study of discourse on *Don Juan*, on children's reading, on radical poetry, or on obscenity. Self-reports of reading experiences are problematic on more levels than is commonly recognized,[15] and cases like this one show that certain kinds of reading experience may be systematically under-reported. Nonetheless, a discourse analytic approach enables us to find much of interest in them, even once a face-value interpretation has become untenable.[16]

We do not have to stop, however, at discourse analysis. A third option is to attempt to understand the processes by which representations of reading experiences are produced, and to take the productive processes (rather than the resulting representations or the reading experiences that they appear to report) as one's object of study. A study of early modern reading, for example, might focus on the textual products of early modern annotation practices more as evidence of how those practices functioned than as evidence of a response to be considered apart from them.[17] Or a study of contemporary reading might focus on literary discussion in contexts such as reading groups, analysing the sequence of conversational turns through which accounts of texts and their reading emerge.[18] One could also investigate the process by which a written account of a text or reading experience comes in some cases to be produced and to be accorded a semblance of stability and definitiveness. In all these cases, one is moving close to the discipline of ethnomethodology.[19] As Michael Lynch writes, ethnomethodologists aim to study 'reflexively organised organisational activities, which are produced and witnessed by the local participants in those activities'.[20] Where these activities are made 'formally accountable' (i.e. transcribed) through a conventional or agreed procedure (as in financial accounting), it is 'the *work* of transliteration, together with its organisational circumstances and consequences' that 'is the phenomenon of interest'.[21] Many reading groups delegate particular members to produce a written record of the group's reading, and an ethnomethodologically-informed approach to these groups can investigate the records' production as a practice, rather than treat the records themselves as a proxy for the group's real reading experiences.

In the research reported in this chapter, we observed the sequential production of reading in one particular reading group's conversational talk, compared this with the written record that subsequently appeared, and asked group members to reflect upon the process that leads from the initial encounter with texts to the 'final' production of a new text in the form of a written report. We thus combined a discourse analytic approach with an ethnomethodological approach to produce the detailed account of the group's reading practices presented below. The extent to which this can be proposed as a model for historical as well as contemporary research is questionable, since historical data is unlikely to be so complete as that with which we worked: we possessed not only the published account of a group's reading (the only source to which a conventional historian of reading would have access), but also audio recordings of the discussion to which the account refers, as well as interviews in which group members discussed the connection between the two. When we encounter textual representations of reading, it will often be too late to observe any of the processes that led to their creation, or to ask the creator to reflect. However, we can still choose whether to take these representations at face value, to analyse their rhetorical construction as texts in their own right, or to consider the material production of such texts as a reading practice taking place amongst others (known or unknown) to produce reading as an accountable, reflexively organized activity in a given context.

The discourse of reading groups

Reading groups should hold considerable interest for literary theorists as a site for the reception of literature. While the conditions of experimental studies inevitably distort and misrepresent their subjects' reading practices, as Geoff Hall has argued,[22] reading groups provide case studies in real-world literary reception (as do the works of academic critics and professional reviewers). It must be recognized that reading group discussion (like criticism, reviewing, and other reading practices) will mediate texts in contextually-specific ways, and not simply unveil the typical responses of a mythical 'ordinary' reader. The spoken discussion of books, such as occurs in contemporary reading groups, offers an opportunity to engage with theoretical debates on such concepts as interpretation and reader response, as well as to investigate the reception of specific texts.

   Reading groups are a significant cultural phenomenon in their own right. Jenny Hartley estimates there to be up to 50,000 of them in Britain today, and up to 500,000 in the USA.[23] Reading group-like phenomena are performed through the entertainment media, with Oprah's Book Club in the USA being the most famous example.[24]

Of potentially equal interest is the degree to which publishers, retailers and librarians appear to view reading groups as the target market for a certain kind of middlebrow fiction, a matter that should be of interest from a 'production of culture' perspective.[25] While survey data that Hartley collected with Sarah Turvey indicate that '[n]o [reading] group would dine exclusively at this table, and some not at all',[26] the commercial incentive to cater to this form of group consumption is clearly a factor in the production of contemporary literary culture. The wealth of recent research into reading groups and other contexts for booktalk thus has the potential to contribute to knowledge of literature as well as of reading.[27]

In this chapter we analyse the practices of one specific reading group. This group was one of sixteen British groups studied as part of the Arts and Humanities Research Council funded Discourse of Reading Groups project at the Open University. Meeting monthly in a book shop in the south of England, this reading group had been running for three years at the time of their recording in late 2007 and early 2008. At that time, it had a membership of fourteen to fifteen people of mixed ages (mostly women), with an average attendance of eight to nine at meetings.

The use of interviews and reading group discussion as data

On a simple interpretation, reading group members could be considered to engage in just two acts of reading: initial private reading and a follow-up discussion where books are collaboratively interpreted and evaluated. Nonetheless, this two-act model can easily be challenged. An individual member's initial reading experience is known to the group (and the researcher) only as a representation in discourse. Some group members participating in our study commented that they were likely to re-read books in the light of discussion. Many also noted that, knowing they were to discuss a book, they were likely to read it differently: for instance, a member of this group stated, in the group interview, that she sometimes makes notes before the reading group meeting 'because if I am ever challenged on a point I do like to refer to the text'. The same member spoke of carrying out research for the newsletter after each meeting, thus presenting her reading of each book not as a single act, or pair of discrete acts, but as a continuous process of reading, re-reading, speaking and writing that runs over approximately three months. In the extract below, she suggests that both the meeting and follow-up research have the potential to add to earlier readings. This participant is identified as speaker A; speaker R is one of the researchers (JS); see Appendix for conventions:

A: yes I like to have my own ideas or my own partly-formed ideas I can't have ideas about everything about the whole book but (xxx) you come to discussion with some (xxx) but you maybe not know quite what em and then in the discussion things come from the back of the brain really for me anyhow and (xxx) enter the arena and they get modified or confirmed or reinforced

R: then you go and do a bit of work

A: and then I go and then I go and I want to see it in writing what other people thought about the book and again the same process you know confirmation mmh or otherwise or new ideas something new that didn't arise in the group for the purposes of the written material of the review

The newsletter provides a vehicle for the recycling and reworking of ideas from the reading group discussion as well as from other sources. Speaker A's reference above to the possibility of ideas (earlier readings) being modified in discussion relates to two themes that are prominent across our data. Members of several groups refer both to the different readings encountered in discussion (always presented in a positive light, as a valuable aspect of meetings) and the potential for their own readings to change or be added to (again, presented positively). The extract below comes from the same group interview as that cited above.

C: . . . when you read them it's very private isn't it it's your thing so then when you do turn up at the book club and people start talking about it I mean most of the time I think my opinion or what I thought about the book will change during the discussion or maybe not change but it will certainly be you know lots more will be added to it because there's loads of things I won't have thought of or whatever certainly for literary criticism that's way beyond me so that's not what you know I don't know much about that so if people do start talking like that it's you know very beneficial to what I've been reading

D: I think that was one of the biggest revelations for me was that not everybody agreed with me about the book
    ((laughter))

D: (xxx) I thought I wonder what we're going to talk about
   ((laughter))
E: oh no that never happens does it
   ((laughter))
D: people think so differently but that's that's kind of the point isn't
   it that everybody has different views

While readings may simply be presented as different (with diversity
seen as valuable in itself), speaker C above points to the benefits of
particular types of reading, in this case literary criticism, which he
describes as 'way beyond me'.[28] The value of particular types or levels
of reading surfaces as a theme (and an occasional tension) in the south
of England group, though less commonly in other groups. The extract
below comes from an earlier (brief and informal) interview, at the end
of the group's discussion of Irène Némirovsky's *Fire in the Blood*. Other
speakers have just commented that, in meetings, 'everyone thinks different things' and 'you find out things you hadn't realized'. Speaker
C continues:

C: you realize you read it in the wrong way or (xxxx)
F: no (it's) not wrong –
C: at a different le – no you've read it at one level and in fact there
     is a way of reading it at a totally different level
Sev: yeah yeah
C: yes ((question intonation))
G: definitely yeah
C: mmh I mean some of us are very used to reading books in a very
     analytical way (where) others of us like myself read them because
     really we want to know what happens next and when we have
     this discussion you get (.)
H: adds richness to it
(*Note*: speaker C here is the same as speaker C in the previous extract;
other speakers are different.)

There is a contrast here between two expressed views of reading:
a notion of readings as potentially right or wrong, and a rejection
of the idea of certain readings as wrong. These alternative discursive positions might be related to different ideological positions,
although wc do not have enough instances across our data to identify

these as a recurring pattern. More interestingly, a closer analysis of the interaction reveals how these positions are negotiated between speakers. Speaker B's initial contention ('you realize you read it in the wrong way') is challenged by speaker F. This is an unusually bald challenge. In reading group talk, challenges are typically accompanied by features such as hesitation, indirectness or other discursive activity that mitigates the potentially face-threatening nature of direct disagreement, for example accounting for a divergence of opinion as the result of different experiences on first encountering the text.[29] Speaker C rephrases his earlier claim in terms of reading at different levels; he receives some interactional support (when speakers say *yeah*) then explicitly solicits agreement (his *yes* with question intonation). Speaker G provides agreement (*definitely yeah*) and speaker C continues, further reformulating his earlier claim. After a brief pause, speaker C's turn is completed by speaker H (*adds richness to it*). Discourse analysis reveals, then, not simply the existence of particular positions on reading, but their collaborative sequential accomplishment (and, as in this case, reformulation) in interaction between speakers.

As one might expect, this also applies to positions on a particular text, and even (arguably) to reading itself. While interview data such as the extracts above provide evidence of how people talk about their reading, group discussion data capture acts of reading on the hoof, showing how these too may be seen as a discursive accomplishment. The extract below, from the meeting discussing *Fire in the Blood*, follows on from talk about the author and/or narrator's representation of relationships between women and men.

I: . . . he does say as well the writer says who does – is it the lover that knows the woman or is it the husband that knows the woman
     <mmh>
I: and I thought that was quite a good question I mean
     <mmh mhh>
     <yeah yeah yeah>
I: I don't know what we're meant to make of that question
     <yes>
I: so it's not like there's the lovers
     <yeah>
I: and there's the uhm (.) the wives

<mmh>

I: uhm y'know it – it's sort of like well w – where is what where
    does the reality lie (.) and I I think that was posed quite well (xxx)
    though in a bit of a disjunctive way

J: I agree with you and I I and I was reading it I said well why does
    this woman writer use a male narrator why does she stick to a male
    perspective
    <mmh>

J: but then when he asked that question I thought that was actually
    you g – you get a sense that there's there's more at stake than just
    a k – kind of conventional male view o – of what's going on that
    that that these women actually he doesn't know how these women
    y'know
    <right>

H: he doesn't understand

A: he doesn't know how women tick [really does he

I: [no but that's not what does
    the writer have a view then

?   (well I don't know)

I: cos I feel [that that's left hanging for us

H: [(xxxx) (anything)

I: as the reader like – wh – who is the real person is it is it the lover
    in Hélène or is it the wife in Hélène
    <yeah yeah>

I: or is it both

J: well I don't – we don't know

I: we don't know

?   (well I started thinking)

L: I think we sometimes want that we want that in a book don't we
    we want to know where our perspective should be
    ((some indiscernible speech around here – alternative floor))
    <yes>

L: and we haven't actually got that perspective I mean even if at the
    end of it when we shut the book we think well actually I don't
    agree with that s – perspective we do when we're reading a book
    have a sort of okay that's where we are and perhaps we don't have
    that here because we're betrayed by this man
    <mmh>

Speaker I refers in her first utterance to a question she feels is posed in the novel – whether it is a woman's lover or husband who knows her. She develops this point with interactional support (minimal responses, *mmh*, *yeah* and *yes*) from others. Speaker J develops a different though related point: her initial question of why the author used a male narrator, then her view that there is more at stake than this – the narrator doesn't actually know the women he's talking about. This new point is preceded by explicit concurrence with I's prior utterance ('I agree with you and . . . '), a common strategy associated with topic development, interpretable as contributing to the management of 'face' between participants.[30] Speaker J's point is collaboratively developed with two other speakers (H and A).

Speaker I then shifts the interaction to her earlier point, asking if the writer has a view on whether the lover or the wife is the 'real person' in the character of Hélène, or whether it's both – a question 'left hanging' for the reader. J comments 'we don't know', a point repeated by I. Speaker L further develops the discussion and rounds off the episode: readers want to know where their perspective should be and don't have that here because they are betrayed by the narrator. Speaker L's *we* ('I think we sometimes want that in a book . . . ') may be read as collaborative (inclusive) or possibly, more critically, as co-optative (i.e. discursively co-opting others into her viewpoint, a strategy sometimes used by speakers such as teachers or meeting chairs). Overall the extract illustrates an aspect of reading group talk that characterizes discussion across our data set: that literary readings (interpretations and evaluations) are interim statements (subject to sequential development and possibly modification), contingent and collaboratively constructed (responsive to prior utterances, developed with interactional support, sometimes jointly developed).

Readings are also interim in the sense that discussion itself is only one part of an extensive complex of interpretative and socially interactional practices, including initial private reading and any further activity such as (private) re-reading, the consulting of other sources, and the composition of reviews or newsletters (discussed above in relation to interview data). Readings can thus be seen as subject to an inter-contextual process of revision, part of which is illustrated below, where a reference to Maupassant in the discussion of the same novel makes its way into the group's newsletter. Following group members' discussions of what they see as cynicism in the book's denouement, one member draws a comparison with this canonical author:

J: I think that was I think she's she's writing in the tradit – it seems to me of Maupassant who wrote short stories and there was the the narrator whether he was just a distanced narrator or whether he was telling a story in the first person the the they almost all had that sting in the tail

H: mn
      <mn>

J: where the the teller of the tale

H: yeah aha

J: and the characters of the tale are ultimately complicit in the in in the immorality of the tale
      <mmh>

J: and I thought she was very much writing in that tradition
      <yeah>

J: and it's really a short story

H: that's good that's good
      <mn>

H: yes it is a short story
      <mn>

As is usual, J's reading is constructed with interactional support and, in this case, an explicit positive evaluation and affirmation from speaker H (although the scope of this evaluation is ambiguous – it is not clear how much of J's interpretation H concurs with). J's reading is subsequently re-versioned in the second paragraph of the concise and carefully-written account of the discussion that appears in the newsletter:

> The novella was very well-received by the group, who thought it to be a damning criticism of the mores of rural France, likening its 'sting in the tail' to the story-telling style of Maupassant.

The contrast between the spoken and the printed reference to Maupassant is striking: the latter represents a group interpretation likening a 'sting' found in the 'tail' of *Fire in the Blood* to Maupassant's 'story-telling style', rather than a comparison made by a single group member, to which other members minimally assented. Different exchanges could have been reported, and the same exchange could have been reported differently: 'one member emphasized the extent to which the characters of the tale were ultimately complicit in its immorality', for example, or (alternatively) 'Némirovsky was deemed to have been writing in the tradition of Maupassant' would have reported the above exchange with approximately equal factual accuracy, and yet with very different implications. The former implies an interpretative approach focused on moral themes, but suggests that this particular interpretation may not have been generally shared; the latter implies an intertextual approach focused on the identification of literary debts, and is ambiguous as to whether it was individual or shared. The statement actually occurring in the newsletter has something in common with both of these two, but also identifies the novel's theme with a critique of specifically French and rural mores: a possibility which is not suggested by the above section of transcript, but which was both raised and contested at other points in the group's discussion.

When we are dealing with linguistic representations of social reality, there can be no question of a uniquely and incontestably true report, and what we find in the newsletter is not, therefore, a mechanical, objectively verifiable, point-for-point record of the group's discussion on one particular occasion. It is, rather, a statement of the group's position vis-à-vis one particular novel (and, cumulatively with other such statements, vis-à-vis the field of cultural production as a whole).[31] This position is constituted in its fine detail by the linguistic choices made by an individual group member, and in its very conditions of possibility by the group's practices of self-representation to the social world beyond the group – including the group's authorization of a specific individual to formulate its position in a text intended for reproduction and external distribution.

Discussion and conclusion

Reading group discussion is a highly specific reading practice, and not a model by which to understand reading practices to which access is less easily attained: the utterances of reading group members are embedded in interpersonal interactions, responsive to earlier utterances, contingent on social structures, and endlessly subject to revision. Nonetheless, the same will be true of other forms of qualitative evidence of reading, from marginalia to diary entries to published autobiography, and the above discussion of this particular group's newsletter should serve to illustrate that reading and reading experiences are constituted on several levels through the mediation of social interactions between readers (and, of course, non-readers).[32]

From one point of view, this diminishes the usefulness of verbal accounts of reading experiences (whether written or spoken), since they cannot be taken to give the researcher a window on the interior lives of readers or their unmediated mental responses. This means that without extensive theorization they cannot be used as a substitute for theory. From another point of view, it redoubles the interest of such accounts, since their production can be seen as an important part of readers' discursive activity and an opportunity for them to take up positions vis-à-vis the field of cultural production. Such an approach enables researchers to see the emotions and interior life of the mind as part and parcel of the exterior life of discourse (a principle of discursive psychology) to such an extent that no firm distinction can be assumed between reading and talk about reading.[33]

The above excerpts from one particular group's discourse show reading in progress: a sequence of readerly acts in which interpretations and evaluations are produced, revisited, reformulated, added to and changed. This picture of reading should remind us that all readerly acts – even those made with an eye to posterity – take place in and by reference to a social context from which they cannot be extricated without loss of meaning. Arguably, attempts to discover readers' 'real' responses to texts are ultimately less interesting than attempts to understand the practices that mediate response.

Appendix: transcription conventions

The following conventions are used in the transcripts above:

(well I don't know)	transcription of text between parentheses is partly speculative as the corresponding speech was hard to discern
(xxx)	'xxx' between parentheses indicates unclear speech that could not reliably be transcribed

((laughter))	text in double parentheses describes nonverbal features such as laughter; or further information about the interaction
(.)	brief pause
[really does he [no but . . .	text in aligned square brackets indicates words spoken simultaneously
<mmh mmh>	text in angle brackets represents minimal responses that do not take up full turns in the conversation

Notes and references

1. Martyn Lyons and Lucy Taksa, *Australian Readers Remember: An Oral History of Reading, 1890–1930* (Oxford: Oxford University Press, 1992), p. 15. This study was made possible by a grant from the Arts and Humanities Research Council. We are also very grateful to the groups who shared their ideas and their time with us and who allowed us to record their discussions. In order to preserve confidentiality, any group or individual whom we refer to or quote has been anonymized.

2. Jonathan Rose, 'Rereading the *English Common Reader*: a preface to a history of audiences', *Journal of the History of Ideas*, 53 (1992), 47–70.
3. Katie Halsey, 'Reading the evidence of reading: an introduction to the Reading Experience Database, 1450–1945', *Popular Narrative Media*, 1 (2008), 136.
4. For example, Lyons and Taksa, *Australian Readers*, Joke Hermes, *Reading Women's Magazines: An Analysis of Everyday Media Use* (Cambridge: Polity Press, 1995).
5. William St Clair, *The Reading Nation in the Romantic Period* (Cambridge: Cambridge University Press, 2004), pp. 332–8.
6. Jonathan Rose, *The Intellectual Life of the British Working Classes* (New Haven: Yale University Press, 2002).
7. Jacqueline Pearson, *Women's Reading in Britain, 1750–1835: A Dangerous Recreation* (Cambridge: Cambridge University Press, 1999), p. 13.
8. St Clair, *Reading Nation*, pp. 335–6.
9. Rose, *Intellectual Life*, p. 2.
10. Ibid., p. 85.
11. Ibid., p. 374.
12. H. M. Burton, *There Was a Young Man* (London: Geoffrey Bles, 1958), pp. 95–7, quoted in Rose, *Intellectual Life*, p. 374.
13. Rose, *Intellectual Life*, p. 374.
14. See St Clair, *Reading Nation*, p. 334 for an amusing list of examples.
15. Ibid., p. 400.

16. For further discussion, see Daniel Allington, 'On the use of anecdotal evidence in reception study and the history of reading', in *Reading in History: New Methodologies from the Anglo-American Tradition*, ed. Bonnie Gunzenhauser (London: Pickering and Chatto, 2010), pp. 11–28.

17. See Alison Wiggins, 'What did renaissance readers write in their printed copies of Chaucer?', *The Library*, 9 (2008), 3–36.

18. See Daniel Allington, '"How come most people don't see it?" Slashing *The Lord of the Rings*', *Social Semiotics*, 17 (2007), 43–62; Bethan Benwell, '"A pathetic and racist and awful character": ethnomethodological approaches to the reception of diasporic fiction', *Language and Literature*, 18 (2009), 300–15; Joan Swann and Daniel Allington, 'Reading groups and the language of literary texts: a case study in social reading', *Language and Literature*, 18 (2009), 247–64.

19. Harold Garfinkel, *Studies in Ethnomethodology* (Cambridge: Polity Press, 1984).

20. Michael Lynch, 'From naturally occurring data to naturally organized ordinary activities: comment on Speer', *Discourse Studies*, 4 (2002), 531–7 (p. 533).

21. Ibid., p. 534.

22. See Geoff Hall, 'Empirical research into the processing of free indirect discourse, and the imperative of ecological validity', in *Directions in Empirical Literary Studies*, ed. Sonia Zyngier, Marissa Bortolussi, Anna Chesnokova and Jan Auracher (Amsterdam: John Benjamins, 2008), pp. 21–34.

23. Jenny Hartley, *The Reading Groups Book, 2002–2003 Edition* (Oxford: Oxford University Press, 2002).

24. See R. Mark Hall, 'The "Oprahfication" of literacy: reading "Oprah's book club"', *College English*, 65 (2003), 646–67.

25. Richard A. Peterson and N. Anand, 'The production of culture perspective', *Annual Review of Sociology*, 30 (2004), 311–34.

26. Hartley, *Reading Groups*, p. 155.

27. In addition to studies already mentioned, see: Elizabeth Long, 'Women, reading, and authority: some implications of the audience perspective in cultural studies', *American Quarterly*, 38 (1986), 591–612; Elizabeth Long, *Book Clubs: Women and the Uses of Reading in Everyday Life* (Chicago: University of Chicago Press, 2003); Katarina Eriksson, *Life and Fiction: On Intertextuality in Pupils' Booktalk* (Linköping: Linköpings Universitet, 2002); Katarina Eriksson, 'Booktalk dilemmas: teachers' organisation of pupils' reading', *Scandinavian Journal of Educational Research*, 46 (2002), 391–408; Daniel Allington, 'Discourse and the reception of literature: problematising "reader response"' (unpublished PhD thesis, University of Stirling, 2008); James Procter, 'Reading, taste, and postcolonial studies: professional and lay readers of *Things Fall Apart*', *Interventions*, 11 (2009), 180–98.

28. An implicit deference to cultural authority among reading groups is noted by Long, 'Women, reading, and authority', pp. 591–612.

29. Swann and Allington, 'Reading Groups', pp. 254–5.

30. Ibid.

31. See Pierre Bourdieu, 'The market of symbolic goods', trans. R. Swyer, *Poetics*, 14 (1985 [1971]), 13–44.

32. On the importance of non-readers, see Daniel Allington, 'How to do things with literature: blasphemous speech acts, satanic intentions, and the uncommunicativeness of verses', *Poetics Today*, 29 (2008), 473–523.

33. For more on discursive psychology, see Jonathan Potter and Margaret Wetherell, *Discourse and Social Psychology: Beyond Attitudes and Behaviour* (London: Sage, 1987), and Derek Edwards, *Discourse and Cognition* (London: Sage, 1997); for discussion of its application to reader study, see Allington, 'Discourse and the Reception of Literature', pp. 113–30.

Part 3
Interpretive Strategies

6
Representing Reading Spaces

Stephen Colclough

Roger Chartier's insistence that reading is a material act which 'brings the body into play' and 'is inscribed in a space and a relationship with oneself and others' has had a profound affect upon historians of reading.[1] As Kate Flint notes in a recent reinvestigation of the evidence presented in her 1993 monograph on *The Woman Reader*, a consideration of the difference between 'consuming a volume in the privacy of one's own room, or sharing the reading with others (as around, say, the Victorian fireside)' has implications 'for our understanding' of the construction of 'individual subjectivity' as well as 'for what one might call the phenomenology of reading: the spatial positioning of the reading body'.[2] If the reader does not only engage with 'the contents, the rhetoric and the conventions' of the text itself, but also with the context in which it is encountered ('a home, a snatched moment at work, the domed space of the old British Museum Reading Room') it is of paramount importance that historians of reading begin to map these spaces.[3] This chapter aims to rediscover some of what Chartier has termed the 'forgotten habits and gestures'[4] of reading in the period 1780–1850 by paying attention to the variety of sources (from promotional tools for commercial libraries to reading diaries) in which images of reading spaces and the positioning of the reading body are recorded.

Reading in public

During the period 1780–1850 a vast array of new spaces designed for reading, including commercial reading rooms and libraries, mechanics' institutes and coffee houses, opened their doors to ever greater numbers of readers. The various visual and written representations of these new contexts which were published in a variety of sources, ranging from newspaper articles to guides to holiday resorts, reveal a great deal about how these spaces accommodated the reading body. Although the images produced to promote the large commercial circulating libraries that sprang up in seaside resorts and spa towns throughout Britain during the 1780s and 1790s are often idealized, they give some sense of how readers used this space. For example, the well-known etching of *Hall's Library at Margate* (1789) promotes the library as a space for walking and socializing with other stylish holidaymakers.[5] The Church Field area in which Hall's Library was located is depicted in *The New Margate and Ramsgate Guide* as part of a leisure zone that included two other libraries, a theatre, meeting house and assembly rooms.[6] The acts of reading that took place here appear of little significance to the author of the *Guide* and are similarly marginalized in the engraving, where the only readers in an otherwise crowded room are two well-dressed gentlemen with newspapers and a fashionable looking woman taking down a volume from the shelves. These male newspaper readers angling their texts to the sun help us to capture one of those lost gestures of reading to which Chartier refers. The engraving also reveals that Hall's contained a shop in which silverware, toys and other goods were sold. If, as Flint suggests, the sights, the sounds and even the smells of such reading places interpenetrated 'the emotional and cerebral affects of the text', the real readers who occupied the space of the commercial library made sense of texts while surrounded by the sights and sounds of friends meeting, families gathering and goods being bought.[7]

Of course, not all of the new commercial library spaces that came into being during this period were as grand as those found in Margate's leisure zone. Most small circulating libraries were located in high street shops, such as that run by Edward Reddell of Tewkesbury in Gloucestershire, whose book labels draw attention to the various other goods sold there, including perfume and patent medicines.[8] However, as Thomas Rowlandson's aquatint (see Figure 6.1) of the interior of a similarly-sized circulating library in the sea-side resort of Scarborough suggests, it was possible for reading to take place in a venue of this size.[9]

The left-hand side of Rowlandson's illustration depicts two men (one of whom clasps a newspaper to his chest) involved in an animated conversation loud enough to be overheard by a black servant

Figure 6.1 Etching by Thomas Rowlandson from *Poetical Sketches of Scarborough* (1813)

waiting in the centre of the shop, who turns to see the source of the disturbance. That the two men are arguing over a newspaper report is made clear by the accompanying text. However, their argument appears to have made no impression on the two young women standing close to them who continue to read from a selection of texts on open display utilizing the light of one of the shop's two bow windows (which are also used to display goods for sale). These women are perhaps being satirized as self-absorbed novel readers, but the accompanying poem's reference to three circulating libraries (Ainsworth's, Scaum's and Whiting's) that actually operated in Scarborough in the early-nineteenth century make it reasonable to assume that this image provides a fairly accurate representation of the reading environment available in smaller circulating libraries at this time. Although some of the stock is available on the open shelves for readers to browse, texts 'just published' are controlled by the shopkeeper who keeps them away from his eager customers behind an impressively wide counter that separates him from the rest of the shop. Although customers are provided with two chairs and a sloping surface near to the window against which they could lean while consulting texts, this space is clearly designed to allow browsing rather than prolonged reading. In even smaller shops, many readers are likely to have been restricted to the consultation of the catalogue or a list of new publications like the one Rowlandson shows displayed behind the shopkeeper's counter.

Because newspapers remained expensive until the 1840s commercial venues for their communal consumption were commonplace. As the *Westminster Review* noted in 1830, 'every large' and 'almost every small town in England' had subscription reading rooms that supplied newspapers to those who could afford 'to pay a guinea or so annually'.[10] The less well off might visit 'smaller scale penny-a-week' subscription rooms, or hire a paper by the hour to read at a news-walk.[11] Like many of the key reading spaces that developed during the nineteenth century, these venues restricted access along class and/or gender lines. In July 1844 the journalist Angus Reach produced a detailed description of the layout and contents of a new sort of coffeehouse that was aimed at a *male* working-class clientele. He claimed that there was 'upwards of two thousand' of these venues in London by the 1840s and that up to 1,600 people regularly visited that in London's Haymarket each day. Unlike many other institutions of reading there was no fee for entry, but coffee was charged at between 1d and 2d per cup. According to Reach the majority could seat up to 100 customers and had a similar layout with a main room 'partitioned off into little boxes with a table in each'. The larger institutions took in a wide range of daily newspapers, monthly magazines, quarterly reviews and weekly periodicals. Small libraries were also relatively common. Reach's remarks about the poor quality of the coffee and the cheapness of the food suggest an element of class-phobic disgust, but this article nevertheless provides an insightful account of the way in which knowledge and food could be consumed together.[12] It was often difficult for working-class readers to find a space within the home in which reading could take place, and although the coffeehouse customer needed to pay at least a penny to read, this guaranteed access to warmth, adequate lighting and a number of modern texts.[13] Reach's account was clearly intended to persuade workingmen to abandon the delights of the gin-palace, but other commentators mocked this attempt to take over a characteristically bourgeois environment (and drink). Although satirical, Richard Seymour's etching of an 'educated dustmen' patiently waiting for another working-class customer to finish the text that he desires to read in 'the Byron Coffee House and Reading Rooms', brilliantly captures what must have been one of the commonest reading gestures in spaces designed to accommodate the communal consumption of texts.[14]

Other new spaces were designed exclusively for reading. James Secord's work on the various contexts in which *Vestiges of the Natural History of Creation* (1844) was consumed reveals that news rooms and reading rooms were particularly important spaces for many working- and lower middle-class readers. For example, Thomas Archer Hirst of Halifax in West Yorkshire 'explored the book in the same way as many other working- and middle-class autodidacts in cities: through discussion with friends at home, in taverns, at work, and at the Mechanics' Institution and his local Mutual Improvement Society'.[15] Hirst read a copy of the *Vestiges* borrowed from the Improvement Society's library in the context of a range of other texts, such as local newspapers and periodicals, also available in the reading rooms of his home town. The practices of private reading and note-making in a shared public reading space recorded in Hirst's journal and the methods of communal text sharing satirized by Seymour show just how important such spaces could be in the everyday lives of those largely excluded from the text buying public, but Secord's work also identifies the correlation between particularly influential communities of readers and the manipulation of reading spaces. For example, as part of an argument that during the early Victorian period 'conversations in London Society' had a profound influence upon a book's success, Secord reproduces an illustration of a fashionable soiree that originally appeared in the *Pictorial Times* in March 1844 (see Figure 6.2).[16]

This image shows that books and other texts were left scattered on tables as conversation pieces at sociable gatherings. It is worth looking at this image again with Flint's questions about how spatial context changes the nature of reading in mind. The solitary woman reading a book to the left of the image may well be using it as a shield, as twenty-first century commuters on the London Underground use a newspaper. But, unlike the commuter, she must know that she is going to be interrupted by someone amongst this fashionable group who will ask her about the text that she is reading. (Readers hide behind texts to impress as well as to avoid and indeed, this very sort of interruption appears to have occurred to the woman sitting behind her.) The presence of texts in this gathering is used to smooth social interaction and the success of such an arrangement is suggested by the man and woman sequestered in the window space glimpsed in the background. The repetition of this image of the interrupted reader on more than one occasion in Phiz's illustrations for *David Copperfield* (1850), even though it is not specified by Dickens's text, suggests that reading to draw or avert attention was an accepted practice at social gatherings in this period.[17]

The representations of reading in public discussed in this chapter help to disrupt what David Henkin has called 'the persistently powerful image of the private reader' and the (often related) thesis that 'the history of reading in the Modern West has been a process of steadily increasing privatisation'. The readers in antebellum New York described in his *City Reading* (1998), for example, were surrounded by texts written 'on buildings, sidewalks, sandwich board advertisements . . . election tickets and two-dollar bills' and he provides evidence that more conventional texts, such as newspapers and books, were often read in the streets.[18] There is something very exciting about the rediscovery of these public readers. Studies such as those by Secord and Henkin have been particularly useful in helping to reconfigure some of the most important reading spaces of the early-nineteenth century, from the Society party through to the advertising hoarding, and of recapturing the sights and smells that surrounded these readers as they made sense of texts.[19]

Figure 6.2 Depiction of a literary soirée from the *Pictorial Times* (1844)

Reading and domestic space

Our excitement at finding new readers scattered throughout the streets and new public spaces designed for reading should not blind us to the continued importance of reading in domestic spaces. Evidence for such reading ranges from the idealized visual images of women and domestic groups particularly common in conduct literature and genre painting, through to autobiographical accounts of reading at home. This evidence needs to be re-examined because it is all too easy to assume that reading within the home was a private experience.[20] Kate Flint's discussion of the phenomenology of reading concludes with her own autobiographical reminiscence of the way in which various reading spaces influenced her early reading. How did readers from the period 1790–1850 represent their experience of domestic reading in their autobiographical writings?

The journal kept by Emily Shore (1819–39) during the 1830s is particularly useful for helping us to think about the role of the body and the relationship of the reader to the other people who shared the same domestic space. Written between July 1831 and May 1839, the edited version published by Shore's sisters in 1891 has been superseded by Barbara Timm Gates's recent electronic edition, which uses the surviving manuscript volumes as its main source.[21] The rest of this chapter will concentrate on the volume compiled between 6 October 1836 and 10 April 1837 as this seven-month period provides a particularly detailed account of the reading practices in the house of the aunt and uncle with whom the sixteen year-old Shore lived while recovering from an illness. Also resident in the house were her brother, Richard, and two cousins, Anna and Phoebe, both in their late teens. Shore was determined to record this new reading environment in as much detail as possible and she often comments upon the performance skills of those who read aloud within the house.

Shore's journal is itself a sign of the significance that the creation and interpretation of manuscript texts played within this reading community. The silent creation of these and other autobiographical writings often took place in the evening if there were no visitors. For example on Wednesday 15 March 1837 she recorded:

> It is now near nine o'clock; we are a perfectly silent party of four. Grandmama is in a bee-hive chair; Aunt Bell is writing a letter, [my brother] Richard and I are writing our journals.[22]

Letter writing was a particularly important activity and Shore records her 'inexpressible pleasure' in reading those from her parents, siblings and cousins.[23] Letters were often read aloud and these and other manuscript texts provided much of the family's entertainment. Shore copied the manuscript of an original poem by Thomas Moore owned by her aunt, wrote 'pencil caricatures' and amusing acrostics, as well as a 'little comedy' on family life, all of which were eagerly consumed by the family.[24] Yet more manuscripts were produced during Sunday reading, or as part of the educational process. Shore tested her own memory by writing abstracts of sections of 'Chalmer's [sic] Evidences', after listening to her aunt read from this text, and abridged passages from several books were turned into a manuscript 'History of Rome'.[25] Shore saw the creation of these texts as an important means to improve her mind and the majority of passages in the journal describe her participation in manuscript culture as a particularly enjoyable part of her life.

The public performance of texts was an important part of family life for Shore and her relatives and she often recorded her reaction to the recitals in which she sometimes took part. During the first few weeks of her stay, she noted that her uncle William would often spend part of Sunday reading aloud from a religious work such as a 'sermon of Chalmers', at the same time making 'remarks on religious and moral subjects' or the style of the text for the benefit of his listeners.[26] However, this combination of reading and discussion was not only practised by her uncle or reserved for religious texts. When Shore responded to her cousin Maria's request to read 'something that will instruct me' she chose an article from the *Penny Magazine*, noting in the diary that 'we conversed as we went along, and I found her very anxious to understand everything thoroughly'.[27] As one might expect, these comments and conversations often led to the discovery or investigation of other texts as when the shared task of reading aloud from Oliphant's *Sacred Poetry* (1828) one Sunday evening led to a reading from Walton's *Life of Hooker*.[28] However, as Shore's journal makes clear, those in the audience did not always concentrate solely on the text, or listen to an entire reading. Some of Shore's own distractions were text based, as in the instance when she 'took up pencil and paper' and sketched the head 'of the Bravo' whilst listening to her brother read from Fenimore Cooper's novel, but for the female members of the group listening was often combined with domestic tasks such as sewing.[29]

Uncle William's reading practices had a profound influence upon Shore during the first few weeks of her stay. Like her father, he was fond of reading Shakespeare aloud, but often chose to select passages from the plays rather than reading them in their entirety. This was clearly a new experience for Shore, who records that she had previously avoided hearing extracts from *King Lear* in case it spoilt her appreciation of the whole.[30] Shore appears to have enjoyed these performances (as did the other listeners) but her journal records an important difference between her uncle and the rest of her reading community over the suitability of prose fiction. After completing a reading of *Macbeth* on 26 November 1836, Uncle William 'expressed his opinion very strongly' that novels were a 'pernicious kind of reading' and referred to Scott 'as one of the most noxious writers of this class'. His audience must have appeared unusually reluctant to join in with the usual post-reading discussion for as Shore records none of them revealed that they had read the first four chapters of *Ivanhoe* (1820) together just two days before, having finished Cooper's *The Water-Witch* (1830) on the same night.[31] Shore's entry invokes the counter-argument of her own father, who occasionally read novels aloud to his family, and she notes that although Anna and Phoebe thought they should give up reading *Ivanhoe* in order to comply with William's thinking the group did not actually take the decision to suspend its progress.[32] It is not entirely clear which members of the family were part of the group reading this novel, as Shore tends to use the phrase 'we were reading', but as the text was halted on 1 December 1836 to allow her brother, Richard, to attend a scientific lecture, it seems to have consisted of Emily, Aunt Bell, Richard, Anna and Phoebe. While Richard was absent they began Shakespeare's *Taming of the Shrew*, Aunt Bell reading the 'greater part' and Anna and Emily contributing 'each a little'.[33] This practice of sharing the verbalization of the text is one that the four cousins and their aunt engaged in as subset of the main reading community of the house throughout Shore's stay.

Patricia Michaelson has argued that when a text is performed the 'social relations between reader and audience' have an impact upon the way in which individual members of the audience interpret the text.[34] For Shore, this certainly holds true for those episodes in which either her father or uncle was the reader. Both men took it upon themselves to give guidance on the text as part of their reading and Shore sometimes made appropriately deferential notes on what they had to say.[35] At other times, however, she disagreed with her uncle's choice and interpretation of Thomas Scott's *Commentary on the Ten*

Commandments (*c*.1820), but appears to have only been able to voice her contrary opinions in the pages of the journal.[36] Shared readings were different, however. Shore often recorded both her perceptions of other readers, and her reactions to text and audience when she was herself reading aloud. For example, after completing a reading of one of her favourite texts, Scott's *Rokeby* (1813) with the assistance of her aunt and cousin Phoebe, she noted that Anna had 'never heard it before'. The diaries make clear that Shore's reading was particularly aimed at Anna, who she wanted to introduce to the delights of Scott's poetry, and she is clearly very pleased by her cousin's 'rapturous admiration' of the text. A long passage that begins 'I never admired Rokeby so much' also suggests that this positive reaction made her rethink her own response to the text.[37] In such instances the audience clearly had as much influence over the interpretive responses of the person verbalizing the text as this performer had over the audience. Similarly, the initial response of individual members of the group must have been rethought and revised by the conversation about the text that followed each performance.

Of course, the manner in which a text was performed also affected its interpretation. On two occasions, Shore notes that her enjoyment of *Ivanhoe* was severely affected by it 'being badly read' by the sub-group and she contrasts their reading skills with her father's captivating performance of Talfourd's verse tragedy *Ion* (1835) ('Papa reads beautifully').[38] Shore's praise of her father clearly reflects the 'social relations' between performer and listener, but in both entries which invoke the poor performance of *Ivanhoe* she is also particularly concerned with the cultural significance of novels – brought forcefully to her attention by her uncle's attack on Scott – and the difference between reading in a group and reading silently for one's own pleasure. When *Ivanhoe* is mentioned for a second time it is part of an entry in which Shore suggests that she is no longer enjoying listening to novels as much as she once did, but she cannot decide whether this results from their poor performance ('Perhaps, if I had read them all to myself, they would have interested me more'), or a 'change in my taste' that will allow 'a greater enjoyment of soberer and more useful reading'.[39] The final words of this entry reflect much that is found in contemporary anti-novel writing, but such passages reflect a tension or conflict in Shore's methods of analysing her own reading. As Thomas Augst has argued, most early nineteenth-century journals were kept to enable the compiler to ruminate on the development of the self and these entries on the novel show Shore attempting to construct a narrative in which as her 'character' develops she rejects the pleasures of communally consumed fiction for 'soberer' silent reading.[40] However, Shore could not fully invest in this narrative of personal development because she was still actively participating in (and enjoying) the communal reading of fiction. Three days after recording her dissatisfaction with *Ivanhoe* for the second time Shore produced a list of four books that she 'regularly read' in private, including Abbott's 'thoroughly Christian' *The Way to do Good* (1836), but her continued participation in the communal reading of *The Bravo* (1831) shows how difficult it was to give up this activity.[41] As these instances from Shore's journal suggest, the reading of printed and manuscript texts was an essential component of sociability in this household.

When Shore's father or uncle read aloud they were usually familiar with the text they were reading and many conduct books from this period advised parents to read only those texts of which they approved.[42] However, in most instances the sub-group that read novels together had no prior knowledge of the text and except in the case of *Ivanhoe*, where some 'profane conversation' seems to have been deemed unfit for consumption, they did not edit the text for performance.[43] The person reciting the text was thus as often surprised by its contents as the audience. Shore records her own excitement at discovering the ending of *The Bravo* as she read:

> I had not in the least expected the conclusion. I was taken by surprise as totally and completely as it was possible to be. This last portion is admirably written, it is so sudden as quite to appal one. I happened to be the reader; till the very sentence which tells the end I had expected a reprieve; and when I read the words,
> 'the head of Jacopo rolled upon the stones as if to meet her',
> it startled me hideously; I felt as if the blood curdled in my heart, my brain swam round, and I was dizzy and giddy from head to foot. I never experienced such a thrill of astonished horror. I could scarcely command my voice to conclude the narrative.[44]

Even if Shore exaggerates the physical effect that the text had upon her in order to make this passage more rhetorically effective, her loss of 'command' must certainly have influenced the way in which her audience perceived this text. But as Shore's depiction of communal reading suggests, while some of those listening might have been as caught up in the reading as she was, others may have cared little because they had anticipated the ending of the text, or been distracted because they thought it badly read, or missed a vital piece of dialogue because they were concentrating on a difficult piece of needlework.

This group reading of *The Bravo* suggests something of the complexity of the domestic reading scene. In common with much recent work on the history of reading the investigation of Shore's journal provides evidence of reading as a sociable rather than private activity. Shared reading and the creation of manuscripts was an important way of reinforcing the social bonds of the group and provided both entertainment and education. Although all of the members of this community also engaged in private reading, often in their own rooms, Shore's journal suggests how difficult it is to make sense of her reading without placing it within the context of the sociable practices of the reading community in which she participated. The fundamental difference between her participation in the performance of texts chosen by the smaller reading group, and of listening as part of a larger group to her uncle reading aloud from a book that he had chosen, shows that domestic reading often helped to reproduce social values and relations by underscoring that men held authority over the text. However, the fact that the female dominated sub-group chose not to report their reading of *Ivanhoe*, and ignored uncle William's advice on the dangers of reading novels, prevents any simplistic understanding of this community as one dominated by patriarchal restraint.

Matthew P. Brown has noted that during the past twenty years or so, historians of reading have tended to promote a paradigm which 'argues that reading habits exist within a dialectic of freedom and constraint, of interpretative play and interpretive control'. However, he goes on to argue, that we need to be careful that 'interpretive play does not stand at one end of a generalized schema that transcends history'.[45] Shore's journal provides a very useful reminder of the various restraints that constrained 'interpretative play' in a typical bourgeois household and in particular the way in which the sociability of reading aloud could influence the creation of meaning both for the person who was enunciating the text and for those listening. Historians of reading still often restrict their focus to the relationship between the reader and the protocols of reading embedded in the text, but as the various examples looked at in this essay suggest, when texts are consumed as part of a social performance both the way in which the reading body is brought into play and the nature of the social relationship between auditor and listener, or solitary reader and venue, can produce meanings that are impossible to recover from the text itself. The further investigation of reading spaces and sociable practices will not only allow us to rediscover Chartier's 'forgotten habits and gestures', but enable us to better understand the way in which reading environments were integral to the creation of meaning.

Notes and references

1. Roger Chartier, *The Order of Books* (Cambridge: Polity Press, 1992), p. 8.
2. Kate Flint, 'Women readers revisited', in *Reading Women: Literary Figures and Cultural Icons from the Victorian Age to the Present*, ed. Janet Badia and Jennifer Phegley (Toronto: University of Toronto Press, 2006), pp. 281–93 (284).
3. Flint, 'Women readers', p. 284.
4. Chartier, *Order of Books*, p. 9
5. Reproduced in Paul Kaufman, *Libraries and Their Users* (London: Library Association, 1969), opp. p. 191.
6. *The New Margate and Ramsgate Guide* (London: Turpin and Wilkins [1790?]), pp. 10–11.
7. Flint, 'Women readers', p. 284.
8. Reddell's book label is reproduced in David Allan's *A Nation of Readers: The Lending Library in Georgian England* (London: British Library, 2008), p. 123.
9. *Poetical Sketches of Scarborough Illustrated by 21 Engravings . . . from Original Designs . . . by J. Green, and etched by T. Rowlandson* (London: Ackerman, 1813), p. 142.
10. 'Provincial newspaper press', *Westminster Review*, 12 (Jan. 1830), pp. 69–103 (69–70).
11. Hannah Barker, *Newspapers, Politics and English Society 1695–1855* (London: Longman, 2000), p. 60.
12. Angus B. Reach, 'The coffee houses of London', *New Parley Library*, 1 (13 July 1844), 293–4. Reprinted in *Victorian Print Media: A Reader,* ed. Andrew King and John Plunkett (Oxford: Oxford University Press, 2005), pp. 246–9.
13. David Vincent, *Bread, Knowledge and Freedom: A Study of Nineteenth-Century Working Class Autobiography* (London: Methuen, 1982), p. 118.

14. This image from *Sketches by Seymour, Volume One* (London: R. Carlile, 1834) is reproduced in Brian E. Maidment, *Reading Popular Prints 1790–1870*, 2nd edn. (Manchester: Manchester University Press, 2001), p. 77.

15. James Secord, *Victorian Sensation: The Extraordinary Publication, Reception and Secret Authorship of Vestiges of the Natural History of Creation* (London: University of Chicago Press, 2000), p. 337.

16. Ibid., pp. 158–9.

17. For a discussion of Agnes Wickfield as reader in Dickens's text, see Catherine J. Golden, *Images of the Woman Reader in Victorian British and American Fiction* (Gainesville: University Press of Florida, 2003).

18. David Henkin, *City Reading: Written Words and Public Spaces in Antebellum New York* (New York: Columbia University Press, 1998), p. 6.

19. See also Sara Thornton, *Advertising, Subjectivity and the Nineteenth-Century Novel: Dickens, Balzac and the Language of the Walls* (Basingstoke: Palgrave Macmillan, 2009).

20. For a discussion of conduct book illustrations, see Stephen Colclough, *Consuming Texts: Readers and Reading Communities* (Basingstoke: Palgrave Macmillan, 2007), pp. 134–6. For mid-Victorian paintings of domestic reading, see Garrett Stewart, *The Look of Reading: Book, Painting, Text* (London: Chicago University, 2006), pp. 21–4.

21. *The Journal of Emily Shore*, ed. Louisa and Arabella Shore (London: K. Paul, Trench, Trübner & Co., 1891); *Journal of Emily Shore*, ed. Barbara Timm Gates (Charlottesville: University Press of Virginia, 1991); *The Journal of Emily Shore: Digital Edition*, ed. Barbara Timm Gates (University of Virginia Press, 2006).

22. All quotations identified by date are taken from Gates's *Digital Edition*.

23. 14 March 1837.

24. 7 December 1836; 11 November 1836; 27 December 1836; 16 December 1836.

25. 18 November 1836 (presumably Thomas Chalmers, *The Miraculous Evidences of Christianity* (1836)); 6 and 12 January 1837.

26. 9 October 1836. See also the entries for 23 and 30 October 1836.

27. 29 October 1836.

28. 13 November 1836.

29. 7 March 1837.

30. 14 and 21 November 1836. On 15 November 1836 Shore noted that *King Lear* was the seventh Shakespeare play that she had heard read aloud. By 21 November William had read *Henry V* and *Lear* to the group in their entirety alongside extracts from other plays including *Julius Caesar*.

31. 24 November 1836.

32. 26 November 1836. On 28 November the group decided to abandon novel reading altogether in favour of 'some book at once instructive and entertaining', but this plan was never put into action.

33. 28 November 1836; 1 December 1836.

34. Patricia Michaelson, *Speaking Volumes: Women, Reading, and Speech in the Age of Austen* (Stanford: Stanford University Press, 2002), p. 175.

35. On her father's reading, see the entry for 19 December 1835.
36. 18 December 1836.
37. 18 February 1837.
38. 3 March 1837; 31 December 1836.
39. 3 March 1837.
40. Thomas Augst, *The Clerk's Tale: Young Men and Moral Life in Nineteenth-Century America* (Chicago: University of Chicago Press, 2003), pp. 19–113.
41. 5 and 6 March 1837.
42. Kate Flint, *The Woman Reader 1837–1914* (Oxford: Clarendon Press, 1993), p. 83.
43. 28 November 1836.
44. 14 March 1837.
45. Matthew P. Brown, *The Pilgrim and the Bee: Reading Rituals and Book Culture in Early New England* (Philadelphia: University of Pennsylvania Press, 2007), pp. 137–8.

7

A Book of One's Own: Examples of Library Book Marginalia

Mats Dahlström

In early 2007 there was an art exhibition in Stockholm by Swedish artist Kajsa Dahlberg,[1] entitled *A Room of One's Own/A Thousand Libraries*.[2] The exhibition included a printed edition of a quite peculiar book the artist had composed. The book and the exhibition triggered some thoughts about book studies and the role of the reader, about bibliography and textual studies, and about marginalia and other kinds of reader interaction in books. But let us begin from the beginning – here is the background of the exhibition and the book.

A couple of years back, Kajsa Dahlberg[3] decided to acquire a copy of Virginia Woolf's *A Room of One's Own* – in Swedish translation as *Ett eget rum* – and to give it away as a present to a friend of hers. *A Room of One's Own*, a collection of essays, was originally published by Hogarth Press in 1929 (the fact that the gallery's press release says 'Hogwarth Press' is, I suppose, a mischievous prank of magic by Harry Potter). Woolf's work was published in Swedish in 1958 and has since been republished in several imprints in both hardback and paperback.[4] To her surprise, however, Dahlberg learned there was currently no edition available in the book stores. She therefore turned to her local public library, borrowed its copy of the book, photocopied the entire contents of the book, had the photocopies bound by a book binder and then presented it as a gift to her friend.

In doing so, she soon discovered there were lots of reader notes, scribblings and underlinings in the library copy – what book scholars refer to as 'marginalia'. It should be pointed out that in this chapter the term 'marginalia' is used in a broad sense. It includes not only reader inscriptions in the margins of a book's pages, but a whole range of physical evidence of reader interactions, from text markings, highlighting, underlining, crossing over, to drawn pointers, arrows or hands. It is further extended to include instances where readers have folded corners (dog-ears) or attached paper clips to single leaves in the book. An even wider understanding of the social interaction of the printed text in a book can include the evidence an owning institution has left behind, e.g. library stamps or anti-theft devices.

As we have all, perhaps, been witness to, marginalia in library books tend to trigger either annoyance or interest. From the perspective of librarians, the former is often the rule. As a case in point, preservational and conservational measures taken by libraries at times involve cleansing copies from unwanted marginalia.[5] As far as Dahlberg was concerned, however, the marginalia she found triggered her immediate curiosity, and I have a feeling she shares that curiosity with the reader of this essay. She began to get in touch with public libraries all around Sweden to find out whether their copies of this particular book also contained marginalia. I know this for a fact as my wife, a small town public librarian, was contacted by Dahlberg as well during this time. Where the library copy did in fact show examples of marginalia – and this was surprisingly often the case – she asked for an interlibrary lending loan, or had helpful librarians photocopy the marginalia pages and send them to her by mail or fax. She borrowed copy after copy – from more than one hundred public libraries. In a later interview, Dahlberg, with tongue-in-cheek, made reference to her increasingly abnormal book loan statistics:

> I now happen to have many library cards . . . And my statistics from borrowing books must look rather strange.[6]

All the time Dahlberg made sure she produced copies of marginalia instances in every book, amassing the 'social evidence' existing in most of the editions of the work available in Swedish public libraries at that point in time. She then sat down by her light board and used a photo-copy of one full copy as base onto which she copied and projected all marginalia, by hand, page by page, from all the other copies. Figure 7.1 gives you an idea of what the result looks like.

If one is prone to seeing similarities between this kind of procedure and that of textual criticism (to which I will refer again below), one might, however, refer to Dahlberg's selected copy as a base document

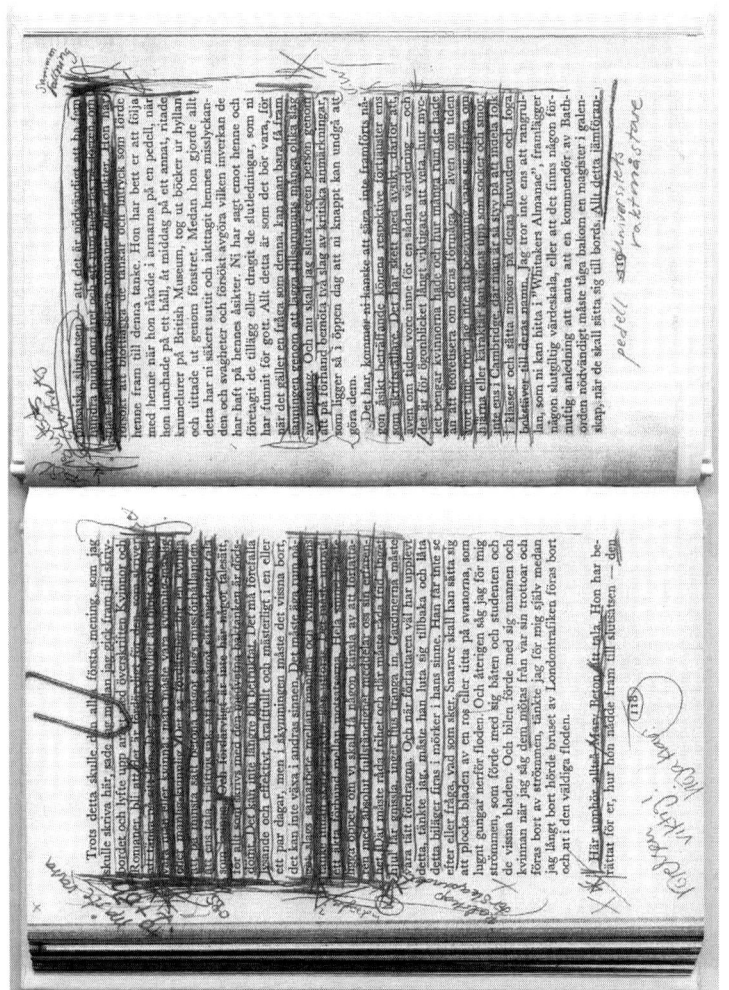

Figure 7.1 Kajsa Dahlberg, *Ett eget rum / Tusen bibliotek* (2006), pp. 118–19

(or 'copy-document') rather than a copy-text, and to the intellectual process as material criticism, rather than textual criticism.[7] The result is, quite literally, a 'readers' edition' of Woolf's work.

Why was this particular work by this particular author chosen by Dahlberg for her project? Was it pure coincidence? I will address this question a little later on in the chapter. One might, however, consider the fact that the method Dahlberg chose, manually copying and projecting marginalia onto a single base document, would have met with severe difficulty if the various copies had belonged to editions with different composition, typography and topography, with the particular text passages appearing at different spatial areas. On the contrary, Dahlberg's projection work using the light board was made much easier by the fact that all Swedish editions at the time were imprints based on one and the same typeset composition from 1958. So the marginalia were collected from a large number of real copies from one composition (although it is unclear precisely which imprints were used at which textual passage).

The book, printed and published as a facsimile edition (of 1,000 copies), could only be bought at the exhibition, but is, thanks to the Swedish national deposit law, duly available in several Swedish public libraries, including the National Library in Stockholm.[8]

There are certainly copyright issues that can be discussed around Dahlberg's project. Well aware that her project involved illegal text copying, she deliberately chose a blank white cover for her book, as an echo of the blank, white-label CDs containing pirated music.[9] Dahlberg goes on:

> My idea is furthermore to return the book to the libraries: I'd like it to be re-registered without being given a certain given place in the shelves. The cover lacks a title, and I am fond of the idea of placing the book in connection to Woolf, but that it actually eventually would disappear among the shelves.[10]

Let us, however, leave aside the aspects of intellectual property rights and devote the rest of this chapter to issues of textuality, materiality and space. To begin with: what kind of work *is* this, really?

Obviously, it is a work of art. With her work, Dahlberg touches upon aspects such as repetition, displacement and the relation between the individually unique and the common. In that sense, the work belongs to an aesthetic movement shared by many art forms, such as Steve

Reich's musical minimalism, Raymond Queneau's pataphysical style variations, or some of the pop art works in the 1960s and 1970s. In another sense, Dahlberg's book has a place in the genre known as 'artist's books', albeit as an odd member: a multiple edition of 1,000 manufactured copies, rather than a unique, handcrafted object.[11] But there are scholarly connections as well, primarily to book history and to literary and textual studies.

There is, as we know, a section within book and textual studies that is engaged in marginalia – but that kind of scholarship is, if you excuse the pun, somewhat in the margin of the discipline.[12] It is usually occupied with the notes and marginalia of canonical authors, and sometimes of famous individual works or documents. At times the marginalia is even subjected to elaborate critical editing and published in a scholarly edition, such as Samuel Taylor Coleridge's marginalia. Other examples of authors whose marginalia have been or are being subjected to scholarly investigation are Charles Darwin, Samuel Beckett, Herman Melville and Paul Valéry.[13] There are, as well, examples of marginalia studies for a particular work – Owen Gingerich's study of readers' notes in various copies of *De revolutionibus* by Copernicus has been much acclaimed.[14] There are also examples of particular document types, genres or periods that have been studied because of their marginalia evidence.[15]

But, to a large extent, the field of marginalia studies is occupied with what we can learn about identified, acclaimed authors in their role as readers. What about the marginalia of 'ordinary' readers? There is in fact such a subsection of marginalia studies, albeit small. Perhaps the best known scholarly work to date is that by Heather Jackson.[16] The reader community being studied is a little difficult to label. Drawing on Dr Johnson, Virginia Woolf herself uses the term 'the common reader' as opposed to the critic, academic or upper-class reader,[17] and that term has been commonly used.[18] Several historians of the book, for example, Stephen Colclough, point to the scholarly awkwardness of using the term 'common reader' as an analytical concept. The ideals of representativeness and generalizability are difficult to attain on the basis of the necessarily particular community of readers being studied.[19] Using Kate Flint's argument, perhaps it is better to talk about the 'historical' rather than the 'common' readers.[20]

Whether labelled historical or common, the readers in Dahlberg's book are also anonymous. Marginalia evidence of modern anonymous readers has scarcely been the object of scholarly study. One example is Greta Golick's investigation of Canadian house wives' marginalia in cookbooks.[21] A potentially interesting empirical material for such marginalia studies could presumably be provided by public library copies, but to my knowledge hardly any work of that kind has been done to date.[22] This is of course due to the difficulty of drawing any scholarly and significant conclusions from the available evidence. We rarely know who made the library book marginalia and what class, gender or community he or she represented. Furthermore, there is little to suggest *why* the marginalia were made in the first place or in what context, whether the persons behind them were deliberately addressing future library patrons or not, or even if the marginalia in a particular copy stemmed from one or several consecutive readers. In consequence, historians of the book have expressed concern about the scholarly value of library book marginalia studies as historical sources.[23] As Stephen Colclough notes,

> [a]nyone making notes on their reading in the margin . . . may well be conscious that their marks are going to be interpreted by a later reader.[24]

This is a particularly important reservation when we are dealing with marginalia in books circulating in a public library system, books that are likely to be borrowed (and possibly annotated) by other patrons using that particular library. In that sense, such anonymous marginalia are messages in bottles.

One could, however, make the *praxis* of marginalia, such as annotating and highlighting, the research object itself (as opposed to the presumed historical readers responsible for them). This is a particular field of study, largely performed by other scholars than those of book history. A fascinating study was done by Catherine Marshall on undergraduate students annotating and highlighting text books.[25] In addition to interviewing and observing students at work, Marshall closely analysed the marginalia evidence available in hundreds of used text books – notes, underlining, text markings, writings in the margin, pointers, drawings etc. – as a way of examining how students go about understanding the work in a book by appropriating and personalizing their copy. By establishing patterns and types of textual interaction, the aim was not only to generate knowledge about the practices of reading and writing, but also to implement this knowledge in the production of tools for digital text annotation later on. Golick's and

Marshall's work can be regarded as instances of bibliographical document analysis with particular social contexts in mind. To some degree, the same can be said of Dahlberg's art project. But the scepticism mentioned earlier in relation to the evidential value of the marginalia in library books is also eminently valid in the case of Dahlberg's book. We have no legitimate evidence of the readers' gender, age or class. Neither do we have any clues as to whether the marginalia from each of the hundred or so original library copies stem from the engagement of one or several consecutive readers, and little to suggest whether marginalia have been made during extensive or intensive reading, leisure reading or study reading (e.g. as part of a course syllabus). Furthermore, the marginalia examined by Marshall were made in copies that were the property of the students themselves. They probably experienced a larger degree (or at least different kind of) freedom to interact materially with their books than did the patrons annotating the borrowed library copies in Dahlberg's project. And we are forced to take Dahlberg's 'evidence' at face value; methodologically speaking, it remains a 'black box'. There are in other words obvious limits as to how much they tell us about what a particular reader 'thought' during reading. Some reader evidence simply remains enigmatic. Dahlberg comments:

> There are a few . . . subtle addendums that unfortunately get lost in my book but that are really nice. In one of the books, somebody had underlined all the times Woolf uses the word wrath, which proved to be quite often. I think eight times on one page. There were also several books that had only a few under linings [*sic*] or words. As in one of books where the only thing that was highlighted were the words *lemon to silver*.[26]

So the various kinds of marginalia studies mentioned above are, if not scholarly siblings to Dahlberg's art project, then at least distant relatives. But there are more: literary and textual studies, for instance.

In the background of the page face in Dahlberg's book we find Woolf's own text, accompanied by a reader community's polyvocal comments and underlinings, together with reproductions of library stamps, dog-ears, drawings, paper clips and much more (see Figures 7.1 and 7.2).

Reception studies, the sociology of texts and scholarly editing have all increasingly discussed the 'social text', pointing to the inherent

122

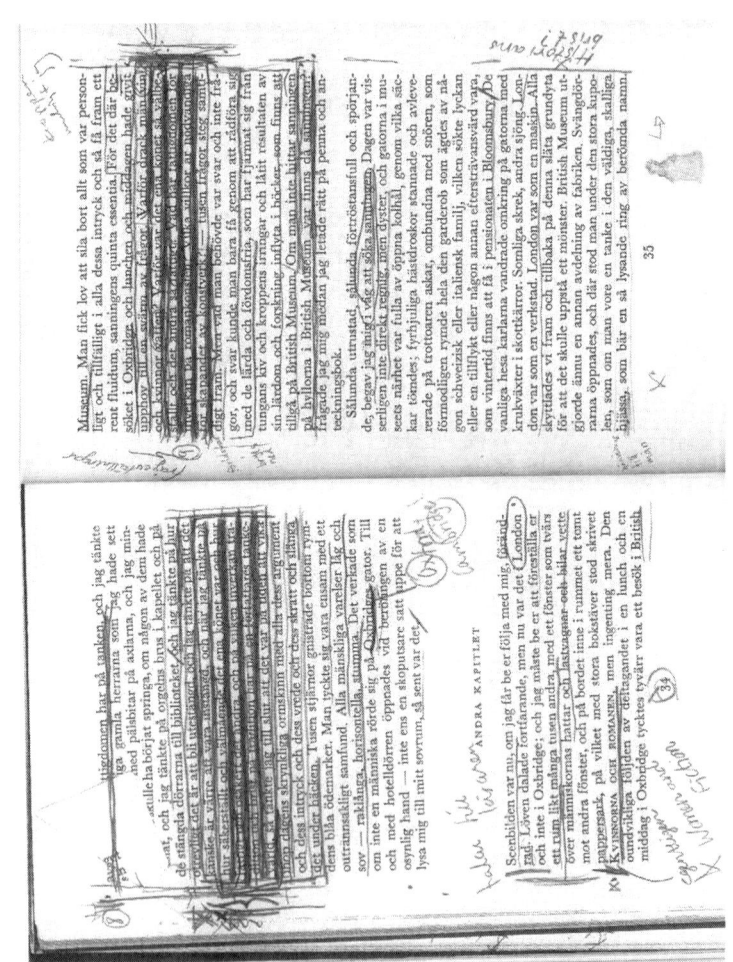

Figure 7.2 Kajsa Dahlberg, *Ett eget rum / Tusen bibliotek* (2006), pp. 34–5

social essence of works, texts and documents.[27] Rather than narrowly focusing on the intention of the solitary author, these scholars stress the need to understand the role of several collaborative actors in the socio-cultural formation of the significance of a work. The text you find in a typical critical edition of a canonical work is to some extent always a socially defined entity. And in a sense, Dahlberg's book makes an illustrative comment to such a concept of *social text*, a tangible example of reception studies and the sociology of texts. When flipping through the pages, one is struck by their ear-splitting (or perhaps eye-splitting) murmur of voices. Some Woolfian passages have escaped the readers' attention rather intact, while others have magnetically attracted their attention to the degree where Woolf's text is virtually unreadable (as in Figure 7.2). One can therefore suppose the book might supply reading evidence for literary scholars in general and Woolf specialists in particular. That would indeed be possible – both qualitatively by closely examining single examples of reader interaction, and quantitatively by counting frequencies and identifying patterns of recurring marginalia types. It would, however, require a thorough and systematic textual and bibliographical analysis of the reader evidence in Dahlberg's book – something that has not been the aim for this chapter. Moreover, there is plenty of reason to be cautious: without being able to ask the annotators themselves, we cannot be sure why certain passages are more interacted with than others.

The project plays with our ingrained boundaries between the private and the public. The thesis in Woolf's lecture, 'A room of one's own', is that women need resources of their own (room and money) to be able to write novels and to be published. Dahlberg's project provides a response to this call by collecting private material and spatial notes and placing them within the public space that both the exhibition and the printed book provide. The fact that legal deposit has made the book a part of the collected national public library also means it has acquired its place in a public room, a memory institution. Dahlberg's 'work about creating a space of one's own within the space of a library book becomes congenial with the content of the book, and with its title'.[28] As Dahlberg states:

I think that is really interesting, how underlining made in a private situation becomes a common reference. In a discussion not only referring to the text itself, but to underlining that has been made over and over again. In this way, the act of reading becomes a part of the text itself.[29]

Perhaps there is also a feminist point to be made. Woolf's work has become a minor classic within feminism. It is striking that marginalia studies, in particular by common readers, seems to be an area populated largely by female scholars. Dahlberg's choice of this particular work is therefore in all likelihood deliberate, particularly if you take into account the topical congeniality discussed above as well as the typographical congeniality between the various imprints making Dahlberg's reproduction endeavour feasible in the first place.

Dahlberg's project also puts the notion and the boundaries of *text* to the test. First, from the point of view of textual scholarship, the degree to which Woolf's authorial and ideal text is posited in the background, while the lectorial and material texts from individual copies are posited in the foreground, is striking. Second, Dahlberg's gaze has wandered off from the printed text to the texts and spaces outside of it. Or as she states in an interview:

My late obsession with this book has been a somewhat inverted experience. That of concentrating, not on the text itself, but on that space which is not the text.[30]

And this is true for more than just the contents of the book. As indicated earlier, the cover, back and spine are all white and devoid of text. In my book shelf at home, the book presents a perfect counter piece to an adjacent book I bought at a stationer's, a note book, perfectly clothed in black leather, an example of how a document can completely lack any typographical text and still be thought of as a book. It is a vessel waiting to be filled with textual notes, while its white neighbour is already brimming with textual notes, way beyond the intentional authorial text we normally expect from a book. The two books extend our habitual scale of expectation on a book's text.

In my own research, I have studied the rationale of textual scholarship and various forms of scholarly reproductions of documents. Of particular interest has been the scholarly, critical *edition* as genre and form. Based on textual criticism, a scholarly editor normally examines different textual versions of a work, selects variants, and presents an established, authoritative and uniform text of the work in a published document: the scholarly edition.[31] Dahlberg's book might be viewed as a form of textual studies and as a kind of edition. But as such, it provides a counterpart, an antithesis, or an *anti-edition* if you will.

Scholarly editing usually has the ideal authorial *text* in its focus. A clean, linguistic text has been chosen or constructed by the editor, while contrasting versions and variants in the sources have been typographically and topographically deported – off to apparatuses at the lower end of the page, or in the back of the volume, or even outside the volume itself. Further, very few editors report on the physicality, condition, materiality and visuality of the source documents. Scholarly editing has a much stronger idealistic than materialistic strand.

Moreover, scholarly editors have the *author's* text in focus. The contributions of other agents such as printers, publishers, co-workers, secretaries, contemporary editors, not to mention *readers,* are regularly excluded. As mentioned earlier, editors in the 'sociology of texts' movement do aim to study literary works as social texts and reception texts, but they talk relatively little about the material interaction between readers and text. Even the scholarly editor's own texts and presence are normally suppressed and largely placed as paratexts in the front or back matter of the edition or even outside of it. Much of the history of scholarly editing is in fact marked by a tug of war between authorial and editorial authority when it comes to visibility and power over the text. Some (indeed most) editors are prone to see themselves as objective uncoverers of The Text, and strive to minimize any visible traces of editorial intervention. Other editions are subjected to the editor's quiddity and ideas to the degree where its main text is editorial rather than authorial. In all this, however, readers do not even get a mention: they are made invisible and mute. Finally, the typical scholarly edition transfers one ideal text from many source documents by selecting or constructing a so-called copytext. It transforms many texts into one text.

As an 'edition', Dahlberg's book is something very different. Technically speaking, it is a *facsimile* edition (or might arguably be thought of as a synoptic variorum edition, which by tradition depicts a work's scholarly reception history by presenting different scholarly readings, scholia and comments in conjunction to the text of the work). As a facsimile edition, it focuses precisely on the idiosyncrasies, the physical and material aspects of documents that textual criticism normally disregards as textually more or less irrelevant. Though one must note that without access to the individual source documents that Dahlberg used it is difficult to ascertain just how faithful and accurate her mode of copying and transferring has been. Cases where the manually copied marginalia spills out across the photocopied book's edges, gutter and binding seem to indicate that the accuracy can be questioned.

It is, furthermore, an edition of both Woolf's text (as the actual text in the composition represented by the chosen imprints) and the readers' texts (as the actual texts in individual copies within imprints of the composition). So the book is an attempt to accomplish a facsimile edition of both a composition (as mirrored by its imprints) and a number of lectorial texts, at one and the same time. But Woolf's work is literally in the background, overshadowed by the lectorial, polyvocal text. And above it all, the artist's own voice floats as editor. If the balance of power in scholarly editing is normally:

(1) author
(2) editor
(3) reader,

Dahlberg's project results in the opposite:

(1) reader
(2) editor
(3) author.

It is an edition that takes its departure from a hundred or so source texts (or documents) and whose very strength lies in visually bringing them out. The result is anything *but* a uniform text. Dahlberg's purpose is not to present a monovocal text but a polyvocal cacophony. It transforms one text into many texts.

Admittedly, we do find an increasingly broad spectrum of counterparts, alternative forms, and experiments with the scholarly edition in the *digital* environment. With a textuality and materiality that is very different from that of the printed medium, digital editions can offer editors radically new opportunities to represent and reproduce texts and documents. But Dahlberg chooses the *printed* codex book form as medium for her 'anti-edition'. That is both poetic and inspirational.

Summing up, there are definite relations between Dahlberg's book and some various fields of scholarly inquiry. However, this does not turn Dahlberg's project into a scholarly endeavour of itself. Almost all of the classic tools and ideals of scientific investigation are simply not there: controlled and controllable empirical data, transparency, reliability, repeatability, generalizability, rigorous methodology, declared theoretical framework, clear and reasonable conclusions logically derived from the empirical investigation, corroboration, validity – you name it. Dahlberg's project has a more than anecdotal character, it remains an art object. Which is, of course, its strength: it aims to question our practices and artefacts and put them in a new perspective. It is able to pose different and valuable questions that scholars are normally prohibited to ask. And that is why I wanted to make Dahlberg's book the centre of this chapter's attention, by virtue of its otherness.

When describing and teaching about the book as media form, one usually highlights the character of the book as artefact by underlining the typical and main features of its form, and framing its most common positions along the scales of, for example, materiality, authority, structure, textual sequentiality, size or shape. But perhaps, in doing so, we tend to forget that the atypical and experimental, even freak examples of books are also instructional for identifying the nature and boundaries of book forms and genres. American media scholar Katherine Hayles has repeatedly illustrated the benefits of studying how artists and authors experiment with material media artefacts that carry texts and images, and how these experiments make us attentive to the delicate balances between material media, performances, readings and texts.[32] If we attempt to delineate some common denominators defining what books as artefacts are, we can learn how book artists and authors have wrestled and played with the materiality of books. Works such as Mark Danielewski's *The House of Leaves*, Lev Rubinstein's *Here I am*, Raymond Queneau's *Hundred Thousand Billion Poems*, not to mention artists' books by, for example, Marcel Duchamp, all have something important to teach us about materiality and form of media and artefacts. They are, if you will, anti-books, deliberate counter-illustrations of 'the typical book'. In their attempts to be anything *but* the typical book, they in fact convey notions of what it means to be, precisely, a typical book. They make us attentive to the regularities, norms and boundaries of our conceptions and urge us to question them. Dahlberg's book has those virtues. Its very idea as well as its textual and material form provide us with an opportunity to readdress those questions that seem to haunt many of us: what is a book, what does it mean to be published and to be public, what is an edition and a scholarly edition, whose voices do we read in printed books, whom do they address, and who is allowed to speak?

Notes and references

1. Kajsa Dahlberg, b. 1973, works with video, text and sound, exploring the construction and mediation of narratives, the relationship between the private and the public sphere, and issues of identity. The exhibition referred to in this chapter ran between 15 November 2006 and 18 February 2007 at the art gallery, *Index: The Swedish Contemporary Art Foundation*. Apart from that exhibition, her work has been shown in several international biennials and group exhibitions, for example at the *Whitney Museum of American Art* in New York in 2009, the *Power Plant* in Toronto in 2008, the *Transmission Gallery* in Glasgow in 2008, the 1st *Athens Biennial* in 2007, the *Royal College of Art* in London in 2007, the *Momentum* Nordic Biennial for Contemporary Art in Moss in 2006, *Sala Rekalde* in Bilbao in 2006, and the *Museum of Modern Art* in Stockholm in 2004.
2. Some parts of this essay have previously been published in Swedish, as: Mats Dahlström, 'En egen bok', in *Bokhistorier: studier tillägnade Per S. Ridderstad*, ed. Kristina Lundblad et al. (Stockholm: Atlantis, 2007), pp. 104–11.
3. *Kajsa Dahlberg in a conversation with Niklas Östholm* [Booklet] (Stockholm: Index, 2007), p. 3, http://www.indexfoundation.se/upload/pdf_Aconversa tionwithKajsaDahlberg.pdf [accessed 24 January 2010].
4. Here are some bibliographical details about the various Swedish imprints. 1958: *Ett eget rum och andra essäer* (Stockholm: Tiden; *Tidens engelska klassiker*); 1965: *Ett eget rum och andra essäer* (Stockholm: Tiden; *Tidens engelska klassiker*); 1965: *Ett eget rum* (Stockholm: Tiden; *Tidens klassiker*); 1977: *Ett eget rum* (Stockholm: Tiden, ISBN 91-550-2109-3; *Tidens klassiker*); 1985: *Ett eget rum* (Stockholm: Tiden, ISBN 91-550-2998-1; *Tidens klassiker*); 1991: *Ett eget rum* (Stockholm: Tiden, ISBN 91-550-3704-6; *Tidens klassiker*); 2004: *Ett eget rum och andra essäer* (Stockholm: Norstedt, ISBN 91-7297-652-7); 2007: *Ett eget rum och andra essäer* (Stockholm: Norstedt, ISBN 978-91-7297-652-8). The composition in the editions contains several essays by Woolf, with *Ett eget rum* on pages 9 to 128. All editions and imprints use one and the same translation by Jane Lundblad.

5. See, for instance, the different points of view by Jonathan Spence and Denis Paz in issue 4 (2005) of the journal *Perspectives*. One can also detect the library attitude in web sites such as the one maintained by Cambridge UL entitled 'Marginalia and other *crimes*' (my italics), http://www.lib.cam.ac.uk/marginalia/ [accessed 24 January 2010]. Greta Golick illustrates how such cleansing can result in the loss of material that is potentially valuable to social historians of the book: Golick, '"one quart milk, five eggs I should say": Marginalia in Anglo-Canadian Cookbooks', *Variants: The Journal of the European Society for Textual Scholarship*, 2–3 (2004), 95–113 (p. 112 f).
6. *Kajsa Dahlberg in a conversation*, p. 3.
7. Book historian Per S. Ridderstad has suggested that the term 'base document', as an alternative to the 'copy-text' (or 'base-text') of textual criticism, emphasizes not only the text of a document, but also refers to the entire material document as potentially significant for the meaning of the text. The focus of this essay on marginalia arguably justifies the use of the term. See Ridderstad, 'Hur dokumenteras ett dokument? Om kravspecifikationer för materiell bibliografi och immateriell textkritik', in *Varianter och bibliografisk beskrivning*, ed. Pia Forssell and Rainer Knapas (Helsinki: Svenska litteratursällskapet i Finland, 2003), pp. 113–30 (p. 127).
8. Kajsa Dahlberg, *Ett eget rum / Tusen bibliotek* (Malmö: The Artist, 2006. Printed in Värnamo by Fälth & Hässler, Pagination: [6], 128, [1]). Available in i.a. the National Library in Stockholm, where its call number is Sv2006 10859.
9. *Kajsa Dahlberg in a conversation*, p. 2.
10. Ibid.
11. Admittedly, there are multiple editions of some 'livres d'artiste' but the unique hand-made object is the norm. See Johanna Drucker, *The Century of Artists' Books* (New York: Granary 1995). Furthermore, Dahlberg's book differs somewhat from other artist's books in the sense that the artist herself takes a step back in the final product, as it were, and lifts the reader evidence to the foreground.
12. Some examples are provided in 'Reading notes', a thematic issue (ed. Dirk Van Hulle and Wim Van Mierlo) of the journal *Variants: The Journal of the European Society for Textual Scholarship*, 2/3 (2004).
13. The Coleridge marginalia were published in five volumes as: Samuel Taylor Coleridge, *Marginalia*, ed. George Walley and H. J. Jackson, in *The Collected Works of Samuel Taylor Coleridge*, 12 vols (Routledge & Kegan Paul and Princeton University Press, Bollingen Series LXXV, 1980), I–V. See also Mario di Gregorio, *Charles Darwin's Marginalia* (New York, Garland, 1990), and Mark Nixon and Dirk van Hulle, *Samuel Beckett's Library* (Cambridge: Cambridge University Press, 2011). From 2006, the Department of English at Boise State University has been working on Melville's marginalia, which is available online: *Melville's Marginalia Online*, ed. Steven Olsen-Smith, Peter Norberg, and Dennis C. Marnon, http://www.boisestate.edu/melville/ [accessed 24 January 2010]. Information about ongoing work on Valéry's marginalia is available at http://www.paulvalery.org/ [accessed 24 January 2010].

14. Owen Gingerich, *The Book Nobody Read: Chasing the Revolutions of Nicolaus Copernicus* (London: William Heinemann, 2004).

15. For example, Matthew Driscoll, 'Postcards from the edge: an overview of marginalia in Icelandic manuscripts', *Variants: The Journal of the European Society for Textual Scholarship*, 2–3 (2004), 21–36; Jonas Carlquist, 'Medieval manuscripts, hypertext and reading: visions of digital editions', *Literary and Linguistic Computing*, 1 (2004), 105–18.

16. Heather Jackson, *Marginalia: Readers Writing in Books* (New Haven: Yale University Press, 2001), and Heather Jackson, *Romantic Readers: The Evidence of Marginalia* (New Haven: Yale University Press, 2005).

17. Virginia Woolf, *A Room of One's Own* (London: Hogarth Press, 1929).

18. By, for example, Anne Fadiman, *Exlibris: Confessions of a Common Reader* (New York: Farrar, Strauss & Giroux, 1998).

19. Stephen Colclough, 'Readers: books and biography', in *A Companion to the History of the Book*, ed. Simon Eliot and Jonathan Rose (Oxford: Blackwell, 2007), pp. 50–62 (53 f.). See also the discussion by Jonathan Rose in his 'Rereading the English common reader', in *The Book History Reader*, ed. David Finkelstein and Alistair McCleery, 2nd edn. (London: Routledge, 2006), pp. 424–39.

20. Kate Flint, *The Woman Reader 1837–1914* (Oxford: Clarendon, 1993).

21. Golick, 'one quart milk', pp. 95–113.

22. See, however, Meg Meiman, 'The anonymous reader: marginalia in library books', talk at the 2005 conference *Material Cultures and the Creation of Knowledge*, arranged by Centre for the History of the Book, University of Edinburgh, and R. C. Alston, *Books with Manuscript: A Short Title Catalogue of Books with Manuscript Notes in the British Library* (London: British Library, 1994).

23. Anthony Grafton, 'Is the history of reading a marginal enterprise? Guillaume Budé and his books', *Papers of the Bibliographical Society of America*, 91 (1997), 139–57.

24. Colclough, 'Readers', p. 54.

25. Catherine C. Marshall, 'Toward an ecology of hypertext annotation', in *Proceedings of Hypertext '98* (New York: ACM Press, 1997), pp. 40–9. This kind of research is to some degree performed in the fields of English and cognition studies as well. See, for example, J. Wesley Miller, 'Functional underlining: an essay in bibliography, criticism, and pedagogy', *College English*, 41 (1980), 575–8, or Sarah E. Peterson, 'The cognitive effect of underlining as a study technique', *Reading Research and Instruction*, 32 (1992), 49–56.

26. *Kajsa Dahlberg in a conversation*, p. 4 f.

27. See, for example, Jerome McGann, 'The socialization of texts', in *The Book History Reader*, ed. David Finkelstein and Alistair McCleery (London: Routledge, 2002), pp. 39–46; Donald F. McKenzie, *Bibliography and the Sociology of Texts* (London: The British Library, 1986); Jack Stillinger, *Multiple Authorship and the Myth of Solitary Genius* (New York: Oxford University Press, 1991). Typically, McGann sees text as: 'an interactive locus of complex

feedback operations. . . . We must attend to textual materials which are not regularly studied by those interested in "poetry": to typefaces, bindings, book prices, page format, and all those textual phenomena usually regarded as (at best) peripheral to "poetry" or "the text as such".' Jerome McGann, *The Textual Condition* (Princeton: Princeton University Press, 1991), p. 13.

28. *Kajsa Dahlberg in a conversation*, p. 4
29. Ibid.
30. Taken from the (anonymous) brochure presenting Kajsa Dahlberg at the Norwegian biennial art festival *Momentum* in 2006, entitled 'Try Again, Fail Again, Fail Better'.
31. Perhaps the best overview of scholarly editing and its various forms is provided by G. Thomas Tanselle, 'The varieties of scholarly editing', in *Scholarly Editing: A Guide to Research*, ed. David C. Greetham (New York: MLA, 1995), pp. 9–32.
32. Most notably, perhaps, in her *Writing Machines* (Cambridge, MA: MIT Press, 2002).

Part 4
Reading the Visual

8
Reading Ephemera

Sadiah Qureshi

In 1847, *Punch* published an announcement of one of the season's earliest and most entertaining exhibitions: the billstickers' 'pictorial embellishment' of Fleet Street Prison's walls (see Figure 8.1). *Punch* argued it offered a 'powerful counter-action' to the other entertainments on offer and even suggested that an enterprising publisher might profit from publishing a catalogue of the wall.[1] The article's humour depended upon the recognition that observing the streets of London was an established practice, both in the imagination and in physical presence. Of particular relevance here is that far fewer people attended an exhibition than knew of its existence, and that the streets were likely to be the first place where consumers were alerted to a new offering. Entrance charges of anything between one to five shillings often proved prohibitive; however, for the unfortunate many there were numerous other opportunities for consumption without attendance. Knowledge of an exhibition potentially extended beyond those attending to any passer-by, since the reproduction and circulation of posters, playbills and handbills enabled their use as highly visible markers pasted up in the streets surrounding the venue and possibly on the entrance door. This visibility ensured that the printed materials used to create and disseminate knowledge of the shows were at least as important as the live performances.

Showmen were acutely aware of the need to attract potential consumers and so were quick to take advantage of the development of advertising into a skilled trade from the mid-nineteenth century onwards.[2] Previously, most advertising took place within the streets and few street-sellers considered it their full time trade. Much of it

Figure 8.1 The billstickers' exhibition, *Punch* (1847)

was oral as sellers 'cried' for buyers, but there was some use of printed materials, especially in the late-eighteenth and early-nineteenth centuries. Billposting was quickly adopted in the early-nineteenth century whilst sandwich boards first came into use mid century. In the late-nineteenth century, specialized advertising agencies were established and there were considerable changes to the visual make-up of printed promotional materials, with more frequent use of colour, images and specialist typefaces. In 1833, a journalist for the *Athenaeum* confidently described advertising as a trade still in its 'infancy', but was uncertain as to whether it was a science or an art.[3] The promotional materials discussed in this chapter have often been ignored or used as isolated pieces of evidence (often of the shows' receptions) with little, if any, analysis of their production, circulation and use.[4] The exception to this general neglect is the literature on photography and anthropology.[5] However, this leaves a wealth of visual material untouched, particularly from the earlier nineteenth century.[6]

In contrast, this chapter explores how the shows' meanings were shaped for both potential and paying visitors through printed promotional material. In particular, it draws on examples from broader research on the commercial exhibition of living foreign peoples in nineteenth-century London. Paying to see living foreign peoples perform was enormously popular. For a shilling or more, the public flocked to see specially imported foreign, often colonized peoples, perform songs, dances and other ceremonies as demonstrations of their 'singular' nature. Not only were such shows common, but they were profitable, publicly accessible and amongst some of the most popular forms of metropolitan entertainment.[7] Despite its focus on such shows, the conclusions drawn in this chapter are of broader significance for histories of reading, not only since reading ephemera was an important activity, but since it has also often been ignored by historians.[8]

Considering showmen's promotional strategies is both revealing and necessary for understanding the ways in which consumers were persuaded to part with their money; however, it is critical to bear in mind that this does not equate to an excavation of consumer responses. Rather, a close analysis of promotional materials provides insights into the varied, and often shared, representational conventions that showmen used to generate public interest and mediate the ways in which the shows were ultimately interpreted. In making such claims, this chapter adds to recent work that has explored the use of guidebooks by working-class visitors to the British Museum and the interpretation of panoramas.[9] Examining promotional material in this vein suggests that it created a publicly accessible network of artefacts and claims that must be considered in discussions of how displayed peoples came to be consumable commodities. Moreover, it draws on the lessons of museological studies which have shown that curatorial decisions regarding the context in which an artefact is placed, as well as its positioning and labelling, can all structure visitor responses.[10] Thus, the importance of promotional materials depended upon the geography of their use; the streets, exhibition venues and the periodical press were all spaces in which showmen laid claim to readers' attention in an effort to secure custom. Meanwhile, promotional materials effectively extended invitations designed to encourage patrons to interpret the shows within diverse frameworks ranging from travel literature to foreign affairs. By employing these strategies, showmen made promotional materials fundamental to shaping the shows' receptions and in the creation of broader attitudes towards ethnic difference.

Reading ephemera also raises issues of broader relevance to histories of reading, particularly for the nineteenth century when such materials achieved a new visibility and commercial importance. Histories of reading have presented an increasingly rich and sophisticated understanding of the material nature of texts, how they were produced, circulated and read.[11] Simultaneously, as this new series suggests, our understanding of reading practices have been transformed as scholars have integrated publishers, printers, readers, critics and authors into accounts of how texts were consumed and understood across diverse spaces and periods.[12] Yet, this work has often been preoccupied with books to the neglect of other kinds of printed material, particularly ephemera. Consequently, the focus has implicitly been directed towards the reading habits of highly literate readers. Moreover, more research remains to be done on the ways in which ordinary people encountered print culture beyond the covers of a book in order to fully open up what reading may have meant across a broad spectrum of contexts. In this light, exploring the production, circulation and uses of printed promotional material opens up new and suggestive avenues for further research. For instance, advertising depended upon printed materials with diverse material forms, including handbills, playbills, posters and admission tickets, whilst also catering for a public with varying levels of literacy. As such, advertising helped to make shows profitable by attracting new kinds of readers who, even if semi-literate, were skilled in deciphering information, such as a show's venue or star attraction, from the palimpsests created by industrious bill-posters. Thus, exploring the uses of such materials and their readers provides a more balanced framework within which to understand reading and its histories.

Advertising humans

Impresarios used a variety of printed promotional materials to encourage people to part with their money: posters, playbills, handbills, newspaper reviews and newspaper advertisements.[13] Unlike newspaper advertisements, printed advertisements, such as handbills, were not subject to taxation and so provided a less costly alternative. Showmen were so eager to take advantage of the streets in lowering costs that billposting, which reached its height in the 1830s and 1840s, prompted parliament to pass an act requiring permission to be sought before pasting any poster.[14]

John Parry's *A London Street Scene* (1835) (Figure 8.2) evocatively captures this remarkable new advertising culture. The sheer wealth of information that street advertising made available to any literate individual is clear. Whilst the use of available walls as an advertising arena is evident, Parry also highlights two problems facing showmen using the streets. Reading is made difficult by the partial visibility of most of the posters. As soon as promotional materials were made public they could be buried under another layer of glue and letterpress. The billposter creates this dynamic palimpsest by pasting yet another announcement onto the wall, whilst the scraps of paper littering the pavement and the tattered posters at street level point towards inevitable destruction. Their transience is juxtaposed with the seeming permanence of St Paul's Cathedral. The direct consequence of this continual turnover means viewers of the painting, and by implication the street scene it depicts, must read carefully in order to discern the boundaries and messages of individual posters; just as posters jostle for space, they also vie for attention.

Since promotional materials were not guaranteed effectiveness by sheer number or presence alone, their efficacy depended upon other innovations. Their visual impact depended upon developments in

Figure 8.2 John Parry, *A London Street Scene* (1835)

advertising fuelled by the needs of promoters in the nineteenth century.[15] Billposting was a relatively new trade and over the century posters increased in size from the early theatre bills (commonly 8"×3") to six-sheet posters (probably 90"×40") which appeared much later. The innovation of special typefaces suited to advertising facilitated their impact. There were three basic varieties. The first were traditional Romans that were exaggerated into fat face by greatly increasing the contrast between thick and thin strokes and were in use by about 1806. The second were the slab serif, or Egyptian, typefaces that quickly became popular after their initial appearance between 1815 and 1817. Larger, bolder and more eye-catching than previous groups, they were characterized by minimal variations in the thick and thin strokes, heavy serifs with squared-off ends, large x-heights and vertical stress in the rounded strokes. The third basic forms were the sans-serifs, or grotesque, and, although they appeared around 1816, were most popular from the 1830s onwards. Any typeface might also have had additional decoration in the form of engraved lines or motifs around the letter.[16]

All three typeface families can be seen in Parry's painting. The artist has used a Roman typeface to sign his name in the centre of the composition whilst the majority of the typefaces he uses are Egyptian. The grotesque family is much rarer but the partially obscured 'Pompeii' on the right hand side is a good example. The new variations in stroke made these typefaces functionally far more suitable for headlines and display type, especially when compared to eighteenth-century conventions. Similarly, the mechanical regularity of newer styles also made them easier to produce; nonetheless, the production of typefaces remained a relatively laborious process until the late-nineteenth century. The combination of new typefaces and writing copy so that individual words could be stressed enabled promoters to consistently emphasize the aspects of exhibitions they considered most enticing or important; there is also the suggestion that this may have reflected the emergence of a semi-literate public who could quickly gain an understanding of the essential meaning of a poster even if they were unable to fully grasp the whole text.[17]

The use of images in promotional materials became far more common in the later nineteenth century: until then, images tended to be either entirely absent, very rare or available as privately produced paintings or prints. The scarcity of images was partly due to the expense of both the production and reproduction until shifting technologies lowered costs in the later nineteenth century. In 1842 the *Illustrated London News* was founded as the first weekly paper to feature images but the first daily to use them was not available until the 1889 launch of the *Daily Graphic*. In the early-nineteenth century, both in the press and in promotional materials, images were much rarer and usually made using cheap woodcuts. Although invented in the eighteenth century, by the 1820s lithography had become commercially viable. The earliest forms of photography, such as daguerreotypes and calotypes, made photography available by 1839 and 1841 respectively. These were quickly used as source material for engraved illustrations from the 1870s and 1880s and by the 1890s were being reproduced in half-tone periodical illustrations.[18] As images became increasingly common, the extent of textual description on posters began to diminish considerably and, in many cases, barely featured more than an exhibition's name (usually indicating the performers' ethnicity), venue and possibly the times of admittance.

Examining promotional materials closely reveals multiple potential uses. The use of primarily large display type and minimal text on some posters suggests they were intended, and certainly suited, for use purely as proclamations. The possible versatility of use is most clearly seen in handbills. They often employed display type in larger point sizes, effectively to form headlines that announced an exhibit's ethnicity and the show's venue. The remainder of the page was then devoted to explanatory text in a significantly smaller point size. Handbills vary in size, but could be as large as 7"×10" (approx. 18 × 25 cm) although they were commonly slightly smaller (A4 approximately equal to 8"×11" or 21 × 30 cm). The presence of headlines suggests that the handbills could easily have been used as posters in the streets or outside venues. Where the explanatory text included the order of play, handbills may possibly have doubled as programmes. Similar versatility may have applied to playbills that detailed the contents of advertised shows. Much of this text was in smaller type which needed to be read carefully. In addition to being pasted in and outside of venues, visitors may also have been able to procure them as programmes. Such versatility is speculative but it would clearly have aided any show's proprietor to reduce costs by greatly lessening the need for a range of promotional material.

Patrons' willingness to accept showmen's invitations to attend the shows is indicated by the number of exhibitions that regularly took place throughout the century and followed London seasons with provincial dates. Scarcely quoted attendance figures bear witness to public appetite. In 1853, one proprietor claimed that 'upwards of three thousand persons' had visited an exhibition of the 'Aztec Lilliputians' in just two days, whilst another claimed that 'upwards of fifty thousand persons' had visited a group of San ('Bushmen') exhibited in 1847.[19] These figures are unsubstantiated and taken from promotional materials; nonetheless, claims that exhibitions were successfully attracting audiences that numbered in their thousands, not hundreds, are indicative of considerable public exposure. Moreover, some venues boasted seating capacities that could have accommodated such figures at a single performance (Exeter Hall, for example, could seat 4,000). For the wealthy thousands able to spare a shilling or more, the significance of promotional material in providing interpretative frameworks continued inside exhibition venues.

Peopling the landscape

Posters and playbills outside reminded queuing patrons of imminent delights. Those who had arranged admission in advance, or reserved seats, were issued with admission tickets that succinctly reiterated promoters' claims and so functioned as more personal mnemonics or even souvenirs. Once inside, patrons frequently heard a lecture in conjunction with the evening's performance. Delivered either before the performance or during special intermissions, lectures were intended to shape the experience of simply seeing foreign peoples.

Patrons' potential lack of relevant linguistic or ethnological knowledge might render any live performance a bewildering display of indistinguishable ceremonies, songs and dances; this created specific needs that effectively invested promotional materials with an easily underestimated role in framing consumers' experiences. Some problems arose partly because most consumers were simply unable to speak the performers' language: one reviewer of the 1847 San exhibition observed that, 'At the conclusion of the lecture the Bosjesmans . . . walked down the hall, and finally entered into an apparently animated conversation on the platform. Of course, what they said was perfectly unintelligible, but they seemed to express themselves with great vivacity and quickness, or, if we may use the expression, natural eloquence.' At a similar disadvantage, another attendee concluded that the shouts were 'very Arabic or Irish in their explosiveness'.[20] The problem was compounded by the lecturer's 'want of physical force' and the 'extreme rapidity of his delivery' which left the audience viewing a 'strange people' with little understanding of their manners and customs because they simply had not heard the explanatory context.[21] The relatively common nature of such incomprehension is reinforced by reviews of an 1853 exhibition of Zulus, managed by Charles Henry Caldecott. The show consisted of acts in which:

> After a supper of meal, of which the Kaffirs partake with large wooden spoons, an extraordinary song and dance are performed, in which each performer moves about on his haunches, grunting and snorting the while like a pair of asthmatic bellows. . . . no description can give an idea of the cries and shouts – now comic, now terrible – by which the Kaffirs express emotions. The scene illustrative of the preliminaries of marriage and the bridal festivities might leave one in doubt which was the bridegroom, did not that interesting savage announce his enviable situation by screams of ecstasy which convulse the audience.[22]

The journalist's derision hints at an audience bellowing with laughter; yet, the review's humour depends upon the assumed incapability of readers, and by extension the show's patrons, of distinguishing between the show's scenes without some guidance. The plausibility of shared incomprehension speaks volumes.

These intriguing glimpses indicate audiences that can be differentiated upon the basis of prior knowledge. Some patrons may have been familiar with the relevant travel and medical literature or have travelled abroad and had first-hand experience of the peoples they chose to see perform. However, between the late-eighteenth and mid-nineteenth centuries, the high cost of travel and the relatively small and falling sales figures of travel accounts suggest that many more are unlikely to have read them and so would have been dependent upon showmen for suitable explanatory contexts.[23] For example, if the playbill named a given scene as a marriage ceremony then many members of the audience may have been unable to contest such a claim, based either on personal experience or substantial ethnological knowledge; witness the frustration of one reviewer of Caldecott's exhibition who grudgingly commented that the 'songs and dances are, as may be expected, monotonous in the extreme, and without the bill it would be difficult to distinguish the expression of love from the gesture of martial defiance'.[24] Showmen evidently understood the importance of these materials. As late as 1884, Robert A. Cunningham, who was exhibiting a group of Australian Aborigines, introduced the show's pamphlet as a 'little work . . . of an uncivilised race of whom but few travellers have given any accounts' and most of which were 'scattered at random through their books; moreover, these notices are distributed through a vast number of works, many of them very scarce, many very expensive, and most of them ill arranged'.[25] Given the likely lack of a mutually intelligible language, falling sales of travel literature and relative expense of foreign travel, especially in the early nineteenth century, the use of promotional materials evidently extended beyond attracting paying customers to playing a fundamental role in providing mutually shared frames of reference that many patrons not only used, but depended upon, to make sense of live performances.

Lectures aside, promotional pamphlets were the most substantial and detailed resources available within exhibition venues. Although relatively neglected by historians, an analysis of their material use and content is revealing.[26] Pamphlets appear to have been adapted for publication from lectures and were related to the guidebooks that were available at museums and galleries. One street trader believed that the 'largest buyers of these [guide] publications were country people, sight-seeing in London, for they bought the book not only as an explanatory guide, but to preserve as a memento of their visit'.[27] More recently it has been suggested that the opening-up of museums to new sections of the public, particularly the working classes, created a new market for teaching resources that was readily filled by enterprising publishers. This role extended the original use of guidebooks in enabling 'country-house visitors to identify items in the painting and sculpture collections when the housekeeper was absent or inadequately informed'.[28] Guidebooks for both temporary and permanent exhibitions most commonly sold for between 6*d.* and 1*s.* and could be bought either officially from the host institution or unofficially from street-sellers. Catalogues, especially for museums and galleries, tended to provide lists of objects in a collection with little or no accompanying text. In contrast, guidebooks were often illustrated and featured more substantial passages that provided explanatory material or even routes designed to maximize the didactic value of the collections.[29] The extensive use of explanatory text marks pamphlets as much more akin to guidebooks than standard exhibition catalogues. However, their adaptation from lectures is likely to be unique, as most visitors to a gallery, museum or theatre are unlikely to have been expected to sit through a lecture contextualizing the prospective displays.

Exhibition pamphlets were short essays providing descriptions of the 'manners and customs' of displayed peoples. Contents varied, but, as a rule, they contained biographical and ethnological histories of displayed peoples. Ranging from twenty to thirty pages each, they most commonly cost sixpence and appear to have been sold within showrooms. They rarely feature in catalogues of printed works of the period and those that do survive are often disintegrating, rarely bound and often housed in collections of ephemera. Their relatively thin paper and weak bindings suggest that they were intended for use during the performance and little else; however, their survival also indicates that they were not always disposed of and may have been kept as souvenirs. The degree of illustration varies, from being entirely absent, to limited to a single title page or running to several plates, as does the subject, from the performers to scenes from their homelands. The text is usually in relatively large point size and divided into short sections with individual subheadings to provide structure. Subheadings often referred to the ceremonies being performed and thus classified the pamphlets' material according to shows' contents. For example, the pamphlet accompanying the 1853 Zulu exhibition contained major sections detailing the characteristics of the Zulus' homelands, laws and government followed by discussions of a 'Zulu marriage', 'witches and witch-finding' and 'hunting and going to battle'. All these sections corresponded to the tableaux detailed on the playbill. Since the material was not necessarily organized according to staged order, the pamphlets are unlikely to have been used as prolix programs; instead, their format suggests that they offered a reference point for the audience to consult during the lecture or performance when a particular scene was being presented.

The pamphlets' descriptive material did not necessarily stem from showmen's personal experience or constitute original pieces of writing;

rather, a close reading reveals that they relied heavily upon well-known contemporary travel literature. Frequently, fragments of the text and, more commonly, substantial sections were either paraphrased or actively excerpted.[30] Likewise, illustrations from travel literature, assumed to be authoritative, were often used for background scenery or as the basis for reworked illustrations in promotional materials.[31]

Travel literature was of fundamental importance in shaping the conventions of representation shared by showmen, consumers and learned men alike. Patrons were clearly encouraged to associate and interpret their experiences within the ongoing discussions set up by travel writers, be they explorers, missionaries, colonial officials, naturalists or tourists. The pamphlets' extensive use of previously published work suggests they were either written relatively quickly or, on occasion, just reprints of substantial sections of other work, perhaps in response to public requests for more information in the early days of a show's run, or simply as a means of keeping costs down by not investing time or money in original research. Such selective excerpting allows us to observe the means through which exhibitors aligned themselves within specific social and political discussions to legitimate their enterprises as accurate representations of foreign peoples and valuable intercultural encounters. It also provides a partial solution to the problem that eye-witness accounts of the shows are woefully rare. Examining the pamphlets, and other promotional material, in detail indicates how showmen used advertising to invite consumers to associate displayed peoples with specific visual and racialist conventions, political activities, and ethnological research.

Whilst the importance of promotional material may be surmised from this brief examination of the individual uses of posters, playbills, handbills and pamphlets, understanding their relationship to each other is also necessary if one is to appreciate fully how contemporary methods of production and circulation created a network of closely related artefacts that, by being so publicly accessible, shaped the shows' receptions.

Promotional exchanges

Promotional materials were not unrelated scraps of paper, but part of a circulating network of claims devoted to successfully creating profitable exhibitions. Textual exchanges and active excerpting between different print forms provides one of the most concrete ways to connect a wide variety of promotional material. Just as showmen relied on travel literature to produce pamphlets, journalists regularly used advertising materials as resources from which to write about displayed peoples. They often based the bulk of their articles on promoters' advertising. For example, in reviews the descriptions of ceremonies were often paraphrased versions of the text appearing on handbills and playbills. Showmen returned the compliment and often employed positive reviews to advertise their wares. Towards the end of an exhibition's run, for instance, showmen might use quotations from particularly approving reviews in the longer advertisements which attempted to encourage visitors during the final weeks. Exhibitors also often collated and reprinted longer reviews alongside a brief description of a show in very short pamphlets, usually only a few pages, which could then be bought by the public.[32] The appropriation of information extended to visual material. Such exchanges demonstrate the movement of information between materially distinct promotional forms and in the wider press (such as handbills, pamphlets and reviews) and so highlight the importance of considering promotional ephemera material as an integrated body of material, rather than isolated scraps of showmen's pomp.

The common use of textual exchanges depends largely on the methods employed to produce newspapers and the nature of journalism as a profession in the nineteenth century.[33] The gap between the production methods of newspapers with larger and smaller circulations can be striking. The smallest papers, for example, might only be produced by an editor and reporter and could not compete with the circulation figures of larger provincial papers or national dailies. Instead, they might offer items of local news, a leading article and digested forms of the larger papers. Freelance journalists may also be a significant source for textual similarity. These 'penny-a-liners' sold written articles to anybody willing to buy them. Frequently impoverished and on the verge of ruin, it is quite likely that they may have sold similar stories, if not exactly the same, to a number of different publications. Although proving how much freelance journalists contributed to a publication is difficult, it is unlikely that they were the sole or even primary source of textual overlaps; but they remain a possible explanation. In addition, many journalists were routinely employed by a number of periodicals. As such, the production methods involved in the production of news in the nineteenth century may account for the extensive use of textual excerpting. Alternatively, newspaper reviews may have been using text from press releases which, with other promotional materials, formed a common framework of claims used to generate paying interest.

In conjunction, publications commonly exchanged whole columns of printed material with the advent of stereotyping. Stereotyping involved setting type into columns and using these to cast plates from which prints could be made. Although invented much earlier it was not in general use until mid century, but, once common, it made textual transfer between publications relatively simple and became especially popular in the 1850s and 1860s as smaller papers attempted to compete with *The Times*. The *Morning Herald* and the *Standard*, for example, cost four pence and a penny respectively yet most of their printed material was not only shared but identical, 'like the Siamese twins'.[34] The development of news agencies in the mid to late-nineteenth century is also relevant.[35] News agencies often supplied text as a package that had been written by journalists in their employment, rather than by the newspaper. This ensured that editors could reliably fill their columns without having to undertake the arduous task of finding a dependable writer; instead, they received material that could be inserted, without alteration, directly into their pages. Similarly, advertising agencies supplied a bridge between clients. They supplied newspapers with press releases and vendors with their required promotional notices. The mutual economic dependence of these parties raises the possibility of arrangements existing between agencies, showmen and the newspapers to benefit each other and may provide an explanation as to why newspaper reviews appear to have been generally positive.

Informational overlaps were not limited to newspapers and promotional material; equally, pamphlets were mined as sources of material for handbills and posters. Advertisements, in the papers and promotional material, are often worded exactly the same as pamphlets and the descriptions contained in reviews are frequently dependent upon, if not paraphrased versions of, the descriptive histories in pamphlets. Informational overlaps could also occur across varying stretches of time. For instance, a handbill for Farini's 1879 exhibition of 'Friendly Zulus' featured an approving review:

THE TIMES (speaking of Farini's Zulus) says – 'The songs and dances are difficult to distinguish the expression of love from the gesture of martial defiance. Nevertheless as a picture of manners nothing can be more complete; and not the least remarkable part of the exhibition is the perfect training of the wild artists. They seem utterly to lose all sense of their present condition: if English actors could be found so completely to lose themselves in the characters they assumed, histrionic art would be in a state, truly magnificent.'[36]

Despite the approbation, the slightly garbled quotation was not a review of Farini's show but Caldecott's 1853 exhibition of Zulus (as above). Evidently, consumers are exceptionally unlikely to have recalled a newspaper review of 1853 in 1879 and therefore discover the misleading claim. Yet, the quotation's use raises the question how did Farini have access to the original review? For instance, did he have copies of some of the original promotional material or did he have access to a scrapbook, or something similar, in which an interested individual, perhaps Caldecott or himself, had collected materials relevant to human display? Either way, his use of the 1853 review provides a pregnant indication of the varied routes and expanses of time that could be involved in textual exchanges.

The importance of textual exchange and appropriation in providing promotional material across such a diverse range of formats may partly depend upon the importance of anthology as a genre during this period. Writers were often anthologized, with or without their permission, and extracts ranged from whole pages to witty epigrams suited to moral commandment. The widespread use of textual appropriation in the form of anthologizing led to writers, for example George Eliot, adapting their writing styles by including passages especially suited to extraction.[37] It is not surprising that in this culture of exchange so much adaptation took place or that the use of accreditation varied considerably.

Textual and visual exchange may be conceptualized as the different levels of a food chain in which text is continually digested, regurgitated and consumed. Within this chain, pamphlets provided the crucial mediating link between travel writing, promotional materials and journalistic accounts. They were also the most common starting point for the circulation of information in London's streets and press as their contents were clipped and used across the most diverse range of promotional material with distinctive functions. Thus, although unavailable, the circulation figures of pamphlets would be unlikely to reflect their importance accurately. Even if pamphlets were only available to audience members, or proved too expensive for those with limited incomes, their use as sources for newspaper articles and promotional materials means the information they contained is likely to have reached a far greater number of people than ever witnessed a show. Thus, they played a pivotal role in the textual and visual representation of exhibited peoples, whether directly or through their use in other print forms.

Conclusion

Promotional material ensured that the shows extended beyond the boundaries of an exhibition venue's walls into the streets. Many could not afford the entrance fees exhibitors charged, but any passer-by could inspect the posters and playbills that were glued onto available walls. Posters, playbills, handbills, newspaper reviews and even entrance tickets carried promises of uniqueness, rarity and ethnic singularity. Using a range of newly emerging techniques exhibitors ensured that their proclamations were as eye-catching as possible. These encouraged passers-by to devote the attention needed to distinguish and read individual posters from the palimpsest that bill-posting produced.

The primary function of advertising for the shows' proprietors was obviously its role in ensuring commercial success, but how did metropolitan observers willing to take another look use these materials? Advertising in the streets enabled individuals who were unable to afford entrance charges or newspapers a form of consumption as long as they were semi-literate. As illustrated promotional materials became common even this prerequisite disappeared (although it required new skills associated with visual communication).[38] The geography of promotional materials' use (close to the venue and even on its walls) also allowed passers-by to know where a show was taking place. For those able to read, advertising was detailed enough for them to know who was being exhibited, where they came from and what they would perform. Although limited, this exposure allowed some measure of participation. Patrons wealthy enough to spare a shilling or more on an evening's entertainment would have found that many of the cues showmen used to frame displayed peoples were ultimately rooted in travel literature. It provided background scenery and the descriptive material that was used in lectures and pamphlets.

Exhibitors' extensive use of travel literature aligned displayed peoples within the discussions set up by the missionaries, government officials, explorers and travellers who wrote of their encounters with foreign peoples. Travel literature has long been acknowledged as critical in creating hierarchical views of foreign peoples which might be used to denigrate their humanity and facilitate the justification for imperial expansion.[39] Showmen perpetuated these perceptions by regurgitating whole passages of such accounts in their pamphlets. Travel literature appears to have provided the script for a significant proportion, if not all, of the promotional material used by showmen (such as posters, playbills and handbills) and provided journalists with a substantial portion of their review material. As such, advertising fashioned a racialist set of expectations which framed the audience's experiences (negative or positive) and thus fundamentally shaped the shows' receptions. Historians have been quick to seize on promotional materials as evidence of the shows' receptions. However, this approach is flawed. As forms of advertising, these materials were wont to emphasize, exaggerate, create or even fabricate ethnic difference for economic gain. They provide valuable evidence for how showmen marketed displayed peoples (and clearly ethnic origin mattered here) and how patrons were invited to frame their experiences using racialist stereotypes; however, advertising cannot be taken as evidence for how paying customers actually interpreted the performances they witnessed.

Consumers are highly unlikely to have adopted promotional rhetoric uncritically; however, examining the promotional material closely still provides clues for possible interpretations. The availability of advertising makes it more than likely that the metropolitan population used the claims of advertising as a measure against which personal experiences could be judged. Attending a performance might provide a basis for rejecting common stereotypes, but an individual doing so would still be employing preconceived notions of how a performer might behave which, ultimately, still depended upon advertising. Showmen capitalized upon this by marketing them as unique educational opportunities. Where patrons failed to make such associations they were made explicit by lecturers who referred to the backdrop of relevant political activity and foreign affairs. Thus, advertising used posters, bills and pamphlets, in which showmen attempted to stereotype displayed peoples into the role of the performing 'savage'; yet, as histories of reading and the shows attest, such hermeneutic control was beyond their grasp.[40]

Notes and references

1. 'The billstickers' exhibition', *Punch*, 12 (1847), 226.
2. For more on early means of advertising see the launch issue of the *Illustrated London News*, 14 May 1842. See also Diana Hindley and Geoff Hindley, *Advertising in Victorian England, 1837–1901* (London: Wayland, 1972); Thomas Richards, *The Commodity Culture of Victorian England: Advertising and Spectacle, 1851–1914* (Stanford, CA: Stanford University Press, 1990) and Michael Twyman, *Printing 1770–1970: An Illustrated History of its Development and Uses in England*, 2nd edn. (London: British Library, 1998). For more on racialist advertising see Jan Piertese, *White on Black: Images of Africa and Blacks in Western Popular Culture* (New Haven and London: Yale University Press, 1992) and Anandi Ramamurthy, *Imperial Persuaders: Images of Africa and Asia in British Advertising* (Manchester: Manchester University Press, 2003).
3. 'Advertising', *Athenaeum*, 13 July 1833, 459–60.
4. For further discussion see Sadiah Qureshi, *Peoples on Parade: Exhibitions, Empire and Anthropology in Nineteenth-Century Britain* (Chicago: University of Chicago Press, 2011). A further exception is the analysis of the Zulu pamphlet in relationship to travel literature and Dickens's journalism in Bernth Lindfors, 'Charles Dickens and the Zulus', in his *Africans on Stage: Studies in Ethnological Show Business* (Bloomington: Indiana University Press, 1998), pp. 62–80.
5. See Elizabeth Edwards, ed., *Anthropology and Photography, 1860–1920* (New Haven and London: Yale University Press, 1994) and Elizabeth Edwards, *Raw Histories: Photographs, Anthropology and Museums* (Oxford and New York: Berg, 2001).
6. This discussion is based primarily upon promotional materials from the John Johnson Collection of Printed Ephemera (JJ), held at the Bodleian Library, Oxford, and the Evanion Collection at the British Library, London. Printed collections of primary materials may be found in Leonard de Vries, *Victorian Advertisements* (London: John Murray, 1968) and Catherine Haill, *Fun without Vulgarity: Victorian and Edwardian Popular Entertainment Posters* (London: The Stationery Office, 1996).
7. Qureshi, *Peoples on Parade*.
8. For a broader consideration of this theme see Michael Twyman, 'The long-term significance of printed ephemera, *RBM: A Journal of Rare Books, Manuscripts and Cultural Heritage*, 9 (2008), 19–57.
9. Aileen Fyfe, 'Reading natural history at the British Museum and the *Pictorial Museum*', in *Science in the Marketplace: Nineteenth-Century Sites and Experiences*, ed. Aileen Fyfe and Bernard Lightman (Chicago: University of Chicago Press, 2007), pp. 196–230; Ralph O'Connor, *Earth on Show: Fossils and the Poetics of Popular Science, 1802–1856* (Chicago: University of Chicago Press, 2008), pp. 263–324; Robert D. Aguirre, *Informal Empire: Mexico and Central America in the Victorian Culture* (Minneapolis: University of Minnesota Press, 2005), especially pp. 35–60.

10. For examples see *Exhibiting Cultures: The Poetics and the Politics of Museum Display*, ed. Ivan Karp and Steven D. Lavine (Washington: Smithsonian Institution Press, 1991); *Colonialism and the Object: Empire, Material Culture and the Museum*, ed. Tim Barringer and Barbara Flynn (London: Routledge, 1998); James Clifford, *The Predicament of Culture: Twentieth-Century Ethnography, Literature and Art* (Cambridge, MA: Harvard University Press, 1988); Peter Vergo, *The New Museology* (London: Reaktion, 1989) and Tony Bennet, *The Birth of the Museum: History, Theory, Politics* (London: Routledge, 1995).

11. For a magisterial example see James A. Secord, *Victorian Sensation: The Extraordinary Publication, Reception and Secret Authorship of 'Vestiges of the Natural History of Creation'* (Chicago and London: University of Chicago Press, 2000).

12. For a seminal work in this respect see Robert Darnton, 'What is the history of books', *Daedalus*, 111 (1982), 65–83.

13. For more on the definitions of posters, handbills, etc. see Maurice Rickards, *Encyclopaedia of Ephemera: A Guide to the Fragmentary Documents of Everyday Life for the Collector, Curator and Historian*, ed. Michael Twyman (London: British Library, 2000).

14. Hindley, *Advertising in Victorian England*, 90.

15. Twyman, *Printing 1770–1970*, p. 10.

16. For more typography see David C. Greetham, *Textual Scholarship: An Introduction* (London and New York: Garland, 1994), pp. 225–70 and Philip Gaskell, *A New Introduction to Bibliography*, 2nd edn. (Winchester: St Paul's Bibliographies, 1995), pp. 207–14.

17. Twyman, *Printing 1770–1970*, pp. 10–14.

18. For the standard account of the history of photography see Beaumont Newhall, *A History of Photography from 1839 to the Present*, 5th edn. (New York: Museum of Modern Art, 1984).

19. 'Aztec Lilliputians', Advertisement, *Illustrated London News*, 16 July 1853, 22 and Anon., *Now Exhibiting at the Egyptian Hall, Piccadilly. The Bosjesmans, or Bush People, from the Interior of South Africa, Who First Appeared at the Exeter Hall, on Monday, 17th May; The only Real Specimens of This Extraordinary and Rapidly Decreasing Race of Human Beings Who Have Ever Visited Europe* (London: Chapman, Elcoate and Company, 1847), p. 1.

20. Anon., *Now Exhibiting at the Egyptian Hall*, 1.

21. Ibid.

22. 'The Zulu Kaffirs, at the St George's Gallery, Knightsbridge', *Illustrated London News*, 28 May 1853.

23. On the falling sales figures of travel literature see Nigel Leask, *Curiosity and the Aesthetics of Travel Writing, 1770–1840: 'From an Antique Land'* (Oxford: Oxford University Press, 2002).

24. 'The Caffres at Hyde-Park-Corner', newspaper clipping dated 18, May 1853, JJ, Human Freaks 4 (83d).

25. R. A. Cunningham, *History of R. A. Cunningham's Australian Aborigines, Tattooed Cannibal Black Trackers and Boomerang Throwers, Consisting of Two Tribes, Male and Female* (London, J. Elliot, 1884), p. 2.

26. Helpful exceptions may be found in Aguirre, *Informal Empire*, particularly pp. 109–11 where he discusses the pamphlet for Maximo and Bartola, and Lindfors, 'Charles Dickens and the Zulus'.

27. Henry Mayhew, *London Labour and the London Poor*, 4 vols (London: Griffin, Bohn and Company, 1861–1862), I, pp. 299–300.

28. Fyfe, 'Reading natural history' p. 214.

29. Ibid.

30. Lindfors, 'Charles Dickens and the Zulus', pp. 62–80; Qureshi, *Peoples on Parade*.

31. For examples of such visual anthologizing see Qureshi, *Peoples on Parade*.

32. See for example, Anon., *Final Close of the St George's Gallery, Hyde Park Corner, Piccadilly. Zulu Kafirs. Last Few Days in London* (London: W. J. Goulbourn, 1853). This short pamphlet is almost entirely a compilation of reviews.

33. Lucy Brown, *Victorian News and Newspapers* (Oxford: Clarendon Press, 1985) and Jeremy Black, *The English Press, 1621–1861* (Gloucestershire: Sutton, 2001). See also, Hindley, *Advertising in Victorian England*, p. 49.

34. Cited in Brown, *Victorian News and Newspapers*, p. 116.

35. See Brown, *Victorian News and Newspapers*, pp. 112–19, and Hindley, *Advertising in Victorian England*, p. 17.

36. 'Farini's Friendly Zulus', Handbill, Evan. 876, Evanion Collection, British Library.

37. Leah Price, *The Anthology and the Rise of the Novel: From Richardson to George Eliot* (Cambridge: Cambridge University Press, 2000).

38. For a superb example of the skills required to read an image see Simon Schaffer 'On astronomical drawing', in *Picturing Science, Producing Art*, ed. Peter Galison and Caroline A. Jones (New York: Routledge, 1998), pp. 441–74.

39. Mary Louise Pratt, *Imperial Eyes: Travel Writing and Transculturation* (London: Routledge, 1992), pp. 15–37.

40. For texts see Secord, *Victorian Sensation*, p. 444. For the shows see Qureshi, *Peoples on Parade*.

9
Books in Photographs

Kate Flint

'Photographs', Susan Sontag tells us near the beginning of her seminal work, *On Photography*, 'furnish evidence. Something we hear about, but doubt, seems proven when we're shown a photograph of it.'[1] She goes on to explore the reasons why this should be the case – even though we know that photographs can distort, be posed, altered, tampered with, recontextualized – and she concludes with a disgruntled lament that 'Needing to have reality confirmed and experience enhanced by photographs is an aesthetic consumerism to which everyone is now addicted . . . That most logical of nineteenth-century aesthetes, Mallarmé, said that everything in the world exists in order to end in a book. Today everything exists to end in a photograph.'[2] But what happens, I want to ask in this chapter, when a book ends up in a photograph; when the material volume is deployed for aesthetic ends – or at the very least, when our interpretation of reading is mediated through a camera lens? What kind of evidence is being offered up?

Books have appeared in photographs ever since the emergence of this new technology at the end of the 1830s. 'A Scene in a Library' is presented as the eighth plate within Fox Talbot's *The Pencil of Nature* (published in part form between June 1844 and April 1846) – allowing us to contemplate the simulacrum of books within a book. This is an image that, from the start, problematizes the question of evidence of reading. As an exhibit, it seems to give us a sense of the mixed nature of Talbot's library: some impeccably bound leather volumes (including three sets of three-volume texts as well as single volumes); some older volumes, their spines cracked and their labels fading and peeling, suggesting that they have been frequently taken down and consulted;

a couple of paper-bound books on the left of the top shelf – maybe from a foreign press; and a collection of pamphlets on the bottom. The lack of regimented neatness indicates, by inference, a library in use. The relatively close-up, cropped frame of the shot points to the personal nature of this book collection: the darkness behind and to the side of the volumes here intimating not just the potential for an unspecified number of other books on other shelves, but the unrecordable interior space of thought, reflection and invention. It is not that Talbot was averse to wider views – the first two plates in *The Pencil of Nature* show street scenes in Oxford and Paris, respectively. Rather, 'A Scene in a Library' belongs alongside the inventory-style images that appear as Plate III, 'Articles of China', and Plate IV, 'Articles of Glass'. Talbot's description of 'Articles of China' shows him speculating about the potential evidentiary status of photography. He writes:

> From the specimen here given it is sufficiently manifest that the whole cabinet of a Virtuoso and collector of old China might be depicted on paper in little more time than it would take him to make a written inventory describing it in the usual way . . . And should a thief afterwards purloin the treasures – if the mute testimony of the picture were to be produced against him in court – it would certainly be evidence of a novel kind; but what the judge and jury might say to it, is a matter which I leave to the speculation of those who possess legal acumen.[3]

Talbot's hypothesis here rests on the assumption that the indexical quality of the photograph – its ability to record, in detail, what is put in front of the camera's lens – carries a truth value, dependent on the presumption that a camera can convey accurate minutiae in an objective fashion. This may, indeed, be true of a Limoges teacup. But it is a line of reasoning far harder to apply to the photograph of his books. The titles on the spines are almost, but not quite, legible, at least in any print made from the $5\frac{1}{4} \times 7\frac{1}{16}$ inch paper negative. Their identification depends upon a knowledge of Fox Talbot's book collection, and through this, recognizing volumes of the *Philosophical Magazine*, *Miscellanies of Science*, *Botanische Schriften*, *Manners and Customs of the Ancient Egyptians*, *Philological Essays*, *Poetae Minores Graeci* and Lanzi's *Storia pittorica dell'Italia*: in other words, a putting together, by Talbot, of his intellectual biography through selected texts, whose influence may be traced through his printed writings and voluminous correspondence. More than that, very probably this is no accurate picture of his library. The intimate grouping of books is most likely the result of the image not having been taken in an actual library at all, but outdoors, maximizing the light in what would still, in these early days of photography, have been a long exposure time. 'A Scene in a Library' helps raise the interpretive question of what it means, and will come to mean, to 'read' a photograph within a book – as does a later plate, Plate IX, when Talbot's 'Fac-simile of an Old Printed Page' points ahead to the bibliographic value of photography when it comes to recording type, and layout – including, in turn, the positioning of plates within Fox Talbot's own ornamental text design.[4] But ultimately, 'A Scene in a Library' belongs to an older tradition of imaging the book: the book as still life, albeit highly emblematic of its owner's status, taste and desired self-presentation; the book as signifying devotion, dangerous frivolity or the brevity of worldly pursuits; books, that is, that manage to be eloquent about the practice of reading even in the absence of any actual reader.

The co-presence of a human photographic subject and a printed text does not, by any means, guarantee that reading has taken, or may take, place. Within photographs, books serve as props in all kinds of ways. As accessories, they were very frequently to be found in early photographic studios, their presence on a table in close proximity to a sitter suggesting, at the very least, not just literacy but bourgeois respectability. As static objects, they could help a subject to keep his or her hands or arms still during a long exposure. Similarly, having a sitter focus on a book, apparently immersed in its contents, was a means of keeping the head motionless – as well, of course, of intimating the reader's capacity for absorption, and their possession of an inner, private, imaginative or intellectual life. Alternatively, to portray, say, a smartly dressed young woman holding an open album indicates that she – like Rosamond Vincy – is to be thought of in conjunction with undemanding objects signifying feminine good taste. Directions as to how to arrange the sitter in relation to reading material could be found in early manuals for the use of photographers. 'The hands of a lady may rest easily on the lap, and should be presented edgewise, neither too high nor too low, which will give them a small, delicate appearance. Or one hand or arm may be laid upon a table, while the other hand may hold a book or some other object, if the sitter so choose',[5] wrote the Philadelphian daguerreotypist Marcus Aurelius Root in his 1864 *Camera and the Pencil*, although the fact that posing with a book had very quickly become a photographic cliché can be judged from the comments of the English photographer Henry Peach Robinson. Writing in 1869 about how to pose people for portraits, he recommends that the photographer think about arranging them with some imagination: 'he should store his mind with incidents suitable to his sitters, and he may then, perhaps, be able to give less occupation to the eternal book we see in the hands of photographées almost as often as a roll of paper is represented in the statues of statesmen'.[6] And yet the book was undeniably an appropriate accompaniment to a writer, and a sign of one's trade in the case of an intellectual editor or journalist, or could be used to convey gravitas, knowledge and statesmanship in a politician. When it comes to indicating inner virtue, a Bible, visibly conspicuous by its very heft, was a very legible sign of piety, and, in certain clearly non-European contexts, of the fact of conversion.

The signifying properties of books were readily available to nineteenth-century photographers putting together composite, and/or staged, narrative pictures. Oscar Rejlander, unpacking the complex 'Two Ways of Life' (the wicked having naked Bacchanalian fun on the left; the pious and virtuous clustered in the right), explained that 'near to Religion is *Knowledge*, personified by a female reading, the book being a sign of human progress'.[7] The Bible, once again, is central to such conspicuously artificial images as the elaborately set up genre piece by Henry Peach Robinson, *When the Day's Work is Done*. This image mimics the style of mid-Victorian genre painting so exactly (one might compare the pious concentration of Robinson's elderly couple to that of the young woman reading her Bible in Frank Bramley's *A Fisherman's Home*, for example) that it forces us to ask, right out, what the difference might be between the appearance of a book in a photograph, and a book in a painting. The tradition is an enduring one: Australian photographer Anne Zahalka, for example, has very consciously modelled her photographic composition on the work of Dutch masters, referencing them within the image itself, using their conventions as a means, as she puts it, 'of bringing into question (or seeking to understand) the influence of European culture and the nature of its incumbent value system',[8] and she continues the seventeenth-century practice of incorporating legible text even into unequivocally modern-day scenarios.

The literary critic Garrett Stewart, in *The Look of Reading*, has written extensively about many aspects of the appearance of both religious and secular books, and their readers; about the capacity of paintings to suggest the absorption and inwardness associated with becoming caught up in a book; and about the erotic charge that so frequently accompanied the depiction of the somatically possessed consumer of printed texts – nothing foreign, here, to those familiar with the role that reading could play in nineteenth-century pornographic photography. Stewart discusses what he calls 'the suffusion of space by private concentration',[9] concentration that in turn makes the painting's viewer reflect on their practices of spectatorship and decipherment in front of the canvas; and the differences – that change over time – between reading a book and reading a painting or work of graphic art. Many of his observations may be borrowed wholesale for the reading of photographs, too, especially when they bear on the dominant visual conventions of a time. Thus, in relation to Berthe Morisot's *Reading*, from 1873, Stewart writes that:

> the impulse to thematize reading as focal and restorative . . . is one of the period's most zealously preserved romantic legacies. This is even more clearly the case when that reading, a disencumberment on its own terms, is further released into nature's open landscape; and released in the form, often enough, of cognitive relief per se. That's the deliberate thematic respite from the urban fray of impressions that the rural idyll so often provides.

Thus we find the pastoral landscape in this painting 'fanned out behind the reader's fan as if by imaginative projection from the comparably splayed book'.[10]

How does Stewart's reading play out alongside a photograph representing two outdoor women readers from the 1890s? Even granted the fact that the landscape is decidedly less comfortable – if probably less damp and productive of grass stains – than Morisot's, they have a good deal in common: the theme of outdoor leisure; the theme of absorption (one woman in her embroidery, the other in the final pages of what appears to be a relatively well-worn paperback); and they refuse all contact with the eye of the photographer *or* subsequent viewer. If there is a view somewhere over the rocks, or if there is leafy shade somewhere among the birch trees, they are oblivious to it. Indeed, their large sunshade shields them from the elements, ensuring the self-contained nature of their world as surely as the mosquito nets protect John Singer Sargent's sister Emily and her friend Eliza Wedgwood in the portrait that he painted of them sitting in Majorca. What distinguishes the two works, of course, is that fundamental difference that distinguishes the photograph from the painting in far broader terms: the photograph's referential qualities. In Roland Barthes's familiar formulation:

> Photography's referent is not the same as the referent of other systems of representation. I call 'photographic referent' not the *optionally* real thing to which an image or a sign refers but the *necessarily* real thing which has been placed before the lens, without which there would be no photograph. Painting can feign reality without having seen it . . . in Photography I can never deny that *the thing has been there.*[11]

Thus we need the external evidence that informs us that the two women in the painting are Emily Sargent and Eliza. Without this information, we would have no means of knowing that this painting were not entirely the product of the artist's imagination. But whoever the two women reading outdoors might be, the very existence of the photographic image is testimony to their actual one-time existence, bringing with them the lacerating emphasis, as Barthes would have it, of the impact of time: 'whether or not the subject is already dead, every photograph is this catastrophe':[12] it carries with it the poignancy of pastness.

And yet, it is the very *posed* quality of this image that points, emphatically, at the limitations of the indexicality of a photograph when it comes to offering up evidence of reading. Suppose we could read the title on the cover of this book: would it offer any guarantee of either of these two women having actually *read* it? Let me take another, far more modern example, Jeff Wall's large, back-lit cibachrome transparency, *Adrian Walker, Artist, Drawing from a specimen in the Dept. of Anatomy at the University of British Columbia, Vancouver.* Here, the artist is at work contemplating, and translating to paper, a severed forearm. There are some files and folders in the cabinet behind him – the kind of printed materials that, shown here in their generic, unidentifiable form, are an ambient part of a laboratory space,

just like the white tiled walls. But there on the window-sill, very identifiable indeed, is a well-thumbed Penguin copy of *Don Quixote*. What
does one do with this? At least one critic has seen it as part of Jeff Wall's
careful construction of the scene. By this criterion, Walker's absorption
in anatomical drawing can be read as an anachronistic, futile activity:
the need for such drawing has been overtaken, from a scientific point
of view, by the role of the camera.[13] Don Quixote has, indeed, long
figured within photography, together with his books, as an emblem of
a man trapped within a whole lumber-closet of anachronisms. But Jeff
Wall's composition would seem to acknowledge the possibility of two
ways of seeing, in that Walker – an artist who uses the human figure
as a starting point in his work, rather than attempting to emulate the
detail of the lens – seems to be rendering up an impression in red chalk
rather than a transcription of the arm: it is the task of the camera to
make the exposed muscles disquietingly clear. In interview, Jeff Wall
has attempted to repudiate any suggestion that the book was deliberately planted as an interpretive clue. 'It's all real', said Wall.

> The Don Quixote just happened to be there. The picture involved
> a performance in that Adrian was working with me, but he didn't
> do anything he didn't normally do. I visited him occasionally dur-
> ing the time he was drawing there. He was a student of mine, and
> wanted to be more involved with drawing the figure. He arranged
> with the department of anatomy that he could work there for an
> extended period. I might have moved the lamp over a little bit, but
> I didn't change anything. The picture is an example of what I call
> 'near documentary'.[14]

But how far can one trust this? Wall is, after all, a photographer
who creates stages for his tableaux as elaborate, and as artificial, as
any movie set designer. And even if Walker was, indeed, carrying
around this battered volume, not only is there nothing to stop *us*
reading the reference to Cervantes in this way, but there is nothing
to say that he himself did not, at some level, understand the knight's
belated standards of reference as providing an analogy for his own
draftsmanship.

Legible titles in images may, indeed, be a snare and a delusion.
Or they may not. Take Eve Arnold's well-known image of Marilyn
Monroe reading *Ulysses*. Nothing could seem more posed, more

calculated to elicit a smile at the apparent incongruity of the quintessence of supposed dumb-blondeness immersed in Joyce's challenging novel – and gripped, no less, by the book's ending, by Molly Bloom's monologue, something calculated to raise the erotic charge of the pose, as, lips slightly apart, she appears oblivious not just to the camera at this highly private moment, but oblivious, too, to the discomfort (and irony) of the playground carousel on which she's perched. The reality lies somewhere in the middle of this. As Eve Arnold recollected:

> As far as I remember . . . I asked her what she was reading when I went to pick her up (I was trying to get an idea of how she spent her time). She said she kept *Ulysses* in her car and had been reading it for a long time. She said she loved the sound of it and would read it aloud to herself to try to make sense of it – but she found it hard going. She couldn't read it consecutively. When we stopped at a local playground she got out the book and started to read while I loaded the film. So, of course, I photographed her. It was always a collaborative effort of photographer and subject where she was concerned – but almost more her input.[15]

Yet even this account leaves open the option that as the two worked together, Marilyn, supremely self-aware of her own status as a highly sexualized icon of popular culture, was a conscious participant in the irony of her apparent absorption in this archetypal signifier of high literary culture. Perhaps it would be safer, when it comes to the matching up of readers and titles in photographs, to stick to what appears to be a documentary exercise – like Harry Pye's Polaroid portrait series, *The South London Book Readers Club*, with each young man shown as caught up in a chosen book – by Anthony Powell, Keith Moon, Michel de Certeau. Yet this turns out to be a conspicuously artificial work: he used his childhood friends to pose for him as members of an imagined organization, in order to highlight the irony inherent in one aspect of book clubs, that their social functions and camaraderie go hand in hand with the most intensely private of activities – one that blocks out immediate social contact and places the reader in a self-enclosed frame.

Do we, then, give up on the idea that the presence of books within photographs might provide some stable kind of evidence of reading? I think not, but this involves extending our understanding of the concept of 'evidence' beyond the factual recording of particular works. Cultural critic Annette Kuhn writes that:

> Photographs are evidence, after all. Not that they are to be taken at face value, necessarily, nor that they mirror the real, nor even that a photograph offers any self-evident relationship between itself and what it shows. Simply that a photograph can be material for interpretation – evidence, in that sense: to be solved, like a riddle; read and decoded, like clues left behind at the scene of a crime.[16]

She reminds us that what the photograph may be taken as evidence *of* is not necessarily visible. In particular, Kuhn is discussing family photographs, reminding us that they 'are supposed to show not so much that we were once there, as how we once were: to evoke memories which might have little or nothing to do with what is actually in the picture'.[17] I want to extend her observation away from intimate records of family life, to suggest that the presence of books within photographs may constitute important evidence not so much about the consumption and ingestion of named, identifiable texts, but about prevalent attitudes towards the practice of reading, and the spaces in which it is conducted. Looked at like this, it matters far less whether a photograph is posed, or depicts an actual moment – the reader indeed wrapped in a text, oblivious of the viewer, devouring words, the fantasy on which so many depictions of reading, photographed or painted, depend. In this way – to take a handful of further examples – a young boy in an image from Simen Johan's 'Images of Things Unseen' series seems to be suffering from nightmares induced by reading the menacing array of books lined up behind him. Turkish photographer Nazif Topçuoglu plays with the very Victorian idea of respectable young girls being simultaneously fascinated and shocked by what they encounter when browsing freely in a library. His images, he says, are very much informed not just with ideas of time and loss, but by the association of these themes with the act of reading. The artist's statement on his website opens with Proust's words: 'On no days of our childhood did we live so fully perhaps as those we thought we had left behind without living them, those that we spent with a favourite book.'[18] Yet this is very late childhood, in which gawky innocence is only a couple of inches away from experience. And, if the idea of textual contagion has been most commonly thought of in relation to women, the poised tension between Anthony Goicolea's precociously formal adolescent boys – in upper-class libraries and drawing rooms – extends the trope in other homoerotic directions.

Other forms of association work in a less cerebral way. Stock photos of people reading – readily available from such sources as www. gettyimages.com, or www.corbis.com, or www.shutterstock.com – rely, to be sure, on associations of leisure, private immersion and concentration, or of using a book to occupy time. Yet each of them depends not just on intellectual knowledge of where and how people read, but on the way in which the postures of reading are encoded within, and recognized by, our neural systems and hence our bodies. It is this somatic identification that comes into play when we look at a (possibly posed, but does it matter?) image of readerly absorption such as André Kertesz's *Paris, Pont des Arts, 1963*, the sense of voyeurism heightened by the elevated view looking down as if over the reader's shoulder. It is this somatic identification with a private experience, I would argue, that helps to make reading such a powerful subject within documentary photography: it encourages identification and empathy through one's shared physical knowledge of what it feels like to sit or lie or slouch with a book; it also relies on our personal and cultural familiarity with the imaginative release that escaping into a book can bring with it.

This somatic knowing also comes into play when we look at the practices of reading recorded by the photographers working for the Farm Security Administration (FSA) between 1935 and 1945. A good deal of the reading that is shown as taking place is of ephemeral material, such as newspapers or comics. Only occasionally is the nature of the reading material specified, most typically a Bible. The photographs tell us, however, a good deal about the spaces, the postures, the *look* of reading, whether out of doors or indoors; at home or in a library; or by children or the elderly. Taken all together – and there are around four hundred images of reading in the collection – they suggest, and in many cases quite probably deliberately, the power of a book to offer up distraction in times of hardship, and to bestow an aura of self-sufficiency, even dignity, on the reader her or himself. Photography's usefulness in providing a record of reading spaces extends far beyond the work of the FSA: it opens up environments where the status of a book seems equivalent to another bibelot, or is a signifier of a rather chilly bourgeois respectability, or, as in one of E. J. Bellocq's images of the room of an early-twentieth century New Orleans prostitute, the presence of literary materials in an otherwise fairly Spartan interior raise unanswerable questions.

Photography feeds our curiosity, moreover, about the private spaces of authors, whether they are present, or absent. The *Guardian* publishes a compelling series of 'Writers' Rooms', which engages us, I think, through playing on a form of covetousness, of projection: if only we had that desk, that view, that *space* – maybe there we would find the secret of productive creativity. There is also the sense, or the illusion, that we are penetrating into private sanctums and that we are thereby learning something intimate and hidden about the personality of the writer – whether we witness the scary chaos of Craig Raine's study, or Antonia Fraser's deliberate, comfortable untidiness: 'I want my mind to be the only orderly thing in the room', she tells the reader; or Andrew O'Hagan's seemingly compulsive neatness: 'I just need to know where everything is before I go in search of things in my own head.' The inhabitants' verbal testimony is, it turns out, crucial to interpreting the visual evidence apparently offered by these rooms. 'Most of the stuff you see in the photograph is redundant', commented Sue Townsend, 'the books go unread, the files are never opened, and the posters are unseen.'[19]

Unopened books, however, have considerable presence, and nowhere is this more apparent than in photographs of libraries. The German photographer Candida Höfer has long specialized in taking pictures of empty institutional spaces: her images of libraries almost always are emptied out of individual readers. Instead, seats, desks, carrels are waiting for their temporary occupants. Whether these library spaces are formal or, on rare occasions, more disorderly, they suggest how knowledge can be accumulated, ticketed, classified, archived, arranged. The underlying taxonomies are not made explicit, but they are part of the numinous presence of these books, located, almost always, in settings that are likewise indicative of an enduring cultural heritage, suggesting, as art historian Monica Alvarez Careaga has put it, that we ourselves 'are just a link in the train of cultural transmission'.[20] If actual readers are visible, the length of Höfer's exposures means that they are just ghostly, transient presences, passing through these rooms that are both spacious, containing the promise of all kinds of factual and imaginative enlightenment – or for that matter, spurious and deluded accounts and information – and enclosed environments, suggesting the library as an all-encompassing universe, like Borges's library, 'unlimited and cyclical. If an eternal traveler were to cross it in any direction, after centuries he would see that the same volumes were repeated in the same disorder (which, thus repeated, would be an order: the Order.)'[21] In that they are records of actual libraries, present and past, Höfer's photographs constitute something of an archive in their own right of actual reading spaces that are or have been, but there is also something of the Borgesian dream of the infinitude of the ideal library in them.

In this, Höfer's locations have something in common with other, composite photographic libraries that are in many ways complete fantasy. Jeff Wall's *The Giant* inserts the imposing presence of a confident, serene, naked elderly woman onto a staircase in what seems to be a busy university library. This is no melodramatic self-exposure: the other library users appear unaware of her presence, leaving one to surmise – but with no answer provided – that she may be some kind of goddess of learning or knowledge, a benign, invisible presence despite the materiality of her statuesque grandeur in this manipulated photograph. It is, Wall has said in interview, rather like Baudelaire's 'art ideal . . . a kind of fusion of reportage with what he thought of as the "high philosophical imagination" of older art'.[22] Even more fantastic is Jean-François Rauzier's *Bibliothèque Idéale* – what he terms a 'hyperphoto', composed of a thousand individual images, most of them taken with an exposure of between one to two hours, the focal length of the lens set anywhere between twelve inches and infinity, seamlessly photoshopped together in order to create a library dreamscape of neatly ordered shelves and a chaos of tumbled books, a baroque ceiling opening onto the sky, corridors receding into an invisible distance, and a number of readers – some of them Rauzier himself, some of them the faces of famous literary figures imposed on his own body, some of them (because he likens these photographs to the products of dreams, products of the unconscious) cats.[23] Like Rauzier's other works, this is a wall-size photo: when he exhibits, he shows the complete work side-by-side with enlargements that bring out even more details than can be seen with the naked eye. Similarly, viewing the image online allows one to scan, to move in, to enlarge: he makes full use not just of the completely inventive possibilities of the photographic medium, but of the technology that can accompany its display. His *Bibliothèque* is evidence not of how any library *is*, but how it *might* be, in the imagination.

In considering these photographic representations of libraries, real and imaginary, books often start to look not so much like individual volumes that might be read on particular occasions, their contents mattering more than their exteriors, but appear as material objects that themselves, in their ordering, can take on an aesthetic valence in their own right. Höfer herself has explored the formalist potential of the book, its shape, thickness, colour and texture, and other photographers have exploited the abstract designs afforded by books on shelves, whether created by their spines (the mosaic of Hong Hao's *My Things No. 7: Knowledge is Power* is a labour-intensive photomontage of his personal library), or by the colours or the forms of their inner edges. Ironies lurk in the arrangements of periodical volumes on shelves, as evidenced by Mickey Smith's *Collocations* project, in which she has set out to photograph library collections waiting to be turned into microfiche. In making one word on the spine do the speaking, Smith's work may owe something to Albert Morell's *Thought Book* (2001). Cuban-American Morell's compositions are the antithesis of Rauzier's elaborate collageing. Often, he takes small details of books, drawing attention to them through lighting that strongly emphasizes the white of a page and the darkness of the surrounding space of reading and thought. Sometimes he is intrigued by their shapes; sometimes he tries, as he said in an interview, 'to get a visual equivalent of what it is to read or to have words be significant';[24] sometimes he positions the books and their openings in order to suggest – 'more than to suggest', he says,

> that most usually the official reading of a book is when it's open and there is a traditional way of getting the official meaning. When they are half-opened (and half-closed) something very interesting is happening as well . . . why not say that a half-open book is as interesting as a fully open book.[25]

Even when a book is damaged, Morell hints at the verbal meaning struggling to escape, in whatever new and transfigured shape, from the sculptural waves of soaked paper. Texas artist Carer Barer takes the transformation, or mutilation, of the book in the service of abstract art a step yet further, soaking her subjects for hours, positioning the pages, curling them over hair-rollers, even fixing them with Velcro. But abstract though the eventual beauty of the image may be, the book's dried corpse set against a studio-portrait black background,

Barer herself acknowledges that the text itself often plays a part in the finished form: that she starts reading whilst she is working; that some of her own titles, such as *Beach Read* or *New Century* or *Roget* reference their origins.

For however objectively a photographer may approach the physical properties of his or her textual subject, it is almost impossible to avoid the implications of its interior, of the signifying properties of the words it contains: not necessarily of the *specific* words, which can look downright surreal on the page once placed under the close scrutiny of the lens, but of what their printed presence implies in more general terms. In the final part of this chapter, I am less concerned with photographs as offering up evidence of reading, or of ideas about reading, as with asking how we might read the evidence of social and cultural assumptions and practices that may be derived from photographs of books: read, in this case, the evidence that may be extracted from the maltreatment of texts. To quote Susan Sontag, again reminding us of what kind of evidence it is, exactly, that photographs offer: 'Photographs are not windows which supply a transparent view of the world as it is, or more exactly, as it was. Photographs give evidence – often spurious, always incomplete – in support of dominant ideologies and existing social arrangements.'[26] It is this incompleteness that allows images of books to be read, in oracular fashion, as pointing towards the future. Thus even Barer's most apparently abstract pieces can be understood as prophetic statements: 'I'm afraid the printed word will become a rarity', she has said, 'and the next generation will rely on the ephemeral word – the digital kind that only exists through a computer monitor, or a sort of virtual book that can hold thousands of titles. I'm not saying that's a bad idea', she continued, but hopes that the paper version continues to exist 'for the people that want the real tactile sensation of turning a page and holding the real thing'.[27]

But if they do not? Nothing is more redolent of cultural destruction and desolation than a discarded book: grubby with dust and rodent droppings in one of Steve Fitch's images of empty houses on the High Plains, or abandoned on a sofa, as when Mark Klett and Toshi Ueshina found, with symbolic serendipity, a volume entitled *Our Nation at Dead Center* in an abandoned house at Logan, Nevada. Such books, discarded and unloved, the print existing only to be read through the meta-commentary of the photograph, are co-opted through photography into a signifying system that greatly exceeds their original use value. They have, in their way, been resuscitated. Abe Morell writes that for him, the 'magic' of his subjects 'lies somewhere between a photograph of a book and the book itself; at times, I have been convinced that books hold all the material of life – at least all the stuff that fits between an A and a Z'.[28] Yet his *Water Alphabet* – the final plate in his *A Book of Books* – conveys, once again, the ephemerality and fragility of the written word, and by extension, of life itself. Hence images of the obliteration of texts, whether this occurs through mutilation, or book-burning or bombing, function as symbols of mass destruction, showing piles of textual corpses, shocking in their numbers, their titular obliteration. In these depictions of biblioclasm, one moves, of course, from the destroyed book as providing the vehicle for an aesthetically pleasing object to the photograph offering up documentary evidence of cultural desecration.

One notable mausoleum of abandoned books is the Detroit Public Schools Book Depository, housing volumes that are the victims not of deliberate violence against particular ideologies or governments, but of neglect. Its interiors have a horrible beauty to them, ravaged by fires, exposed to the elements, so that mushrooms grow in the damp ashes of charred and rotted workbooks. James Griffioen is the most prominent and articulate of the photographers who have returned to this spectacular scene of desolation over the past twenty years, not just recording the wreckage of textbooks and teaching materials, but investigating the history behind this long-term neglected building, once a post office, then used to store books for the Detroit Public Schools system until a fire – and the water used to fight it – badly damaged the warehouse in 1987. But many books and stationery supplies were left undamaged, never, however, to be salvaged. The building has been part of a reclusive billionaire's real estate portfolio for some years now; in depressed downtown Detroit, its demolition and redevelopement hardly seems imminent.

Griffioen ends his investigation of the Book Depository's history with an apocalyptic prophecy:

> Here we get to see what the world will look like when we're gone. We see that the world will indeed go on, and there is a certain beauty to nature's indifference. Someday the books will tumble from the shelves at the Bodleian and there will be no one to replace them. Someday even sooner than that, books themselves may

become an anachronism, like scrolls or cuneiform tablets. It is the book lover, I think, who is most pained by these images. Even as we sit here at our computers, we pine for the feeling of pressed pulp between our fingers. We have a hard time accepting that all our words and knowledge might one day feed the trees.[29]

His photographs are evidence of catastrophic mismanagement and waste when it comes to educational resources, of the ugliness of urban poverty, and, he tells us, have been the prompts for all kinds of racial ugliness, too. Since their publication, commentators have also seen in them evidence of what happens when African Americans are empowered and run city government, of why taxes earmarked for education are wasted, and of why America's public education system is a failure. One of his most eloquent and beautiful photographs, of a tree growing in the wreckage of the book depository, has been lifted into a blog called keepitwhite.com, and labelled 'This is what blacks do with books.' 'And I,' says Griffioen of his photographs, with just a touch of self-irony, 'just thought they were beautiful.'[30]

But a photograph of a book, or a shelf of books, or even an entire warehouse full of decayed volumes, can never be simply 'beautiful' – such an adjective is a denial of the knowledge of the passage of time that each photograph brings with it. 'The contingency of photographs', as Sontag reminds us, 'confirms that everything is perishable', and this must be as true of the fragility of paper and print and glue just as much as it is of books' mortal readers. She continues her sentence, moreover, by dwelling on the instability of the photographic image, writing that 'the arbitrariness of photographic evidence indicates that reality is fundamentally unclassifiable'.[31] Arbitrariness rests in the moment the shutter was pressed (or the length of time it was left open), in the framing of a shot, in the available light, and, of course, in the uses to which photographs are put. The differing readings of images of the wrecked repository certainly bear this out: one person's evidence of culpable administrative incompetence is someone else's wasted tax dollars.

Any picture of a book, like the words it contains, is open to different contextualizations, different readings. But because it is *of* a book, its metatextuality is foregrounded: we are propelled into considering the types of reading in which we engage when we interpret a photograph. In other words, the evidence that is offered up by such images vastly exceeds the circumstantial. In the end, it is far less about books themselves than it is about our varied emotional, somatic and scholarly investments in the idea and practice of reading itself. When Cara Barer changes books into sculptures, and then photographs them, she is deliberately showing, she says, 'a common object' in a state of flux. For her, the way in which we research and find information today – the ways in which we look for evidence – are also in evolution. What she aims at in her photographic project holds good for the project of looking at books in photographs as a whole: 'to raise questions about these changes, the ephemeral and fragile nature in which we now obtain knowledge, and the future of books'.[32]

Notes and references

1. Susan Sontag, *On Photography* (New York: Farrar, Straus & Giroux, 1977), p. 5.
2. Ibid., p. 24.
3. Fox Talbot, *The Pencil of Nature* (London: Longman, 1844).
4. See Carol Armstrong, *Scenes in a Library: Reading the Photograph in the Book, 1843–1875* (Cambridge, MA: MIT Press, 1998), pp. 107–78 for an illuminating discussion of Fox Talbot's volume.
5. Marcus Aurelius Root, *The Camera and the Pencil, or The Heliographic Art.* (Philadelphia: M. A. Root, 1864), p. 106.
6. Henry Peach Robinson, *Pictorial Effect in Photography* (London: Piper & Carter, Moll, 1869), p. 92.
7. O. G. Rejlander, 'On photographic composition; with a description of "Two ways of life"', *Journal of the Photographic Society* (21 April 1858), 191–7 (p. 193).
8. Anne Zahalka, 'Reading pictures', *Exit*, 23 (2006), 88.
9. Garrett Stewart, *The Look of Reading: Book, Painting, Text* (Chicago: University of Chicago Press, 2006), p. 152.
10. Ibid., p. 201.
11. Roland Barthes, *Camera Lucida: Reflections on Photography* (*La chamber Claire*, 1980; trans. Richard Howard (New York: Hill and Wang, 1981), p. 76.
12. Barthes, *Camera Lucida*, p. 96.
13. See, for example, Michael Newman, 'Towards the reinvigoration of the "Western tableau": Some notes on Jeff Wall and Duchamp', *Oxford Art Journal*, 30 (2007) 81–100 (p. 83).
14. Robert Enright, 'The consolation of plausibility: an interview with Jeff Wall', *BorderCrossings*, 19 (1) (2000), 50.
15. Eve Arnold to Richard Brown, 20 July 1993, quoted in Brown, 'Marilyn Monroe reading *Ulysses:* goddess or post-cultural cyborg?, in *Joyce and*

Popular Culture, ed. R. B. Kershner (Gainesville: University Press of Florida, 1996), p. 175.

16. Annette Kuhn, *Family Snaps* (London: Verso, 1995), p. 13.
17. Ibid.
18. Marcel Proust, 'On reading', quoted on http://naziftopcuoglu.com [accessed 12 July 2008].
19. 'Writers' rooms: Craig Raine', *Guardian*, 15 February 2008; 'Writers' rooms: Antonia Fraser', *Guardian*, 16 March 2007; 'Writers' rooms: Andrew O'Hagan', *Guardian*, 30 March 2007; 'Writers' rooms: Sue Townsend', *Guardian*, 7 September 2007.
20. Monica Alvarez Careaga, 'Candida Höfer: Timespaces.' Notes to exhibition at the Kukje Gallery, Seoul, Korea, August 30 – September 30 2005, http://www.artnet.com/Galleries/Exhibitions.asp?gid=633&cid=78711, accessed 11/28/2008.
21. Jorge Luis Borges, 'The library of Babel' (1941) in his *Labyrinths: Selected Stories and Other Writings*, trans. and ed. by Donald A. Yates and James E. Irby (New York: New Directions, 2007), p. 58.
22. David Shapiro, 'A conversation with Jeff Wall', n.d. http://www.columbia.edu/cu/museo/3/jeffwall.htm [accessed 13 July 2008].
23. For this image, see 'Voyages extraordinaires.' http://www.rauzier-hyperphoto.com/category/galeries/ [accessed 22 May 2010].
24. 'Abelardo Morell. Cuban-American photographer talks with Robert Birnbaum,' 2 January 2003, http://www.identitytheory.com/people/birnbaum80.html [accessed 15 July 2008].
25. Ibid.
26. Susan Sontag, *Where The Stress Falls: Essays* (New York: Picador, 2002), p. 220.
27. Elizabeth Wadell, 'The book art of Robert The, Cara Barer, and Jacqueline Rush Lee', *The Quarterly Conversation*, 12 (2008), http://quarterlyconversation.com/the-book-art-of-robert-the-cara-barer-and-jacqueline-rush-lee#cara-barer [accessed 28 November 2008].
28. Abelardo Morell, 'Afterword', in his *A Book of Books* (New York: Bulfinch Press, 2002), p. 103.
29. James D. Griffioen, 'Detroit Public Schools Book Depository', http://www.jamesgriffioen.net/index.php?/depository/the-story/ [accessed 28 November 2008].
30. Ibid.
31. Sontag, *On Photography*, p. 80.
32. Cara Barer, http://www.carabarer.com/gallery2.php [accessed 28 November 2008].

Part 5
Reading in the Digital Age

10
Filipino Blogs as Evidence of Reading and Reception

Vernon R. Totanes

The first two books printed in 1593 in what is now known as the Philippines were sold for two and four reales, respectively. Other details about these books – how they came to be written and printed in Spanish, Chinese and Tagalog; the personal lives of their authors and printers; and even how the printing press arrived on Philippine shores – have either been proven conclusively or at least speculated upon based on existing copies (one for each book) or other, related evidence.[1] No evidence, however, has turned up regarding what readers thought about the books. Did they love the books? Did they hate them? Who were these readers? No one really knows.

The same is true for most books published in the Philippines since then. Personal correspondence, interviews, diaries and marginal comments in books have been used by Western scholars as evidence that certain books were read, and what readers thought of them. But Filipino scholars, unfortunately, rarely have access to similar resources for various reasons, including environment-related and man-made disasters. The few studies that have been conducted on the reading habits of Filipinos have relied on surveys, and quantified, among others, just how many Filipinos were reading specific *kinds* of books, not specific *titles* or their opinions about what they read.[2] Fortunately, the rise of the Internet – specifically the growing popularity and ubiquity of blogs, which some call 'online diaries' – has made it possible to gather evidence of the reading and reception of books published in the Philippines in the twenty-first century. This chapter will show how blogs can be searched to identify evidence of reader reception, and that differences in the way bloggers write about books can be used as indicators of the nature and quality of their reading experience. It must be noted, however, that bloggers are *not* necessarily representative of the entire population – especially in the Philippines, where Internet access is still very limited. The use of blogs as evidence of reading and reception will be illustrated in this chapter through the analysis of blog posts about two history books written by Filipinos and published in the Philippines. The first is *Pasyon and Revolution* by Reynaldo Ileto, which was based on the author's PhD dissertation at Cornell University, and the second is *Rizal Without the Overcoat* by Ambeth Ocampo, which is a collection of newspaper columns written by someone who started as a journalist, but is now better known as the most popular Filipino historian in the Philippines.[3]

It must be noted, though, that both books were written in English, and not in Spanish, Tagalog or any other Filipino language. Despite almost three-and-a half centuries of Spanish rule over what the Spaniards then called 'las Islas Filipinas', very few Filipinos ever learned to speak or read Spanish. When the Americans began their colonization of 'the Philippine Islands', they mandated that English would be the medium of instruction in schools.[4] This is the reason most books published in the Philippines – officially the Republic of the Philippines after 1946 – are in English. It should not be surprising, therefore, that much of what is written about these books, as well as the blog posts quoted in this chapter, are primarily in English – even though most Filipinos prefer to converse with one another using one of the many languages of the Philippines, such as Tagalog or Cebuano.[5]

The 'Pasyon' that Ileto writes about in *Pasyon and Revolution* refers to the text of a popular Tagalog adaptation of a standard work used by Spanish missionaries to educate Filipinos about Jesus Christ's passion, death and resurrection. Ileto argues that the Pasyon inspired what historians had previously thought were unrelated revolts and, ultimately, the Philippine revolution of 1896. Ileto's book is one of the best-reviewed history books about the Philippines, and one of the most frequently cited by Filipino and non-Filipino scholars.[6] In fact, it has recently been declared one of the fourteen most influential books in the field of Southeast Asian Studies – one of only two published in Asia, and the only one about the Philippines.[7]

Ocampo's work, meanwhile, has been all but ignored by the scholarly community, even though more Filipinos have likely benefited from the fresh perspective he brought to the subject of his book.[8] José

Rizal, whose best-known works were written in Spanish, is the *de facto* national hero of the Philippines, and the overcoat in *Rizal Without the Overcoat* refers to the one Rizal is usually depicted as wearing in the numerous monuments, photos and coins bearing his likeness that Filipinos see every day. This image, however, led Ocampo to wonder as a child why Rizal would don such a warm garment in a tropical country. It turns out Rizal only wore it outside the Philippines. Appropriately enough, the different covers of Ocampo's book do not show Rizal as he is usually imagined (see Figure 10.2).

Pasyon and Revolution has had the same cover for more than thirty years, while each new edition of *Rizal Without the Overcoat* has been accompanied by a new cover; the 'Expanded edition' even had two covers. The most significant differences between editions involved the addition, deletion and reinstatement of content. Covers used with permission (see Figure 10.1).

Both *Pasyon and Revolution* and *Rizal Without the Overcoat* are very likely two of the bestselling history books published in the Philippines. Comparing sales figures – or perhaps even the number of editions and covers – shows that more copies of the latter have been bought than the former.[9] And though books purchased are not necessarily read by their buyers, further evidence to support the conclusion that Ocampo's compilation of columns has had more readers than Ileto's scholarly monograph may be found in blogs, where the two books are reviewed or discussed extensively, and their titles are mentioned in passing or included in lists and bibliographies. The method by which these blogs were identified and classified, as well as the quantity and quality of the references to each book, will be the focus of this chapter. Examples of blog entries, as well as comments left by blog readers, will be provided.

What is a blog?

The word 'blog' is the more commonly used term for 'weblog,' a specific kind of website. Weblogs were originally 'logs of links to websites that people thought were interesting and wanted to share with others'.[10] The term 'log' implies that a weblog is a repository of entries – maybe a list of items received, a record of visitors, or even a diary. But unlike entries in most logbooks, the posts in a blog are arranged in reverse chronological order. And this is the reason why the most

Figure 10.1 Cover illustrations of Reynaldo Clemeña Ileto, *Pasyon and Revolution* (1979) and Ambeth R. Ocampo, *Rizal Without the Overcoat* (1990, 1995, 2001 and 2008)

recent post is the first one that is read on a blog.[11] The word 'blog' is now used as a noun – the blog itself – and a verb: if someone says s/he is going 'to blog' about a subject, this means s/he is going to write about it on a blog. People who own blogs are called 'bloggers'. The community of bloggers is called the 'blogosphere'. And though some blogs are now routinely cited in mainstream media, this has not always been the case (see Figure 10.3).

In 2005, Michael Gorman, who was then-president of the American Library Association, wrote that, 'A blog is a species of interactive electronic diary by means of which the unpublishable, untrammeled by editors or the rules of grammar, can communicate their thoughts via the web.'[12] While it is true that some – or maybe even most – blogs are 'unpublishable,' Gorman was obviously comparing blogs unfavourably with published materials like newspapers, journals, books. Danah Boyd, on the other hand, believes that blogs are more properly compared to paper:

> Some people use paper to write insightful articles; the same is true on blogs. Some people use paper to write grocery lists; the same is true on blogs. Paper has been used for journalism, diaries, scribbling, gossip, passing notes, writing letters, bookkeeping, collages, photographs, and all sorts of other practices. The same is true on blogs.[13]

One huge difference, however, between paper and blogs is that what is written on paper is not always published. Much of what is written down on paper is, in fact, intended to be read only by its author or perhaps a few others. A blog post, on the other hand, may be viewed by just about anyone surfing the Internet once its author clicks 'Publish'.[14] There are, of course, ways by which certain posts or even entire blogs can be kept private, but unlike scribblings on paper, which may then be submitted for publication if their authors so desire, the default mode for blogs is that anyone can read them.[15] Unlike mailing lists and social networking sites – most of which require readers to register with a username and password – readers can usually access blogs without having to disclose any information about themselves. Thus, the ethical issues that confront researchers when studying private, online exchanges do not apply to this study on the use of blogs as evidence of reading and reception.

Method

Various search engines may be used to search blogs, but this chapter will rely on Google's blog search capability to identify the posts to be studied. While it is possible to go directly to Google's dedicated site for searching blogs (http://blogsearch.google.com/), the method discussed below will use the site familiar to most people. The steps enumerated below were executed on 21 May 2009 using 'pasyon and revolution' as the search term.

How to search Google for blog posts with the words 'pasyon and revolution'.

1. Go to http://www.google.com/.[16]
2. Type search term enclosed in quotation marks (i.e., 'pasyon and revolution'). Hit 'return' or 'enter' to see the list of results from all websites indexed by Google.
3. Click on 'more', which may be found at the end of the list of links on the upper left-hand corner.

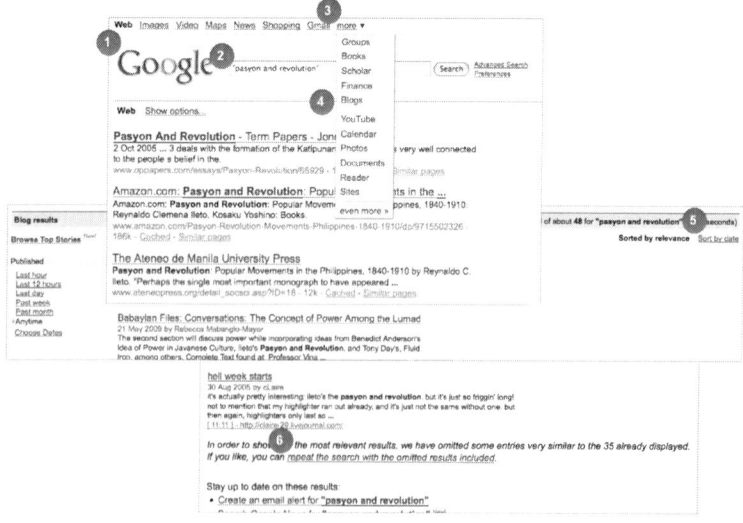

Figure 10.2   Google search results for blogs with the key term 'pasyon and revolution'

4. Choose 'Blogs' on the drop-down menu, and a list of blog posts will appear.
5. Click on 'Sort by date' on the upper right-hand corner of the page to arrange the results from the most recent to the earliest.[17]
6. Go to the end of the list. Click on 'repeat the search with the omitted results included', which leads to a list similar to the one used in this study.

The same steps were followed for 'rizal without the overcoat' on the same day.[18]

The process described above produced 48 entries for 'pasyon and revolution,' and 67 results for 'rizal without the overcoat.' Each of the entries was examined, and it was determined that three of the latter results were not found on blogs, as defined in this chapter.[19] The 112 blog entries were posted between March 2005 and May 2009. In some cases, the same text appeared on two or more distinct blogs, which meant that either one blogger posted the same text on different blogs or several bloggers reproduced the same newspaper article, for instance, on their blogs. There were also a few cases where the book titles were mentioned on the same blog – but on different blog posts – more than once, which means that there were actually less than 112 unique blogs examined for this study (see Table 10.1).

The results for each search term were classified into three groups:

1. Scholarly voice, if much of the post was written in a formal manner, as if the blogger was writing a school report.
2. Personal voice, if the post appeared to have been written informally, as if the blogger was conversing with a friend.

Table 10.1 Comparative search results for blogs on *Pasyon* and *Rizal*

	Pasyon	*Rizal*
Blog search results	48	67
Actual blog posts	48	64
Scholarly voice	25	7
Personal voice	4	41
Bibliographies and lists	16	12
Duplicate posts	3	4

3. Bibliography or list, if either search term was cited in a bibliography or included in a list of favourite books, for example.

This classification shows that those who blogged about the two books wrote in very different ways. For instance, 25 of those who mentioned *Pasyon and Revolution* in their blogs wrote about it in a scholarly voice, against only four who used a personal voice. In contrast, 41 blogged about *Rizal Without the Overcoat* in a personal voice, with only seven writing in a scholarly voice. The quality of the difference in voice will become apparent in the next two sections.

These are merely statistics, however. The rest of this chapter will be devoted to what bloggers have written about *Pasyon and Revolution* and *Rizal Without the Overcoat*. The excerpts quoted in the next two sections were selected to serve as examples of what may be found online, not necessarily because they were representative of all the blog posts found.[20]

Pasyon and Revolution

One of the two bloggers who devoted an entire post to *Pasyon and Revolution* begins this way:

> I first became familiar with Reynaldo Ileto's *Pasyon and Revolution* as a freshman . . . Ileto's book, as with many other readings in that class, gave me a much richer understanding of history, one that went beyond the stories of the elite, powerful, ilustrados of Manila.[21]

Not only does this reveal that the blogger read the book as a class requirement, it also alludes to the significance of Ileto's work as a history from below. The next example is even more specific – and scholarly:

> Ileto's book presents the correlation between the *pasyon*, folk religious traditions and the revolution, putting emphasis on the agency of the masses. The book's springboard is the Lapiang Malaya . . . which according to Ileto, is one of the many examples of the continuity of the unfinished business of the Katipunan's struggle toward independence.[22]

The next quote illustrates one of the important differences between a blog and a traditional diary. It was not written by the blog's owner, but by one of the readers who left a comment:

> In the book 'Pasyon and Revolution', Reynaldo Ileto investigates the beliefs of the 'masses' of Filipino Christians. Their beliefs were a blend of orthodox Christian and indigenous spiritual beliefs.[23]

This comment is not unlike many of the other blog posts that were scholarly in tone. They were not really writing about *Pasyon and Revolution*, but just citing it. The next example is actually about another book by Ileto, but the lone comment is significant because it demonstrates just how blogs facilitate interaction between readers and writers. The following comment was written by Ileto himself:

> I welcome your critique of the essay on Rizal that I wrote in 1979 . . . Looking back at the things I wrote more than thirty years ago, including Pasyon, I can see how they were the product of their time and my youth.[24]

Aside from discussing a book's text, some bloggers also mention details that tell us about their knowledge of the publishing industry. This amateur book collector shares a little about the realities of publishing in the Philippines:

> Philippine publishers do not usually publish a new edition of a certain book unless the title is very popular like Reynaldo Ileto's '*Pasyon at Revolution*' . . . Sad to say but it is very rare for Philippine books to be reprinted once its first edition is off the press.[25]

Yes, Ileto's book is popular, especially considering that most scholarly books like it are lucky to sell more than a thousand copies in several years. Note, however, that this blogger is confusing 'new edition' with 'reprint'; and when he speaks of 'Philippine books' he ignores the romances and other books, which the literati usually disregard, but sell more copies in one year than even the most popular scholarly books sell in several decades.

It is worth noting that none of the excerpts quoted thus far reveal any kind of emotional connection to the book or its author. The next three are ones that were classified as having been written in a 'personal voice'.[26] The following post, incidentally, is the second of the two – out of 45 – that were devoted to *Pasyon and Revolution*:

> required reading for EN 12. just finished with the first two chapters. kids, you know me. 73 pages is nothing to me. but it becomes a pretty heavy job when you have no clue what the book is about. it's like the freaking da vinci code of philippine history. problem is, i cannot decode it. haha.[27]

The next one actually tells us more about the blogger's study habits than the book itself:

> It's actually pretty interesting: Ileto's The Pasyon and Revolution. But it's just so friggin' long! Not to mention that my highlighter

Figure 10.3   Blog posts on Ileto's *Pasyon and Revolution*
Note: Clockwise, from top left: Mark Andrew Lim, 'Pasyon and Revolution', *Philosopher King*; Sherwin Mapanoo, 'Of Class and Crass', *Antibiotyx*; Camille Maria Layug Castolo, 'Pasyon and Revolution', *Sponge Cake*. Please see 'Endnotes' for URLs and other details. Screenshots used with permission.

ran out already, and it's just not the same without one. But then again, highlighters only last so long with me. Over *naman kasi ako mag-highlight e.* [I actually highlight too much.][28]

And finally, there was one post that actually had a sentence in ALL CAPS:

> 4. pasyon and REvolution – I HATE THIS BOOK. HISTORICALLY IMPORTANT BUT I HATE IT![29]

Rizal Without the Overcoat

While more blogs mention *Rizal Without the Overcoat* than *Pasyon and Revolution*, this difference is probably not statistically significant. But it is worth noting that there were many more interesting excerpts to choose from for this section than the previous one (see Figure 10.4). The following examples demonstrate just how warmly readers have embraced Ocampo's book, in contrast to the more formal reception accorded *Pasyon and Revolution*.

> Sprinkled with witty comments and laughable remarks, college students can now heave huge sighs of relief and offer prayers of thanks to the Almighty for the creation of this book that spared them the burden of enduring the subject that is P.I. 100: Rizal.[30]

Rizal is so revered in the Philippines that a law was actually passed in 1956 requiring all university students to take a course about him and his works. Some professors, instead of asking their students to read one of the many scholarly biographies available, have resorted to recommending Ocampo's compilation of columns. The rest of the examples in this section – most of which were written in a personal voice – provides an indication of the possible reasons behind not only professors' recommendations to students, but also why the book is read voluntarily even outside the classroom.

> I have finished Ambeth Ocampo's *Rizal Without the Overcoat*. I really loved it. Unlike other books on Rizal, Ocampo's was light on the eyes and the mind. What Ocampo did was he 'undressed' Rizal, painted a picture of a human Rizal. And it was a fresh and welcome perspective. Because after years of studying Rizal, this was the only time

Figure 10.4   Blog posts on Ocampo's *Rizal Without the Overcoat*. Clockwise, from top left: Jason Tabinas, 'Bridging Literature Gap', *Beer at Booksale*; Melissa Villa, 'What I am Reading Now: Rizal Without the Overcoat', *Bloggera Ako!*; Valerie Barcinal, 'Of Ambeth Ocampo, and Learning to Love Our History [Naks!]', *Reach for the Stars*. Please see 'Endnotes' for URLs and other details. Screenshots used with permission.

I realized that he has feelings like all of us. He was always portrayed as invincible. But Ocampo showed that Rizal was not. He made mistakes like the rest of us. And this endeared me more to Rizal. It made me admire him more. It almost made me fall in love with him![31]

Some bloggers do not write as well as others, but their posts are worth noting, too:

I love, love, love, love, love ! I think every Filipino should read this book – specially the young filipinos who have no clue who Rizal is.[32]

The next example was written in Taglish, a combination of Tagalog and English.

Ito ang opisyal na libro sa mga hindi masyadong opisyal na detalye ng kanyang buhay. Totoo, history is just too serious to be left to historians . . . Boring masyado si Rizal pag naka-Amerikana. Tara tanggalin natin ang overcoat nya. Dahil once nahubaran mo na sya, you'll never look at our national superhero the same way. Ever again.

[This is the official book on the not-so-official details of his life. True, history is just too serious to be left to historians . . . Rizal is too boring in his suit. Come let's take off his overcoat. Because once you've unclothed him, you'll never look at our national superhero the same way. Ever again.][33]

What does he mean by 'Ever again'? Perhaps the next blogger can provide a clue:

So what is interesting about Rizal? Well actually the book revolves around him and about his lovers, books and Rizal as human (not the heroic type). I learned that he eats tuyo [dried fish] in breakfast and his 'kargada' or penis was placed in the right. Peculiar? Well it is just to remind us that he is also human![34]

The reference to Rizal's penis may be traced to a sculptor who examined Rizal's clothes and determined that he was a "rightist" because one side of the crotch area of his pants was looser than the other. The next blogger describes her work at a call centre and how she was able to buy books before she was employed:

Thanks to my job that requires nothing but for me to eat american insults and get paid for it, i can now afford to by books and can still have some penny to spare for drinking sessions and food trips. Unlike in college when buying a book means eating below my means.[35]

But one more way in which this post is significant is that the book's author also dropped by:

Thanks for reading my books and posting your impressions in your blog. I do appreciate it. Having readers like you makes the toil of research and writing worth it. I hope to get more books out this year.[36]

The following post is remarkable because it reveals how the blogger was inspired to pursue a career in history, at the age of 11, after acquiring his first copy (implying perhaps that he has more than one copy) of Ocampo's book:

> noong tag-init ng 1995, nang ipabili ko sa National Book Store Ever Gotesco Grand Central ang aking unang kopya ng Rizal Without the Overcoat ni Ambeth Ocampo . . . at mabasa ko ito, napagtanto ko na nais kong maging bahagi ng disiplina ng kasaysayan bilang historyador at guro . . .

> [in summer 1995, when my first copy of Rizal Without the Overcoat by Ambeth Ocampo was purchased for me at National Book Store Ever Gotesco Grand Central . . . and I read it, I realized that I wanted to become part of history, the discipline, as a historian and teacher . . .][37]

There was a grand total of one dissenting blogger:

> In comparison to original Rizal documents, it also has *too many* original speculations and what-ifs of Ocampo that my feeble brain (after 6–7 reads) couldn't take it anymore.[38]

It is possible that there are others like her, but there is no guarantee that their posts can be found through the use of search engines. For instance, searches conducted at different times do not always yield the same results. The next two excerpts were discovered in earlier searches in December 2007 and April 2008, but did not appear in the May 2009 search. One of these posts reveals just how readable Ocampo's books are, and makes an observation regarding another way in which books circulate:

> My boardmates are naturally readers but they usually do not read my books. They do not touch my poetry books all lined up on my desk. Even novels and some short fiction anthologies are hardly borrowed. So far, they read *Centennial Countdown* and *Rizal Without the Overcoat*, two books of Ambeth Ocampo that I have . . . It's actually fascinating to see how books change hands unlike those books which just gather dust in bookshelves.[39]

And finally, one blogger provides evidence that some who are perceived as non-readers make an exception for Ocampo's books:

> ever since i was a freshman in high school, i HATED history subjects: the dates, the UNrelevant places, events . . . blah, blah, blah . . .
>
> but thank goodness, my dad has this collection of Ambeth Ocampo's books . . . and my elder brother, of all people who i know would choose television and computer over books, *reads* them, and even *enjoys* reading them . . . [40]

Conclusion

While the examples cited in this chapter are specifically about Filipino history books, and thus unique to the Philippines, the method by which they were found is not. The process described here may be used to search blogs for evidence of reading and reception of all kinds of books written and published in different languages around the world. The same process may, in fact, be used to identify feedback from readers on just about any kind of site indexed by search engines, including customer reviews on Amazon.com, fleeting mentions on Facebook, and even religious condemnations on random websites. It is much more difficult to obtain evidence of reading through these sites – due to intrinsic limitations, privacy settings, or just plain volume of results (like numerous auction listings) – but it can be done.

One significant difference between blogs and all the other sites mentioned above is that blogging platforms allow users to do more than just provide input in a predetermined manner. Bloggers can actually customize their own blogs beyond colour and font much more easily than on conventionally-designed websites, which usually require specialized knowledge of web design languages or software. Partly because of their user-friendly interface, blogs are much more varied and candid as a source of evidence than scholarly journals, magazines and newspapers – many of which also have their own websites. In fact, it is more likely that bloggers have already shared their opinions about books – or just about anything, for that matter – that would not normally even be mentioned in mainstream media.

Comparing and contrasting the quantity and quality of the search results for at least two books, as demonstrated in this chapter, is important in contextualizing any conclusions that may be drawn from the available evidence. Though Ileto's *Pasyon and Revolution* is obviously more widely known and esteemed in scholarly circles, the evidence from the blogs shows very clearly that Ileto's book does not provoke the same kind of passion that Ocampo's *Rizal Without the Overcoat* inspires.

But the analysis need not be limited to the number of blog posts and what readers say about specific books. The blogs themselves – from design to content to grammar to photos used – may be used as indicators of readers' personalities, the kinds of books they read, their reading habits and other details that cannot normally be obtained through surveys or interviews. In addition, the public nature of blogs makes it easier for researchers to examine data that would have been almost impossible to obtain as recently as the 1990s.

Four centuries have passed since the first two books were printed in the Philippines in 1593. It is still not possible to determine what readers thought of those books then, but perhaps evidence obtained from blogs about which books – whether print or electronic – were read and the reception they were accorded early in the twenty-first century will give researchers more to work with in the decades and centuries to come than those before them.

Notes and references

1. See P. van der Loon, 'The Manila incunabula and early Hokkien studies', *Asia Major,* 12 (1966), 1–43.
2. The most recent and most comprehensive of these studies is the '2007 NBDB Readership Survey' commissioned by the National Book Development Board.
3. Reynaldo Ileto, *Pasyon and Revolution: Popular Movements in the Philippines, 1840–1910* (Quezon City: Ateneo de Manila University Press, 1979); Ambeth Ocampo, *Rizal Without the Overcoat* (Pasig City: Anvil, 1990).
4. Vicente Rafael, 'Taglish, or the phantom power of the lingua franca', in his *White Love and Other Events in Filipino History* (Quezon City: Ateneo de Manila University Press, 2000), pp. 162–89 (167–70).
5. This does not imply, however, that most Filipinos are fluent in English. It is very likely that those who can afford Internet access are also the ones who are able to read books in English and write about them in their blogs.
6. ISI's Web of Knowledge lists 98 citations for *Pasyon and Revolution* as of 20 June 2009.

7. Hui Yew-Foong, 'The most influential books of Southeast Asian studies', *Sojourn*, 24 (2009), vi–xi.
8. ISI's Web of Knowledge lists three citations for *Rizal Without the Overcoat* as of 20 June 2009, significantly fewer than *Pasyon and Revolution*'s 98.
9. Based on figures provided by the Ateneo de Manila University Press and Anvil Publishing – the publishers of Ileto's and Ocampo's books, respectively – 9,223 copies of *Pasyon and Revolution* were sold from 1979 to 2008, and 26,262 copies of *Rizal Without the Overcoat* from 1990 to 2008.
10. Dan Cohen, 'Creating a blog from scratch, part 1: What is a blog, anyway?', *Dan Cohen* (16 December 2005) http://www.dancohen.org/blog/posts/what_is_a_blog_anyway [accessed 21 May 2009] (para. 2 of 6).
11. Rebecca Blood, 'Weblogs and journalism: Do they connect?', *Nieman Reports*, 57 (Fall 2003), 61–3.
12. Michael Gorman, 'Revenge of the blog people!', *Library Journal*, 130 (15 February 2005), 44.
13. Danah Boyd, 'Blogging outloud: Shifts in public voice', *Danah Boyd's Publications* (1 October 2005) http://www.danah.org/papers/LITA.html [accessed 21 May 2009] (para. 15 of 52).
14. This is the most common term used on popular blogging platforms. Other terms used are 'Post' and 'Save'.
15. In fact, whether a blog is so popular that it has millions of daily readers or so obscure that its author is its lone reader, all bloggers write for an imagined audience. They do not always know or care if they have readers, but none will be surprised – and most will probably even be delighted – to learn that someone is reading their blog.
16. Other blog search engines are http://technorati.com/ and http://www.icerocket.com/.
17. Preferences may be set so that up to 100 results are shown on each page, ensuring that numerous clicks on 'next page' will not be necessary.
18. It is worth noting that these simple searches are possible only because both books have unique titles, which eliminates the need for further searches to exclude books with similar titles. Not all blog posts, however, about the two books will be discovered through this method. Many will not be found simply because the bloggers did not explicitly cite the books by their titles or, if they did, misspelled certain words or recalled the titles incorrectly. Also, due to a variety of reasons, Google does not index all blog posts.
19. The others led to Flickr, a photo sharing site; Symbianize, an online forum; and BookMooch, a community for exchanging used books.
20. The blog posts, it must be noted, were not primarily about the books themselves. In many cases, the books' titles were mentioned only in passing. In fact, only two of the results were primarily about *Pasyon and Revolution*, but a more significant number were exclusively about Ocampo's work, including eight that used 'Rizal Without the Overcoat' as the post's title. The great majority of blogs were owned by individuals, but there were also a few institutions that were using blogging platforms – instead of traditional websites – and were thus more likely to use a scholarly voice. Most posts were in English, but some were written in Filipino

languages, with two in Japanese and one in Russian. Many did not use capitalization at all.

21. Mark Andrew Lim, 'Pasyon and Revolution', *Philosopher King* (18 May 2009) http://philosopherroi.blogspot.com/2009/05/pasyon-and-revolution.html [accessed 21 May 2009] (para. 1 of 2). Except for the addition of ellipses to indicate that certain passages were shortened, excerpts are reproduced – typos and all – as they appeared in the original posts. Translations of words or excerpts written in Tagalog or Taglish are enclosed in square brackets. The bibliographic information for blog posts quoted in this chapter was obtained from the blogs themselves. Aside from the bloggers from whom permission was obtained to reproduce screenshots for this chapter, no effort was made to ascertain the authors' identities beyond what is disclosed on their blogs.

22. Sherwin Mapanoo, 'Of class and crass', *Antibiotyx* (28 June 2007), http://antibiotyx.blogspot.com/2007/06/of-class-and-crass.html [accessed 21 May 2009] (para. 2 of 3).

23. Anonymous, Comment on 'What we Filipinos should know', *The Filipino Mind* (7 November 2005), http://thefilipinomind.blogspot.com/2005/11/what-we-filipinos-should-know-upang.html [accessed 21 May 2009] (comment 4 of 6).

24. Rey Ileto, Comment on 'Notes on Ileto's "Rizal and the Underside of Philippine history"', *Joseph Scalice* (19 November 2007), http://josephs calice.com/index.php/2007/11/19/notes-on-iletos-rizal-and-the-under-side-of-philippine-history/ [accessed 21 May 2009] (comment 2 of 2).

25. James Esguerra, 'A collector's psyche', *Thinking Things Through* (22 October 2007), http://jvmesguerra.blogspot.com/2007/10/collectors-psyche.html [accessed 21 May 2009] (para. 1 of 4).

26. A fourth merely noted that, 'we didn't have the quiz for pasyon and revolution'.

27. Camille Maria Layug Castolo, 'Pasyon and Revolution', *Sponge Cake* (11 September 2005), http://mypacey11.blogspot.com/2005/09/pasyon-and-revolution.html [accessed 21 May 2009] (para. 1 of 3).

28. Claire, 'Hell week starts', *[11:11]* (30 Aug 2005), http://claire-29.livejournal.com/104492.html [accessed 21 May 2009] (para. 1 of 15).

29. Baby_nemi, 'Top Grey's quotes and the strange "RE"'s . . . ', *The Baby's Journal aka Bloggy!* (24 September 2006), http://baby-nemi.livejournal.com/3058.html [accessed 21 May 2009] (para. 5 of 14).

30. 'Rizal Without the Overcoat: a review', *White Noise* (25 May 2007), http://aiys.vox.com/library/post/rizal-without-the-overcoat-a-review.html [accessed 21 May 2009] (para. 5 of 5).

31. Hailie, 'Surveys, Rizal, and dicta license', *Hello Kitty Visiting the Zen Garden* (3 April 2006), http://ulzzanghailie.blogspot.com/2006/04/surveys-rizal-and-dicta-license.html [accessed 21 May 2009] (para. 1 of 6).

32. Melissa Villa, 'What I am reading now: Rizal Without the Overcoat', *Bloggera Ako!* (1 March 2009), http://villavilla.wordpress.com/2009/03/01/

what-i-am-reading-now-rizal-without-the-overcoat/ [accessed 21 May 2009] (para. 1 of 3).

33. Frencelt, 'Rizal Without the Overcoat', *Frenz Kiss* (6 March 2007), http:// frencelt.multiply.com/reviews/item/19 [accessed 21 May 2009] (para. 2 of 2).

34. Jaymar, 'Rizal Without the Overcoat', *Retro* (20 July 2006), http:// iampopular.multiply.com/reviews/item/43 [accessed 21 May 2009] (para. 2 of 3).

35. Superwebsurferforcrafting, 'What I'm currently feeding my fried brains', *What's in My Messy Bag?* (10 February 2008), http://meandmyfriedbrain. blogspot.com/2008/02/what-im-currently-feeding-my-fried.html [accessed 21 May 2009] (para. 1 of 2).

36. Ambeth Ocampo, Comment on 'What I'm currently feeding my fried brains' (comment 1 of 1).

37. Michael Charleston Chua, 'Si Ambeth at ako: Isang foto-sanaysay', *Ang Tarlakin* (30 June 2008), http://michaelxiaochua.multiply.com/ photos/album/361/SI_AMBETH_AT_AKO_Isang_Foto-Sanaysay_Bilang_ Pagpugay_sa_Paggawad_sa_Kanya_ng_Officier_de_lOrdre_des_Arts_et_ Lettres_26_Hunyo_2008 [accessed 21 May 2009] (para. 3 of 6).

38. Beeya, 'The most lamest paper Ive done . . . for now,' *Beeya* (18 November 2007), http://beeeya.livejournal.com/2213.html [accessed 21 May 2009] (para. 1 of 6).

39. Jason Tabinas, 'Bridging literature gap,' *Beer at Booksale* (12 May 2007), http://saldang.multiply.com/journal/item/44 [accessed 2 December 2007] (para. 2 of 8).

40. Valerie Barcinal, 'Of Ambeth Ocampo, and learning to love our history [Naks!]' *Reach for the Stars* (13 March 2008), http://seventhhorcrux. multiply.com/journal/item/63 [accessed 12 April 2008] (paras. 3–4 of 24).

11
Reading the Book of Mozilla: Web Browsers and the Materiality of Digital Texts

Alan Galey

Rediscovering the browser

If dirt is simply matter in the wrong place, it may be that digital texts can bear the marks of the world around them in ways we have yet to understand.[1] In defiance of the conventional wisdom offered by hypertext theorists of the 1990s, who installed a vaguely defined immateriality into their arguments about new media, digital texts today seem to insist on being troublesome in the same ways as material documents: they may change in form and content when migrated from old formats to new ones; they manage to get themselves lost (think of White House email records); they demand embodiment and constant attention in expensive mobile devices; reading them at injudicious times even causes automobile accidents. Digital texts were supposed to be above the messiness of the world, but scholars of electronic textuality, like David Levy, have dragged them back down to earth:

> Digital documents are *not* immaterial. The marks produced on screens and on paper, the sounds generated in the airwaves, are as material as anything in our world. And the ones and zeros of our digital representations . . . are embedded in a material substrate no

This research was supported by a grant from the Social Sciences and Humanities Research Council of Canada and was presented at the conference of the Society for the History of Authorship, Reading and Publishing in Toronto, 2009. I am grateful to Sarah Brouillette, Travis DeCook and the audience members at that event for their comments, especially Michael Winship, and to the many classes and audiences who have shared their insights on the Ramelli image with me.

less than are calligraphic letterforms on a piece of vellum. It may be true that digital representations can move around extremely quickly, that they can be copied from one storage device to another, even when they are separated by thousands of miles. But at any one moment, the bits for a particular document are somewhere real and physical.[2]

The best testimony to the truth of this statement may be the Patriot Act (2001), which authorizes the US government to monitor acts of reading and writing based on the territorial location of servers. A more encouraging investment in the idea of digital materiality is the turn toward media-specific analysis and granular reading of digital technologies exemplified by Katherine Hayles, Matthew Kirschenbaum, Lisa Gitelman and others who bridge between science and technology studies, digital humanities and the history of books and reading.[3] Their attention to the material specificities of digital texts points toward the valuable middle ground that textual scholarship occupies, where we make a virtue of the tensions between the opposing tendencies to generalize or to particularize – in other words, between the knowledge that comes from our encounters with artefacts, and the framing assumptions we bring to those encounters.

How, then, can this renewed attention to the materiality of digital texts provoke new ways to think about the study of reading, past and future? To work through that question, I offer the example of the web browser as a vital yet unacknowledged agent in the sociology of texts in the present. This chapter considers the relationship between browsers as software and browsing as a mode of reading, then turns to a well-known moment in the iconographic history of reading machines, and concludes with a reading of certain contradictory tendencies within the Firefox web browser itself and what they reveal about digital texts' elusive materiality.

Few historical developments have invigorated and challenged the study of reading as much as the renewed viability of the e-book and digital reading devices. Yet the proliferation of Amazon Kindles, Sony Readers, Apple iPhones, and similar devices reminds us that for years we have been using even more ubiquitous devices, but in the form of software with names like Firefox, Internet Explorer, Netscape, Opera and Safari. Web developers have always followed the unfolding history of browsers with intense interest, but academic discussions of browsers focus mainly on economic and policy questions, especially the legal disputes over Internet Explorer in Microsoft's operating systems.[4] It is worth remembering that when Steve Jobs first rolled out the iPhone, one of his chief selling points was that it ran the *same* web browser, Safari, as every other Mac notebook and desktop computer. The same is now true of the iPad, and the flexibility of browsers as venues for many kinds of interaction will likely increase in importance as mobile reading devices proliferate. While it is true that textual scholars have begun to examine how software such as word processors and hypertext authoring systems affects the nature of texts, the web browser itself has tended to remain transparent in humanists' engagements with digital textuality. This is an unfortunate omission in our field of study, since it leaves the analysis of browsers to fields like computer science and business in which scholars tend to lack a bibliographic understanding of textual transmission.

We can see the putative transparency of browsers whenever web pages are represented in scholarly publications in print, where screenshots tend to show either the page itself detached from context, or the page with the browser window around it (which is usually enough to identify the operating system, browser and sometimes browser version), or, less often, the browser window in the context of the author's desktop. The latter instances may inadvertently capture details of the article's composition, such as the clock showing when the screenshots were taken, other open applications, and unrelated files on the author's desktop. All of these visible traces connect the text to the site of scholarly labour that generated it. The web browser becomes even more implicated in that labour as browsers become a platform not only for viewing web pages, but also for using tools like Zotero to manage and share sources, citations, and notes (Figure 11.1).

These markers of digital materiality stand as modern counterparts to the iconographic tradition of the scholar's study in the early modern period, in which the *mise-en-scène* of the life of the mind reveals the embodiment of readers and texts.[5]

What, then, can the history of books and reading reveal about web browsers, and how in turn can that inquiry prompt us to reconsider our understanding of reading, especially its future in online environments? We could begin by considering browsing itself as a readerly activity, one which links humanists of the past and present. A recent study of humanists' research patterns in different kinds of libraries

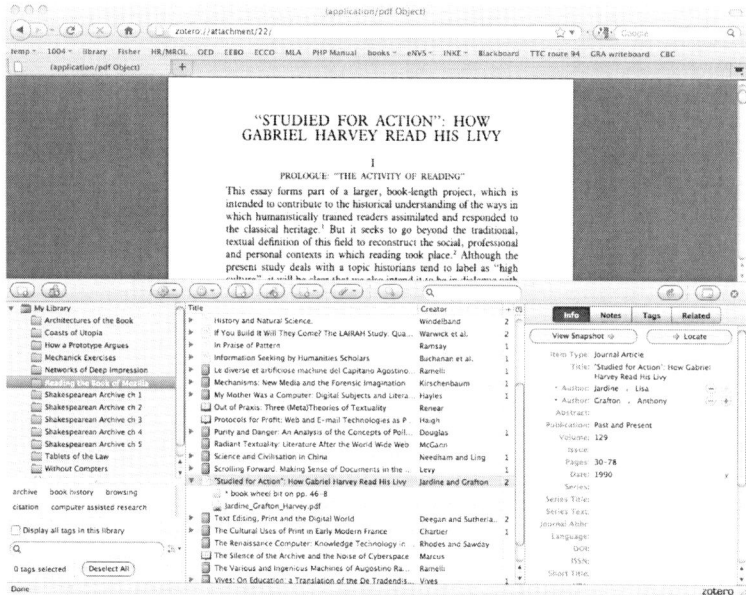

Figure 11.1   Zotero running in the Firefox web browser

highlights the importance of browsing – as opposed to, say, searching or aggregating – as a way of interacting with materials that characterizes the humanities disciplines in particular.[6] This owes partly to a major strength of the interpretive aspect of the humanities, in which inquiry is rarely dependent on notions of complete data sets: one need not read every Victorian novel in order to make a valid argument about, say, textual labour and subjectivity in *David Copperfield*.[7] Yet the design of digital libraries has tended to reflect the information-seeking habits of the sciences, with the database search form as the domain of searching scientists, and the library stacks as the natural habitat of browsing humanists – a habitat increasingly under threat in times of scarcity.[8]

The pleasure that humanists derive from browsing may well result from the moments of serendipity that arise when one makes a connection because of material constraints like the arrangement of books on a shelf, or the original order of archival materials. Interface design has been slow to reckon with the distinctive power of humanistic modes of reading, but researchers are beginning to influence design traditions and to use digital interfaces as occasions to think about the nature of materials.[9] However, as Claire Warwick and her co-authors point out, the power of serendipity depends upon being able to trust what one finds, and the philological instinct to interrogate the provenance and transmission of texts is alive and well in humanists' experience of digital libraries.[10] Browsing is not so much about overcoming constraint – by, say, enhancing access or efficiency – as about making a virtue of the often incomplete and fragmentary state of our materials: the gaps in the archive that remind us that the human record is formed as much by loss as by preservation.

Books, browsing and machines: the case of Agostino Ramelli

In considering the web browser we might also look to browsing as an activity throughout the history of the book, a topic that deserves a study unto itself. The role of machines as mediators between browsing scholars and their materials would be an essential topic in such a study, and there has of course been a great deal of book historical studies of moving bookshelves and other physical aids to reading. These lines of inquiry sooner or later tend to arrive at the image shown in Figure 11.2, the book wheel depicted by the Italian engineer Agostino Ramelli in his 'theatre of machines' volume published in *Le diverse et artificiose machine del Capitano Agostino Ramelli* (Paris, 1588).[11]

Commentary on the book wheel often points to it as a distant ancestor of the web browser and its implementation of hypertext.[12] There are even some similarities between this machine and Vannevar Bush's Memex from 1945, another of the modern web browser's conceptual ancestors.[13] A twenty-first century digital humanist might well see hints of Zotero in this image.

It is the strangeness of this image, however, that has made it an emblem for machine-assisted modes of reading. Of the 195 machines pictured in Ramelli's book, most have military or infrastructure applications, for tasks like assaulting cities or moving water over distances, so this lone figure is an odd standout.[14] Ramelli's vertical book wheel seems to have caught on more as an imaginative pursuit than as a real engineering project. Just three decades after its first printing in Paris, a version of this image shows up in a book printed in China in

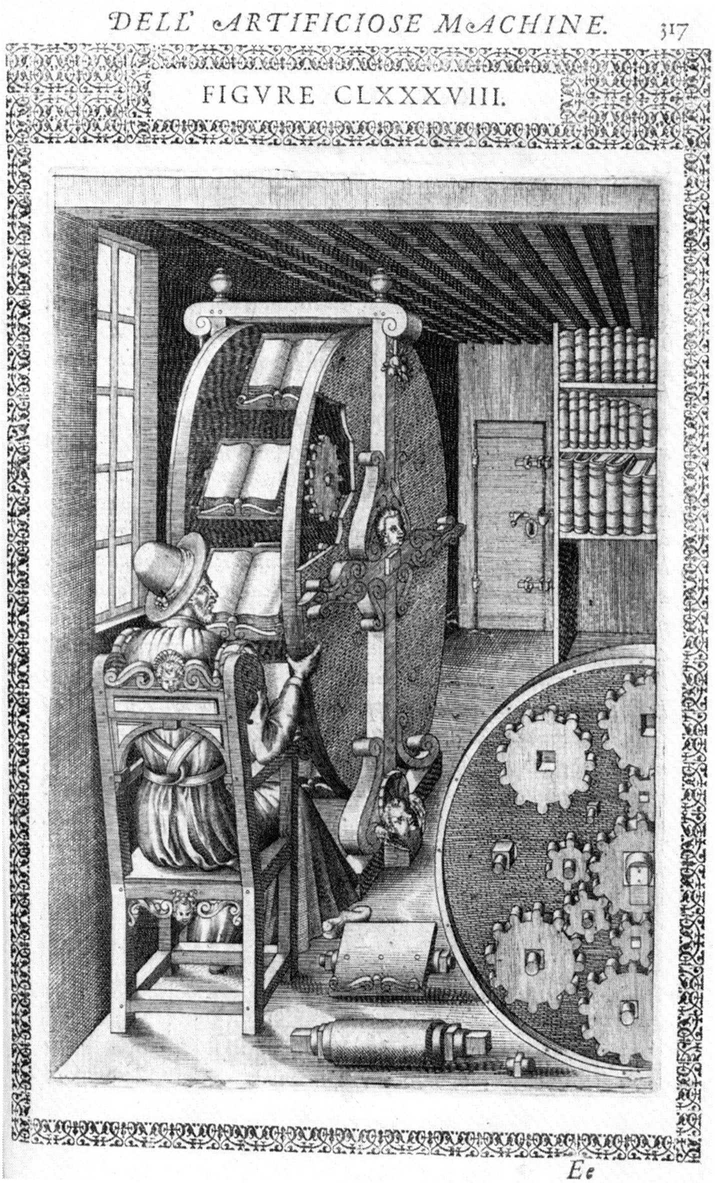

FIGVRE CLXXXVIII.

Ee

Figure 11.2 Agostino Ramelli's book wheel from Agostino Ramelli, *Le diverse et artificiose machine del Capitano Agostino Ramelli* (1588), plate 188

1627, *Chhi Chhi Thu Shuo* ('Diagrams and explanations of wonderful machines'), by Jesuit missionary Johann Schreck and Chinese scholar Wang Chen (Figure 11.3).[15]

Most of the same elements are present: the wheel, the scholar (now Chinese), the bookshelf, the locked door, and the exploded view of the gearing system. Note that the books on the wheel have changed in format to become vertically lined scrolls. We see Ramelli's design showing up a century later in Figure 11.4, in another *theatrum machinarum* by Nicolas Grollier de Servière (*Recueil d'ouvrages curieux de mathematique et de mecanique*, Lyon, 1719).

Grollier has removed the exploded view of the gearing and instead uses gravity to stabilize the book cradles, but again the essential elements of the reader, chair, and well-stocked bookcase remain along with the wheel. Even in the Ramelli wheel's popular film debut in Richard Lester's 1973 version of *The Three Musketeers* – a film stocked with machines seemingly drawn from Ramelli's book – the emphasis is on the strangeness of the device in its context, as Michael York's D'Artagnan spills books on the floor when he fails to realize that the wheel moves if he leans on it.[16] Ramelli's original interest may not have extended beyond demonstrating the planetary gearing system we see in the exploded view, as Bert Hall speculates, but in its subsequent representations the book wheel itself is never depicted as technology in isolation, as though the machine was the sole source of agency over the materials.[17]

To modern eyes the Ramelli book wheel tends to signify the interconnectedness of information itself, and the multitude of paths that radiate outward from single books and together constitute a so-called docuverse. In such a reading, the researcher figured here becomes a kind of explorer or navigator of the world of Renaissance books. To Lisa Jardine and Anthony Grafton, the reader here exerts a new kind of power over texts, acting as a facilitator and intermediary of the textual energies of others, resulting in what they call a centrifugal mode of reading that amounts to information retrieval on a new scale.[18] Ramelli's own description limits the wheel's innovation to serving scholars suffering from gout, for whom movement to and from the shelves would be difficult. But, as Terry Harpold suggests in one of the few sustained readings of Ramelli's machine, this image is about more than the convenience afforded by the machine; rather, 'it is instead the topology of reading realized by the wheel's rotations that marks it

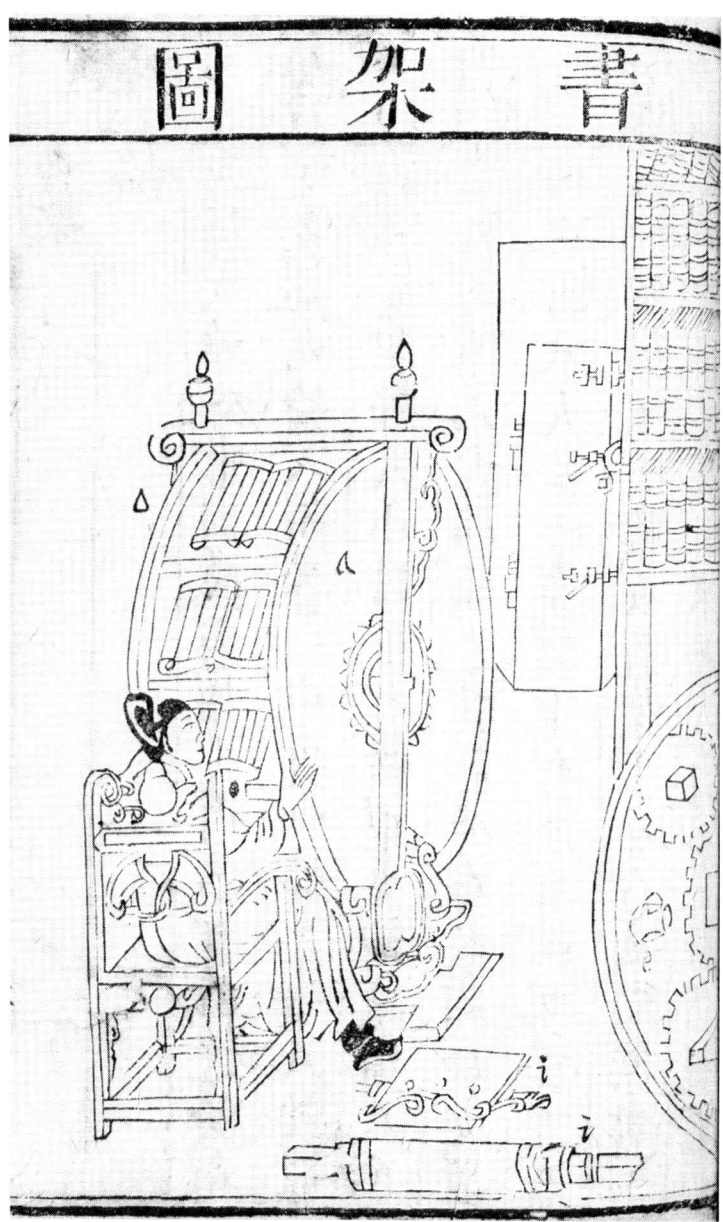

Figure 11.3 A book wheel from Johann Shreck and Wang Chen, *Chhi Chhi Thu Shuo* (1627, plate 104)

Figure 11.4 A book wheel from Nicolas Grollier de Servière, *Recueil d'ouvrages curieux de mathematique et de mecanique* (1719), plate 85

as an authentic precursor of the digital field'.[19] The wheel also represents a form of human–machine interface, a relationship accentuated by the common decorative flourishes on both the wheel and the chair.

Aesthetically the two items are of a piece, just as the wheel, scholar, books, shelves and window together constitute a system.

For humanists, it is this 'topology of reading', as Harpold calls it, which characterizes a given technology, often more so than its efficiency. But even the topology metaphor suggests a level of abstraction – like the topological map on the cover of 'distant reading' advocate Franco Moretti's most recent book – which selects as it represents, omitting the level of detail associated with materialist analyses of reading.[20] By now Ramelli's wheel has become a standard think-piece in scholarly accounts of the history of reading, and the 1588 image functions not just as historical evidence of synoptic or discontinuous reading, but also as an occasion to think through the difficulties of making sense of new reading technologies. Hypertext enthusiasts have tended to cite this image for its proleptic qualities: for them this is an emblem for browsing that allegedly transcends historical distance – despite the fact that 'the book' for this early modern scholar was, in many respects, not the same object it is for us.

A different way of looking at this image would view all of the elements in the picture as part of a single system, encompassing not just the wheel and the scholar, but also the room itself and the many symbolically loaded details of *mise-en-scène* it contains. I propose that we take Ramelli's image as an emblem for the contestability of historiography itself, and especially for the tendency to recruit pre-modern technologies to naturalize modern ones. The presence of other elements in the images – the bookshelves, the scholar, the chair (reminding us of the embodiment of readers), the enclosed and privileged space of the study – all remind us that the book is never just an ideal object in isolation, but always contextualized by the systems that surround it, whether those systems are social or mechanical.

One such contextualizing system is evoked by the circular shape of the wheel, which contains the books within a shape that alludes both to Platonic perfection and to the organization of knowledge into an encyclopedic continuum – a structure that privileges connectivity and topic-based browsing. That browsing structure is encoded in the very architecture of the massive circular reading rooms such as the one Antonio Panizzi designed for the British Museum Library, which we could imagine as though it were Ramelli's wheel set on its side and amplified to the scale of the British Empire. The Web itself is sometimes figured as an ideal universal library – or at least one still under construction – but the linked symbolism of the Ramelli wheel and Panizzi's reading room troubles that ideal. In the latter's case, its circular space of ordered knowledge sits a few floors above its shadowy counterpart, the British Museum basement, whose chronic disorder Thomas Richards identifies as symptomatic of the epistemological crisis of the imperial archive.[21] In the case of the British Museum, we can imagine the circular reading room above and the chaotic basement below as integral parts of the same system existing in tension with each other.

The encyclopedic ideal is under threat in Ramelli's figure, too. Against the far wall we can see part of the library from which this scholar draws his books, but where the reading wheel suggests an encyclopedic round of knowledge contained within a circular form, this irregular mass of books extends beyond the frame of the image, exceeding both the organizational capacity of the wheel and the representational capacity of Ramelli's illustration. We could think of this library in the context of the humanist Juan Luis Vives's assessment of the problem facing Renaissance humanists: in his treatise on education published in 1531 he says, 'if everything written by those old philosophers, historians, orators, poets, physicians, [and] theologians, had reached this age, then we could put nothing but books in our houses; we should have to sit on books; we should have to walk on the top of books; our eyes would have to glance over nothing but books'.[22] This absurd excess of material documents lurks just beyond the frame of Ramelli's illustration.

Another unsettling detail is the locked door at the back, with a formidable trio of bolts to keep the outside from getting in. What is the door's function in this representation of machine-assisted reading? (Notably, the Chinese version of the image retains the door even though it omits the window, no less vital to reading.) On a practical level the locks accentuate the value of the books and machine within, but the locks serve a figurative purpose as well: in the ideal library they would mean that threats like error, textual corruption and the distractions of the world are excluded from the protected space within, like the idealized studies described by humanists such as Machiavelli and Montaigne. But we can also invert that reading and see this as a space that needs protection, one whose integrity is threatened by whatever might be on the other side of that door. One imagines something like Edmund Spenser's bibliographical monster, Error, who vomits books and ink, or perhaps the invading *dance macabre* skeletons from the first surviving image of a printing press from 1499, breaking in to steal the volumes, or to rip out leaves for sale at auction, or to vandalize Wikipedia entries.[23] Ramelli's image thus shows us an interior space for knowledge that presupposes and even generates an exterior space. The book wheel may serve as an emblem for document browsing, but the full illustration depicts an epistemological structure in its attempt, not altogether successful, to enforce a separation between the knowledge within and the disordered world outside.

'View source': reading the web browser

The tensions at work within the Ramelli image serve as reminders of similar ones at work in technologies of reading today. Web browsers link us to an outside space of texts beyond our immediate surroundings, like the bookshelf extending beyond Ramelli's frame. However, the scale and diversity of digital textuality on the Web also frustrates any encyclopedic fantasies of epistemic mastery: a digital environment like Wikipedia gives us connectivity but not necessarily continuity. Book historians have long understood how books may reflect and negotiate tensions like these, and indeed one of the field's inaugural works was a study of how the encyclopedic project of Denis Diderot took shape within the material constraints of publishing and the book form.[24] It was D. F. McKenzie, however, who prompted the related domains of textual criticism and bibliography to extend their scope from manuscripts, books and ephemera to digital texts, software, images, film and the other kinds of artefacts that McKenzie grouped under the term 'non-book texts'.[25]

Far from being transparent windows to the content of digital texts, browsers are themselves agents in the sociology of texts that Darnton and McKenzie outlined, and can shape reading in subtle but consequential ways. So what, then, should historians of books and reading look for in web browsers? For the sake of space I will focus on two aspects of browsers which, like the Ramelli image, expose contradictory tendencies in the framing assumptions we bring to materiality and materials. Specifically, these examples represent the poles of the ideal and the material – or perhaps the rational and the irrational – which define the continuum where all texts have their place.

To take the rational side first, all major browsers today overlay a kind of central nervous system upon documents, called the Document Object Model (DOM), which connects every part of a digital document, right down to strings of text, to a single tree structure. The DOM provides tremendous advantages for web programmers by rationalizing the messiness of texts into computationally tractable order, making every part of the document accessible to scripted queries. Yet the DOM's structural centrality within browsers makes them ubiquitous implementations of the controversial neo-structuralist hypothesis that all texts, no matter their provenance, conform at some level to a structure known as the Ordered Hierarchy of Content Objects (OHCO). Allen Renear, the most eloquent champion of this position, promoted a school of thought within humanities computing during the 1990s which praised the computational usefulness of designing electronic texts as trees of containers.[26] In the OHCO worldview, a document contains paragraphs which contain sentences which contain words, with none of these elements overlapping their hierarchies. This chapter, for example, would conform to an OHCO model in terms of its structure, and my word processor, MS Word for Mac 2008, is saving it as an XML file as I write (a remarkably messy XML file, if one looks at the source code, but an OHCO structure nonetheless). Much of the OHCO way of thinking influenced the Text Encoding Initiative (TEI), whose encoding guidelines form the standard – albeit an evolving one – in the digital humanities today.

The complication, however, was that proponents of the OHCO thesis took the further step of inferring that *all* texts, everywhere, must embody the OHCO structure. As Renear describes the inferential leap, 'the comparative efficiency and functionality of treating texts *as if* they were OHCOs is best explained by the hypothesis that texts *are* OHCOs'.[27] This dubious logic – a form of the fallacy of arguing from consequences – was opposed by textual scholars like Jerome McGann for its potential chilling effect on the digital humanities' conception of the field's materials, and those who lined up to refute it tended to invoke the materiality of texts in some form.[28] Although it is fair to say that the OHCO thesis failed to win over mainstream humanists, its structural principles nonetheless form the very essence of the DOM and XML (and TEI). The Firefox browser even included a feature called the DOM Inspector in its first two versions (available as an add-on for version 3), which would display the markup structure of any web page in a manipulable tree structure.[29] Like the idealistic tree diagrams of Diderot and the encyclo-pedist tradition, web browsers in this regard treat the world of texts and knowledge as fundamentally rational.

If the OHCO thesis and its implementation in the DOM embodies a thoroughly rationalized worldview, implying a reverence for structure and authority, its opposite also lurks within one browser in the form of a so-called Easter egg: a joke or other message deliberately hidden in software by its designers. The bibliographic analogy for software Easter eggs might be the errant bits of waste paper one sometimes finds within the bindings of books. The Firefox browser since its first release has used Easter eggs to conceal within every copy of itself an account of its struggle with its giant competitor, Microsoft's Internet Explorer, as did many versions of its predecessor, Netscape Navigator. This account is known as the Book of Mozilla, after the Mozilla project which began within Netscape and from which the lighter and faster Firefox browser emerged as a side-project in 2004. The Book of Mozilla may be viewed in any installation of Firefox by typing 'about: mozilla' into the location bar; one need not be connected to the Web, as the code is built into the browser itself. Typing this into the current version of Firefox (4.0.1) produces a screen containing part of an allegorized account of the recent history of the browser wars:

> Mammon slept. And the beast reborn spread over the earth and its numbers grew legion. And they proclaimed the times and sacrificed crops unto the fire, with the cunning of foxes. And they built a new world in their own image as promised by the sacred words, and spoke of the beast with their children. Mammon awoke, and lo! it was naught but a follower. (emphasis removed)

In this quasi-Spenserian language, 'the beast' is the Mozilla project as personified by its Godzilla-like mascot, and 'Mammon' is unmis-takably Microsoft, who became 'naught but a follower' after other browsers like Firefox and Safari exceeded Internet Explorer in stan-dards-compliance, speed and interoperability.

This is just the most recent entry in an ongoing sequence of chap-ters and verses from the Book of Mozilla. One can read the whole narrative at Wikipedia, though to be bibliographically rigorous one would need to do installations of every single version of Firefox and Netscape Navigator from their first releases, and on different operating systems.[30] An annotated edition of sorts may be found on the Mozilla website, though appropriately enough the annotations are readable only as comments in the source code, accessible by means of the browser's View/Page Source feature.[31]

Part of the significance of the Book of Mozilla is that it is simply there, hidden inside the binding (so to speak) of every copy of Firefox for those in the know to find. But the form and content of the Book of Mozilla also work together as a comment on the materiality of digital artefacts and the labour that goes into them, left there by their makers and using the book as a source of metaphorical power. The Book of Mozilla is clearly modelling itself on the Book of Revelation, which, in addition to being a prophecy, was also a letter written to an embattled minority promising eventual liberation. Here, the language of market-driven competition is sublimated into the language of liberation theology, hidden from view and revealed only a piece at a time with each release, like the liturgical cycle of readings in the church calendar. The Book of Mozilla represents a strand of continuity, albeit an ironic one, between digital web browsers and printing itself as a supposedly providential technology, bestowed by God upon the world to negotiate between divine order and the messy materials of human affairs.

Reading digital materiality

I suggested at the outset that textual scholarship does its best work in the messy middle ground. Web browsers have become the most potent sites where documents and algorithms merge into hybrid forms: they are threshold spaces where we may observe the changing materiality of texts. For the purposes of, say, textual criticism, a digital textual scholar might trace how the transmission and presentation of a text changes between different browsers, or different versions of the same browser, or the same browser on different platforms. Examples of this level of studying the materiality of digital texts may be found in Kirschenbaum's analysis of electronic literature, or Greetham's of word-processor files.[32] Alternately, for the more sociological purposes of book history – the kind based on Darnton's well-known communications circuit – one might consider how browsers enable or prevent different populations' access to information depending on constraints of language, political control of infrastructure, economics of operating systems and support of character sets.[33] The point is that the materiality of digital texts means that they change and act in the world in ways that are knowable – at least more knowable than humanists generally realize – and which respond to the kinds of analysis that have developed out of the study of books, manuscripts and other more familiar forms of material texts.

That said, textual scholars should not entirely let go of the estrangement that new technologies bring to our experience and understanding of reading. As a counterpart to Ramelli's emblematic image for reading, I will close by suggesting another as a think-piece for digital reading: Robert Hooke's illustration of a period as seen through a microscope and reported in his 1665 work *Micrographia*.[34] Hooke's illustration brings together the themes I have been discussing here; like Ramelli's book wheel, it embodies a particular response to the irregularity and imperfection of material texts. In Hooke's commentary on the many periods he examined, inscribed with a range of means from manuscript to print to copperplate etching, he expresses his surprise that a perfectly round period on the page appears under the microscope as, in his words, a 'great splatch of *London* dirt', made irregular by factors such as the unevenness of the paper or imperfections of the type or engraving.[35] Unlike things created by nature, such as the tip of a bee's stinger, human artefacts become disturbingly flawed when you look closely enough. Hooke shows clear disgruntlement at the secret ugliness and geometrical chaos hiding within even the most innocent-seeming of punctuation marks – and the one most important in the web's addressing system, along with the solidus.

As Adrian Johns suggests in his insightful reading of this image, Hooke also realized that the 'postlapsarian disproportion of the senses to nature, and their alliance with the passions and imagination, were both necessary and precisely sufficient to allow human beings to read'.[36] Far from the circular perfection of Ramelli's encyclopedic book wheel or Panizzi's great reading room, this great splatch of dirt shows a circle coming apart, taking a shape only recognizable as a period when we use our unaided human vision, which is imperfectly calibrated to the world. As tempting as fantasies of ideal texts and knowledge environments might be, they must be tempered by the reality that all material inscriptions will at some level look like Hooke's period, and hold the same implications. Those implications are the rationale for digital textual scholarship in the coming decade, which is well-equipped to recognize that digital texts are made of the same kinds of matter as James Joyce slyly claimed, that 'papyr is meed of, made of, hides and hints and misses in prints'.[37]

Notes and references

1. See Mary Douglas, *Purity and Danger: An Analysis of the Concepts of Pollution and Taboo* (New York: Routledge, 1984), p. 173.
2. David M. Levy, *Scrolling Forward: Making Sense of Documents in the Digital Age* (New York: Arcade Publishing, 2001), pp. 155–6; emphasis in original.
3. See N. Katherine Hayles, *My Mother Was a Computer: Digital Subjects and Literary Texts* (Chicago: University of Chicago Press, 2005); Matthew G. Kirschenbaum, *Mechanisms: New Media and the Forensic Imagination* (Cambridge, MA: MIT Press, 2008); Lisa Gitelman, *Always Already New: Media, History, and the Data of Culture* (Cambridge, MA: MIT Press, 2006).
4. See Thomas Haigh, 'Protocols for profit: Web and e-mail technologies as product and infrastructure', in *The Internet and American Business*, ed. William Aspray and Paul Ceruzzi (Cambridge, MA: MIT Press, 2008), pp. 105–58.
5. See Henry Petroski, *The Book on the Bookshelf* (New York: Vintage, 1999), esp. his chapter 'Studying studies', pp. 100–28; and Dora Thornton, *The Scholar in His Study: Ownership and Experience in Renaissance Italy* (New Haven: Yale University Press, 1997).
6. Jon Rimmer et al., 'An examination of the physical and the digital qualities of humanities research', *Information Processing & Management*, 44 (2008), 1374–92.
7. Stephen Ramsay makes this point in his 'In praise of pattern', *Text Technology*, 2 (2005), 177–90 (p. 181).
8. Rimmer et al., 'An examination', p. 1385.
9. To let two examples stand for many, see Claire Warwick et al., 'If you build it will they come? The LAIRAH study: quantifying the use of online resources in the arts and humanities through statistical analysis of user log data', *Literary and Linguistic Computing*, 23 (2008), 85–102; and Margaret Hedstrom, 'Archives, memory, and interfaces with the past', *Archival Science*, 2 (2002), 21–43.
10. Warwick et al., 'If you build it', pp. 99–100.
11. For an English translation, see Agostino Ramelli, *The Various and Ingenious Machines of Agostino Ramelli (1588)*, trans. Martha Teach Gnudi (Baltimore: Johns Hopkins University Press, 1976), p. 508.
12. Roger Chartier, *The Cultural Uses of Print in Early Modern France*, trans. Lydia G. Cochrane (Princeton: Princeton University Press, 1987), pp. 222–3; Leah S. Marcus, 'The silence of the archive and the noise of

cyberspace', in *The Renaissance Computer: Knowledge Technology in the First Age of Print*, ed. Neil Rhodes and Jonathan Sawday (London: Routledge, 2000), pp. 18–28; Lisa Jardine and Anthony Grafton, '"Studied for action": how Gabriel Harvey read his Livy', *Past and Present*, 129 (1990), 30–78.

13. Vannevar Bush, 'As we may think', in *From Memex to Hypertext: Vannevar Bush and the Mind's Machine*, ed. James M. Nyce and Paul Kahn (Boston: Academic Press, 1991), pp. 85–107 (first published in different versions in *Life* and *Atlantic Monthly* in 1945). See also Alan Galey and Patrick Finn, 'Digital humanities and the networked citizen', *Text Technology*, 15 (2007), 11–26 (pp. 16–18).

14. Terry Harpold suggests that this image and the four plates that precede it, which depict moving ornaments and mechanical birds driven by water- and air-pressure, are united by the theme of simulation; Terry Harpold, *Ex-Foliations: Reading Machines and the Upgrade Path* (Minneapolis: University of Minnesota Press, 2008), p. 215.

15. On this example and the one following, see Bert S. Hall, 'A revolving bookcase by Agostino Ramelli', *Technology and Culture*, 11 (1970), 389–400; on the Chinese example specifically, see Joseph Needham and Wang Ling, *Science and Civilization in China* (4 vols., Cambridge: Cambridge University Press, 1965), II: *Mechanical Engineering*, p. 547.

16. For two other modern replicas of the Ramelli wheel, one built by Dante Gnudi and the other by Daniel Libeskind for the 1985 Venice Biennale see respectively Hall, 'Revolving bookcase', pp. 397–400; and Harpold, *Ex-Foliations*, pp. 210, 216–18.

17. Hall, 'Revolving bookcase', p. 392.

18. Jardine and Grafton, 'Studied for action', p. 48.

19. Harpold, *Ex-Foliations*, p. 215; see also pp. 209–20.

20. Franco Moretti, *Graphs, Maps, Trees: Abstract Models for a Literary Theory* (London: Verso, 2005).

21. Thomas Richards, *The Imperial Archive: Knowledge and the Fantasy of Empire* (London: Verso, 1993), pp. 16, 74.

22. Juan Luis Vives, *Vives: On Education; a Translation of the De Tradendis Disciplinis of Juan Luis Vives*, trans. Foster Watson (Totowa, NJ: Rowman and Littlefield, 1971), p. 45.

23. The *dance macabre* image is reproduced in David C. Greetham, *Textual Scholarship: An Introduction* (New York: Garland, 1994), p. 83.

24. See Robert Darnton, *The Business of Enlightenment: A Publishing History of the Encyclopédie, 1775–1800* (Cambridge, MA: Harvard University Press, 1979); and Darnton, 'Philosophers trim the tree of knowledge: the episte-mological strategy of the Encyclopédie', in his *The Great Cat Massacre, and Other Episodes in French Cultural History* (New York: Basic Books, 1984), pp. 191–214.

25. D. F. McKenzie, *Bibliography and the Sociology of Texts* (Cambridge: Cambridge University Press, 1999), p. 13; see also McKenzie's chapter, 'The broken phial: non-book texts', in his *Bibliography*, pp. 31–53.

26. See Steven J. DeRose et al., 'What is text, really?', *Journal of Computing in Higher Education*, 1 (1990), 3–26; Allen H. Renear, 'Out of praxis: three (meta)theories of textuality', in *Electronic Text: Investigations in Method and Theory*, ed. Kathryn Sutherland (Oxford: Clarendon Press, 1997), pp. 107–26; and Renear, 'Out of praxis', in *A Companion to Digital Humanities*, ed. Susan Schreibman, Ray Siemens and John Unsworth (Oxford: Wiley-Blackwell, 2004). For an overview of the positions, see Susan Schreibman, 'Computer-mediated texts and textuality: theory and practice', *Computers and the Humanities*, 36 (2002), 283–93.

27. Renear, 'Text encoding', p. 118.

28. See Jerome J. McGann, *Radiant Textuality: Literature After the World Wide Web* (New York: Palgrave – now Palgrave Macmillan, 2001), p. 185; Hayles, *My Mother*, pp. 89–116; Peter Robinson, 'What text really is not, and why editors have to learn to swim', *Literary and Linguistic Computing*, 24 (2009), 41–52; Paul Eggert, 'The book, the e-text and the "work-site"', in *Text Editing, Print and the Digital World*, ed. Marilyn Deegan and Kathryn Sutherland (Farnham: Ashgate, 2009), pp. 63–82; and David Golumbia, *The Cultural Logic of Computation* (Cambridge, MA: Harvard University Press, 2009), pp. 105–19.

29. See 'Introduction to DOM Inspector', *Mozilla Developer Center*, http://developer.mozilla.org/en/DOM_Inspector/Introduction_to_DOM_Inspector [accessed 15 February 2010].

30. 'The Book of Mozilla', *Wikipedia*, http://en.wikipedia.org/wiki/Book_of_mozilla [accessed 15 February 2010].

31. 'The Book of Mozilla', *Mozilla.org*, http://www.mozilla.org/book/ [accessed 15 February 2010].

32. See Kirschenbaum, *Mechanisms*, pp. 213–48; and David C. Greetham, *Theories of the Text* (Oxford: Oxford University Press, 1999), pp. 254–5; and Greetham, *Textual Scholarship*, pp. 290–1. For a more general overview see David L. Vander Meulen, 'Thoughts on the future of bibliographical analysis', *Papers of the Bibliographical Society of Canada*, 46 (2008), 17–34.

33. For example, try using any recent version of Internet Explorer to visit a website like un.org, enter the version of the site in Arabic or any other language read right-to-left, and watch what happens to the browser's scroll bar.

34. Adrian Johns, *The Nature of the Book: Print and Knowledge in the Making* (Chicago: University of Chicago Press, 1998), pp. 430–1.

35. Robert Hooke, *Micrographia, or, Some physiological descriptions of minute bodies made by magnifying glasses with observations and inquiries thereupon* (London, 1665), p. 3.

36. Johns, *Nature of the Book*, p. 431.

37. James Joyce, *Finnegans Wake* (New York: Penguin, 1999), p. 20.

Further Reading and Weblinks

Selected books

Altick, Richard D., *The English Common Reader: A Social History of the Mass Reading Public, 1800–1900* (Chicago: University of Chicago Press, 1957)

Birkerts, Sven, *The Gutenberg Elegies: The Fate of Reading in an Electronic Age* (London: Faber, 1996)

Bloom, Harold, *How to Read and Why* (New York: Scribner, 2000)

Collinson, Ian, *Everyday Readers: Reading and Popular Culture* (London: Equinox, 2009)

Darnton, Robert, *The Case for Books: Past, Present and Future* (Philadelphia: University of Pennsylvania Press, 2009)

Dehaene, Stanislas, *Reading in the Brain: The Science and Evolution of a Human Invention* (New York: Penguin, 2009)

Flint, Kate, *The Woman Reader 1837–1914* (Oxford: Clarendon Press, 1993)

Gunzenheimer, Bonnie (ed.), *Reading in History: New Methodologies from the Anglo-American Tradition* (London: Pickering & Chatto, 2010)

Hartley, Jenny, *Reading Groups* (Oxford: Oxford University Press, 2001)

Hayles, N. Katherine, *Electronic Literature: New Horizons for the Literary* (Notre Dame: University of Notre Dame Press, 2008)

Henkin, David, *City Reading: Written Words and Public Spaces in Antebellum New York* (New York: Columbia University Press, 1998)

Hermes, Joke, *Reading Women's Magazines: An Analysis of Everyday Media Use* (Cambridge: Polity Press, 1995)

Hofmeyr, Isabel, *The Portable Bunyan: A Transnational History of the Pilgrim's Progress* (Princeton: Princeton University Press, 2004)

Jackson, H. J., *Marginalia: Readers Writing in Books* (New Haven: Yale University Press, 2001)

Kirschenbaum, Matthew, *Mechanisms: New Media and the Forensic Imagination* (Boston, MA: MIT University Press, 2008)

Leavis, Q. D., *Fiction and the Reading Public* (London: Chatto & Windus, 1932)

Long, Elizabeth, *Book Clubs: Women and the Uses of Reading in Everyday Life* (Chicago and London: University of Chicago Press, 2003)

Lyons, Martyn, *A History of Reading and Writing in the Western World* (Basingstoke: Palgrave Macmillan, 2009)

McHenry, Elizabeth, *Forgotten Readers: Recovering the Lost History of African-American Literary Societies* (Durham: Duke University Press, 2002)

Moretti, Franco, *Graphs, Maps and Trees: Abstract Models for a Literary Theory* (London: Verso, 2005)

Nafisi, Azar, *Reading Lolita in Tehran: A Memoir in Books* (London: Random House, 2004)

Nord, David Paul, *Communities of Journalism: A History of American Newspapers and Their Readers* (Urbana: University of Illinois Press, 2000)

Raven, James, Helen Small and Naomi Tadmor, eds., *The Practice and Representation of Reading in England* (Cambridge: Cambridge University Press, 1996)

Rose, Jonathan, *The Intellectual Life of the British Working Classes*, 2nd edn. (New Haven and London: Yale University Press, 2010)

Secord, James, *Victorian Sensation: The Extraordinary Publication, Reception and Secret Authorship of Vestiges of the Natural History of Creation* (London: University of Chicago Press, 2000)

St. Clair, William, *The Reading Nation in the Romantic Period* (Cambridge: Cambridge University Press, 2004)

Stewart, Garrett, *The Look of Reading: Book, Painting, Text* (Chicago: University of Chicago Press, 2006)

Wevers, Lydia, *Reading on the Farm: Victorian Fiction and the Colonial World* (Wellington: Victoria University Press, 2010)

Wolf, Maryanne, *Proust and the Squid: The Story and Science of the Reading Brain* (New York: HarperCollins, 2007)

Selected articles

Aubry, Timothy, 'Afghanistan meet the *Amazon*: reading *The Kite Runner* in America', *Proceedings of the Modern Language Association*, 124:1 (2009), 25–43

Crone, Rosalind, 'Reappraising Victorian literacy through prison records', *Journal of Victorian Culture*, 15 (2010), 3–37

Esbester, Mike, 'Nineteenth-century timetables and the history of reading', *Book History*, 12 (2009), 156–85

Eubanks, Charlotte, 'Circumambulatory reading: revolving sutra libraries and Buddhist scrolls,' *Book History*, 13 (2010), 1–24

Fuller, Danielle, 'Listening to the readers of "Canada reads"', *Canadian Literature*, 193 (2007), 11–34

Gerrard, Teresa, 'New methods in the history of reading: "Answers to correspondents" in *The Family Herald*, 1860–1900', *Publishing History*, 43 (1998), 53–66

Gutjahr, Paul, 'No longer left behind: Amazon.com, reader-response, and the changing fortunes of the Christian novel in America', *Book History*, 5 (2002), 209–27

Halsey, Katie, 'Reading the evidence of reading: an introduction to the Reading Experience Database, 1450–1945', *Popular Narrative Media*, 1 (2008), 123–37

Kawana, Sari, 'Reading beyond the lines: young readers and wartime Japanese literature,' *Book History*, 13 (2010), 154–84

Piroux, Lorraine, 'The Encyclopedist and the Peruvian Princess: the poetics of illegibility in French Enlightenment book culture', *Proceedings of the Modern Language Association*, 121:1 (2006), 107–23

Smith, Erin A, 'How the other half read: advertising, working-class readers, and pulp magazines', *Book History*, 3 (2000), 204–30

Warkentin, Germaine, 'In search of 'The word of the other': Aboriginal sign systems and the history of the book in Canada,' *Book History*, 2 (1999), 1–27

Weblinks

Beyond the Book: http://www.beyondthebookproject.org/

British Fiction, 1800–1829: A Database of Production, Circulation and Reception: http://www.british-fiction.cf.ac.uk/

China Publishing Today: http://www.cptoday.com.cn/En/Index.aspx

Devolving Diasporas: http://www.devolvingdiasporas.com/

International Reading Association: http://www.reading.org/General/Default. aspx

Mass Observation Online: http://www.amdigital.co.uk/

North American Women's Letters and Diaries, Colonial to 1950: http://solomon. nwld.alexanderstreet.com/

The Reader Organization: http://thereader.org.uk/

The Reading Agency: http://www.readingagency.org.uk/

The Reading Experience Database (RED): http://www.open.ac.uk/Arts/reading

Scottish Archive of Print and Publishing History Records: http://www.sapphire. ac.uk/

What Middletown Read: http://cms.bsu.edu/Academics/CentersandInstitutes/ Middletown/Research/MiddletownRead.aspx

Women Writers and their Audiences: http://neww.huygens.knaw.nl/

Index

Page numbers for illustrations are given in bold. References to tables are indicated in brackets.